R

# NORTH SPIRIT

## Also by Paulette Jiles

**POETRY**

*Waterloo Express*

*Celestial Navigation*

*The Jesse James Poems*

**FICTION**

*The Late Great Human Road Show*

*Sitting in the Clubcar Drinking Rum and Karma-Kola; or,*
*A Manual of Etiquette for Ladies Crossing Canada by Train*

**NON-FICTION**

*Cousins*

**COLLECTIONS**

*Blackwater*

*Song to the Rising Sun*

# NORTH SPIRIT

Travels Among
the Cree and Ojibway
Nations and Their Star Maps

PAULETTE JILES

Doubleday Canada Limited

**Canadian Cataloguing in Publication Data**
Jiles, Paulette, 1943–
    North spirit

Hardcover ISBN 0-385-25499-7; Paperback ISBN 0-385-25539-X

1. Jiles Paulette, 1943–    – Journeys – Ontario, Northern. 2. Cree Indians – Social life and customs.
3. Ojibwa Indians – Social life and customs.
4. Indians of North America – Ontario, Northern.
5. Ontario, Northern – Social life and customs.
I. Title.

E99.C88J5 1995    971.3'112004973    C94-932716-6

Cover design by Tania Craan
Text design by Heidy Lawrance Associates
Printed and bound in the U.S.A.
Printed on acid-free paper

Published in Canada by
Doubleday Canada Limited
105 Bond Street, Toronto
Ontario M5B 1Y3

Portions of this book first appeared in *Celestial Navigation* (Toronto: McClelland & Stewart, 1984), the *Southwestern Review,* and *The Quarterly.*

The Cree writing and drawing on page (127) is by Noah Atlookan and translated by Joan QueeQueesh.

*This book is dedicated to*

*Mrs. Mindemoya and*

*all the respected elders*

*of the north*

# Preface

This is a book of creative non-fiction and therefore many liberties were taken in rearranging events, places, times, and the construction of composite characters, including my own. Most of the people in this book are, in fact, composites. The village of North Spirit Lake is based mainly on Big Trout Lake, but also on the village of Sandy Lake, both communities where I spent many happy times. All the incidents are true.

I have used the words "Indian" and "native" as I heard them used in my years in the north.

My thanks to the Canada Council, without whose support this book would not have been possible. An "A" grant freed me for an entire year to write the initial draft. I am deeply grateful.

Neither would this book have been possible without the support, patience, and good cheer of my husband, Jim Johnson. He read and reread the manuscript time and again, and his editing and suggestions have been invaluable. My thanks and gratitude.

And many, many thanks to my editors John Pearce and Susan Folkins for their patience and suggestions, and Ginger Barber fo all her help.

And thanks to old friends who are far away and yet near in my thoughts: Jim Morris, Ruby Cutfeet Morris, Pat Ningewance, Garnet and Margaret Angeconeb, Victoria Maxwell, Tokyo Rose, Mary Alice Morrison, Margaret and Innis Fiddler, Donna Pace (Rahda Krishnananda), Ifka Filipovich, Peggy Saunders, Don Plemel, the Flying Friesans, Hannah Achineepiniskum, the Beardy family of Muskat Dam — Virginia, Emasiah and Lucy, Frank, Arthur and Stan, and Eli and Sarah Beardy, who have passed away but whose wisdom is still with us. To the memory of Chief Aglace Chapman and John-George Morris, wise men and accomplished storytellers. My thanks especially to elder Jemimah Morris. Thanks to Emmanuel Desveaux for sharing stories. Thanks, also, for the presence and energy of the children of the north who are now young adults: Matt and Teesa Angeconeb, Spencer Morris, Maeengan Ningewance, Jesse and Willow Fiddler, Ato and Little Girl Sitting Among The Flowers Fiddler, Joe Linklater, Alicia Pace and Forrest Chisel.

Thanks to Kathy and Tim Chisel for advice and help and three days of summer peace at Whitefish Bay, and to those who survived two northern theater tours with such good spirits: Doris Linklater, Graham Greene, Robert Lac Seul, Keith Turnbull, Jerry Wootton, Rick Gorrie, Doug Rodgers, Eric Nagler, and many others.

And to all those in the northern villages who offered help and hospitality through all my years in the north; *gahkenah ni-nakomenawah.*

# 1.

A Twin Otter moves through the uncertain air of February, pressing through low clouds freighted with snow. It is flying at an altitude of 1,500 feet and the pilot is watching the landscape unreel beneath him, keeping his plane and passengers over the Pipestone River, feeling his way from landmark to landmark, toward the village of Muskrat Dam. At the horizon line, an immense being waits at the entrance to the upper world.

The Twin Otter is loaded with actors and sets. The actors and I, the writer, smoke and stare out of frosted windows with subdued fright. Nobody really trusts the air but the pilot. The pilot is named Gary Kakekeyash. Kakekeyash means Forever Seagull. The air is a sort of material in rough weaves, we are in its textures. Tall, draining columns of snow-squalls are marching across the world in spectral steps without noise or any other indication of their passing.

Forever Seagull and the copilot are handling the aircraft with all four arms; they look like Hindu spider dancers. We are flying over a landscape without roads, without railroads or towns. These are the endless, uncut forests of one of the last great wildernesses of the world.

One of the actors is named Graham Greene. He's Oneida, from the Six Nations reserve near Toronto. He has glossy black hair down to the middle of his back and is wrapped up in a red Hudson's Bay Company blanket-coat.

He says, "What are you writing, Jiles? That's not the script is it? You're not writing in *new* stuff on that script, are you?"

"No, no, it's my journal."

"It better not be the script."

"I swear. Look. J-O-U-R-N-A-L."

"If it's any of my parts in that script you're dead."

The stage manager has to yell over the noise of the engines. He's near the front. He shouts, "Hey Doris? Do we get white cake in this place or what?" Doris Linklater, one of the actors, is a young Ojibway woman with a thin, taut body and black-brown hair in a heavy braid.

Doris yells back, "Spork. Spork steak."

Doug Rodgers says, "Hey Doris? How do you say 'projectile vomiting' in Ojibway?"

Doug Rodgers is a red-headed white guy from Hamilton, Ontario. He is an amiable man whose character in the play is a ranting bureaucrat. He plays the part in a three-piece suit and toe rubbers; he performs it with juicy relish.

"If I ever have another piece of Spork I'll throw up onstage."

Spork is a Spam-like substance. It is bright pink, comes in Spam-can-shaped cans, and as a food it is slightly better than United Nations emergency relief stuff like tofu. It is full of pork fat. Just the sort of food you need when your body is emptying itself of vital energy in the deep cold and you don't have anything else to eat. It is cheap and it is everywhere. It is welfare food. I never travel without it.

Doris says, "You say *bleaccchhhh.*" She is tired of translating for people who don't speak Ojibway. Doris is from Manitoulin Island, that grand, graceful island in a blue inland sea six hundred miles to the southeast of here.

They have been to four villages so far this tour. It is the middle of February, 1981, and the temperatures would jell whiskey. We are flying over Anishinabe-Aski, the Indian Nation. It is the country of the northern Ojibway and the Cree peoples, who call themselves Anishinabek, which means the Spontaneously Created People. Somewhere to the southeast, in the sky just below the edge of dark, a great being outlined in stars is lifting his sparkling paddle and plunging it into galaxies and nebulae, they foam up like rapids.

The Cree and Ojibway of remote northern Ontario, inland from the great Bays, remain on their ancestral homelands. It is a country of extreme temperatures and frosted tundras, black-spruce forests dense as fur, where poplars shine lemon-yellow in the fall over old burns and the Canadian Shield granites are overwritten with glacial scarring that resembles wiring diagrams.

The Spontaneously Created People have never been pressured out of their country by white populations. They have been here for eleven thousand years, they have been here since the tall cliffs of the Wisconsin glaciers melted back in ice-water floods. For all practical purposes God made them right here on the premises, six hundred miles north of Minneapolis. The Great Spirit spontaneously created them in a moment of joy and enthusiasm for life, at this particular latitude of Turtle Island, and so they arose, and put on their snowshoes, and began to argue about which way to go, and nobody could make anybody else see reason, and so they stayed here.

Here is where everything important happened that ever happened to people. Here is where the Thunderbirds foam up into spectacular cumuli in the spring, and send down bolts of lightning to electrify the earth into pincherry blossoms, here is where Wolverine was blinded and made his way to the salt water, here is where Wiskejac killed a beaver big as a boxcar and its blood runs yet in brilliant streams on the stones of the Vermillion River. Here, in this country. It is a country of stories, myths, and legends. The legends, like the blue gems of landfast ice, are alive in subtle ways. It is a land of tales. It is a word-of-mouth imaginative planet, where stories will be told about the hero Kahyana as well as you, if you stay long enough to establish a sort of stage presence.

The Twin Otter rises and falls on the stiff columns of subzero air, drawn forward by its double propellers; it is like being dragged over railroad ties. The interior is blue with smoke. White-knuckled people gaze out of frosted portholes, longing for mother earth.

I am jammed in a rear seat with a packet of Players, a knapsack full of notebooks, a nightgown in flowered lawn, tiny binoculars, a leather writing case with a fountain pen and rag paper. I am traveling with the theater group because I wrote the play. We're an ad hoc invention, a native theater in search of a native writer. I wrote this thing because there wasn't a native playwright immediately available. I wrote it just to have a play to play. They say everything will happen in good time. I have been in the north five years now and things do happen, though not always in good time. It depends on what a person means by time.

I am thirty-eight and I like to think of myself as an old maid. I have a little book light that clips on book covers and runs on batteries. I take this with me when I travel into the villages north of the rail lines. Then I can sit up late in my sleeping bag and read, and listen to the tinking noises as the fire dies down, and then the cold, the pure, transparent cold, like a personality from the legends, comes stalking up out of the floors and through the little eight-paned windows to crisp the nail heads in the logs and settle down onto the pages of my book. Sometimes I write things down in the blank front pages of the paperbacks that later turn into poems.

That's how I wrote this play. It's not much of a play, however. It doesn't have plane crashes or murders in it. There are no piercing emotions or losses. It is light and amusing, a little goofy.

Keith Turnbull and Jerry Wootton, the producer and the director, are in a sleep like a coma, their loose bodies jiggling in the rough air, packed in army-surplus parkas.

Forever Seagull has been watching the landscape below intently. We have left the Pipestone River and picked up the broad river-lake called the Severn River. He suddenly straightens up and pulls himself loose from his intense searching. He turns and looks back at the passengers, the motley crew of actors and sets.

"No puking," he says. "Did I hear somebody talking about puking? Not allowed."

"How long are we going to be in the air?" asks Graham. "Maybe we should break up the sets and set them afire for tea."

"We need more quarters," says Forever Seagull. "Your time has run out."

The quarters joke only gets a mild laugh. The sets are another matter. They were put together in Sioux Lookout and must be unbolted, loaded, unloaded at the new villages, and then bolted together again.

They are, like the little theater company itself, constructed with the minimum amount of expense and the maximum amount of skill and hope. The sets have been specially constructed to fit on a Twin Otter, although they have been crammed into a Beechcraft and have banged around in the big cargo spaces of a DC-3. The props sometimes get confused with their equivalent objects in real life. For instance, the fake papier-mâché caribou hindquarter and the real moose hindquarter. The actors have been lugging the real hindquarter along from village to village on this tour in order to have moose steaks. They saw off great frosty chunks with a hacksaw. Several times they have lost the hacksaw. They all accuse one another in fierce voices of having lost it.

Then someone finds it. The fiddler looks the other way and sighs. He is a thin, pale man, a strict vegetarian, and is wasting away in the northern cold on a diet of oatmeal and canned peas. The Indian actors have tried to deprogram him with frankfurters and Spork but nothing works. They don't want to lose him. His rousing rendition of "Ste. Anne's Reel" brings down the house every night.

Scattered around the smoky interior of the Twin Otter are copies of the *Wawatay News*. Normally, I work for the newspaper. It is the only bilingual Ojibway-English newspaper in the world, and it is printed in two different scripts. I have a long chronicle of stories about flying on bush planes in search of news. I love to astonish people with them when I am safe on the ground, but when I am in the air I don't like being astonished. This is why I am sitting as far to the rear as I can manage. But if anything untoward happens, here we are with a load of unsecured cargo. By now the actors are bored with my stories. By now they have plenty of their own.

I didn't put any of these stories in the play and now I am regretting it. The Thunderbirds and their cosmic artillery that can explode tents and people; bush planes running into radio towers in the dim, snowy air; the charged hatreds that simmer in a bad marriage in a trap-line camp; the loss of a child; gambling tales and heroic rescues; the dense, fictional tapestry of the legends. The more I think about the play, the sillier it is.

"Graham, there's a lot better stories up here than what I have in this script."

"If you change one word, you go out the cargo door."

"But look, what if you took all the maps of the migration routes. Migrations of caribou and the geese, it would make a kind of pattern."

"That's a thought." Graham looks back over his seat back, considering. "But that's a wall decoration, not a script."

"There'd be a story in it."

"What story? Name one."

"It would make a pattern. There'd be stories about the roads where things happened."

"Story roads." He lights a cigarette and pours smoke on his window and defrosts a hole. "The pattern would make a face. Crazy Horse. Wovoka. Chief Joseph. Almighty Voice."

"So you could make a set with the pattern on it."

"Not *this* script, Jiles. You changed it too much already."

Keith comes awake out of his dreams or stupor.

"Is she changing something?" he cries, alarmed.

"Nah," says Graham. "We were just having a serious philosophical conversation. You wouldn't understand."

Doris says, "*Asha!*" Now. Already.

Below us, appearing and disappearing beneath breathy rags of clouds like airborne frost, is the peninsula of Muskrat Dam. The village is down there; I see one house, a wisp of smoke, another house, a snowmobile crawling across the lake. Forever Seagull and the copilot let themselves go into the mechanical demands of an earth fall. It is as if they were being absorbed by their instruments, servants of flight. The tune of the propellers becomes coarse and the whine of their pitch changes.

I wrench out a copy of the script in order to take my mind off the landing process. Don't think about it. You, the reader, are on this story road as well. You may wonder what got you into this, this journey into the temples of snow. You may be in search of wise elders, the ancient mysteries of shamans, but here you are, in an unforgiving climate, suspended in a flight machine that is pouring itself in a deep slant toward snowpacked ice.

They told you there were ancient secrets here, and healing mysteries. But you realize that you are going to have to sleep on a plank floor, carry water from a hole in the ice, lay an ax into the iron surfaces of frozen green birch. They said, *you have never seen anything like the cotton grass in the spring, fields of it, or the poppies flooding out over the tundra, or the aurora and its midnight light shows.* How, you ask yourself, did I get into this? We jam through veil after veil of flying snow, we are caught between the two engines in a polyrhythmic crossfire of thunders.

But don't worry; I will make smooth the way; we will get down in one piece. There is a vessel larger than all our imagining moving through the deep song of time, and at its stern the immense being plunges his paddle again and again into the river of stars.

We are now grinding with blunt determination on a downward slant toward the snowpacked ice in front of the village. Muskrat Dam is on a long peninsula that thrusts out into the Severn River, which at this place is miles across. It is a sort of lake, white as marble.

I think madly about changes. For instance, I could have the protagonist suffering from an incurable disease, which he reveals to the female lead at the last moment. I could write it in right now, as a matter of fact.

"What are you doing with the script? Eh?" says Keith. He's alert. "You're changing something."

"What if Graham's character had an incurable disease?" I say.

"I'll slash my wrists," says Keith.

We descend out of the blue dusk in a long glide. Landing on snowpack in white weather is a kind of fainting out of the air. We sink into the foaming ground-blow, and then touch, batter and jerk, and then charge toward the village on skis.

Muskrat Dam is a group of log cabins and Indian Affairs-built prefab houses. It is strung out among the pines on a long point. It is at the northern limit of pines, and telephones, and the English language. It is a storybook village, with lamplight glowing in buttery bars out of eight-paned windows, the tin-pipe chimneys are puffing smoke, the light, warbling voices of excited children pipe and grace note the air.

We stumble down the steps, and then Forever Seagull throws the cargo door open. They begin heaving out baggage and sets.

Doris yells, "There's Sarah!"

Sarah Winnepetonga waves over the heads of people crowding around. She is tall, with blue-black hair and black eyes, pale skin, and red cheeks. Her hair is cut short straight around. She looks like a tall China doll.

"Puanets!" she yells. "Doris!"

It seems all two hundred and fifty villagers have come out to meet the plane, dropping saws and fishnets and pots and pans and books and tools. Over the crowd rises a kind of communal breath, clouding the frigid air, steaming and evaporating and reforming. Plates of new snow drop off the drooping arms of pines. The Spontaneously Created

People stretch out hands in caribou mitts, wanting to take some baggage, shake hands, help out, offer a ride on a snowmobile. They ask the actors to pose for photos, and there is the constant flash of Instamatics.

The kids tangle around the feet of the actors like kittens. Graham Greene is taller than everybody else, his ponytail down to his waist, his red blanket-coat frosted with snow. He has the frozen moose hindquarter over one shoulder and the papier-mâché caribou hindquarter over the other. He puts down the papier-mâché one to shake hands with the little boys. They take his hand and mutually lift it once up and once down with their puffy, beaded mitts, and then inspect the fake caribou hindquarter. They begin to tear tentatively, experimentally, at a loose strip.

Sarah Winnepetonga and I shake hands.

"Ah, Puanets!" she says.

"What the hell is a PUANETS?" says Graham.

"That's Jiles," says Doris. "That's her Indian name."

Sarah and I are delighted at seeing one another again. She has been at home for the past two years. She slaps me on the back.

"We were worried, you guys are late, what took you so long? I got whitefish from my nets for you!"

"What does Puanets *mean*?" says Doug, the redheaded guy.

"It means 'projectile vomiting,'" says Graham. "And if you took all the patterns of the upchuck, it would make a story puke, or the face of Almighty Retch."

"Okay Graham," says Doris. "Enough puke jokes."

By the time we finish unloading, stars are beginning to come out in orderly progression. The lamps are lit all over the village. There is the dense, brilliant blue of Colemans and brassy yellows of coal oil. Herds of children are chasing each other around the tail of the airplane, clever and quick. I watch them. Two years ago I was uncomfortably close to a plane crash in this village, and the windshield popped out, and within minutes the kids had the windshield and were using it as a toboggan to slide down a snowbank. While people were still picking up wheels and smashed baggage.

"*Ahte awuss!*" yells Forever Seagull. "You kids get out of here, all of you. We're going."

Two little girls stand behind Doris, staring up at her.

"Are you a play person?"

"Yes," says Doris.

"Are you on the movies?"

"No."

The Twin revs up, snow-clouds erupt behind the props, and it jumbles off down the bumpy snowpack, into the dark. There will be a lighted runway at Sioux Lookout.

Jerry and Keith look as if they had been dragged through a knothole. I say, "Go with Sarah. They'll feed you at the Winnepetonga house."

"Eat what?" says Jerry. "Winnepetongas? I thought I'd eaten everything."

"Whitefish. Come on."

Graham says, "What about us wagon burners?"

"There, down the hill to the nursing station. You can put up in the nursing station. It's got oil heat and beds. Luxury." Somebody points him in the right direction, and the tall, dusky pines bend and sigh and make a deep, beautiful noise. Snowmobiles and their speary headlights are racketing all over town. A play, an entertainment, a celebration! The stage manager, Rick Gorrie, walks up with his arms full of things.

"Where's the community hall?"

"Follow those people."

In the log community hall, a world is under construction, a world of the imagination. The actors don't even wait to eat, the frozen hindquarter is left on the little emergency operating table down at the nursing station, they are bolting the sets together and hooking up lights. They set down their props right where they know to lay their hands on them, not one is out of place.

The play is about a little radio station in a northern village, where amusing things happen and everything turns out all right in the end. There are broad jokes and a fiddler and some square dancing. The sets the people of Muskrat Dam will be looking at are a reproduction of the small one-watt FM radio station they have here in their own village.

I sit in a corner of the hall and watch the actors go about their business. The Honda generator is outside in the snow, crashing with combustive, mechanical noises and flooding the hall with miraculous electrical light. Doris moves fast, laying out her props: the toilet seat, the missionary box, the five-by-seven-inch playing cards. Graham and Doug are having at the sets with wrenches and screwdrivers. The fiddler draws his fragile violin out of its case and gazes down on it as a mother gazes into her baby's eyes, riveted, fascinated.

I wonder why these people want work like this. This tour is a sort of endurance contest. The actors sleep anywhere, eat anything. For the natives the answer is that they want to act. They want to act so badly, and the task of becoming an actor is so difficult that they must endure living conditions and stress that would discourage people of less stamina. Graham has told amusing stories about playing Chinese characters, Hawaiians, Métis — anything but an Oneida. Doris has just begun. But this part at least is familiar to her; the wood stoves and water buckets, the grinding hard work.

"Hey guys, cards at me and Doug's place after the show," says Graham. "At the nursing station. We found *drugs*. We can play poker and get wrecked on Tylenol."

"What a fun evening," says Doris.

I pick up the oversized playing cards. Their stiff, armorial bearing is somehow comforting and familiar. They are like the characters of legends and fairy tales, the briefest sketch of personality types, a preliminary study of the humors, and then they are thrown into the world of action, fate, and chance. They are nothing if they are not in movement. This is how legends work, and fairy tales, and the *Bhagavad-Gita*.

"Puanets, give me those cards," says Doris. I hand them to her. She is slim, grave, focused. She places them behind the tin stove, stage left. "Calm down. People are going to like the show. Don't worry."

"BUT WHAT ABOUT THE CRITICS IN TORONTO??!!" shrieks Doug.

"I was thinking about making a little change in the script," I say. "Nothing major. To make it more serious."

Ellen Sands says, "Okay. Make my character skinny and rich."

"Nooooooooo," says Robert Lac Seul. "You change it all the time already."

I start scribbling on the script, holding it on my knee.

And this is where I will leave the play, in the little log community hall in Muskrat Dam, leave the actors placing their props in the right places, the sets in their proper relationship, Sarah looking for more gas for the generator, Keith and Jerry fallen forward onto their plates in sheer exhaustion, asleep in their fish. They fall still and enchanted, perhaps, and a thick forest of spruce and poplar grows up around them until the writer returns.

From now on, the book is a flashback beginning in 1973. It too is an artificial construct, as are all tales. But I will tell you there is a deep place in our minds where stories find a reception, a certain struck chord that produces image hypnosis. It is an enchanting and perilous gift. The backdrop for this story is the presence of the boreal forests of far northern Ontario, the country of the Cree and Ojibway, the Indian Nation, a place where the moon is called the sun of the night sky, in whose language stars are alive, stones are alive, and December is the Moon of Little Spirits. The musical score is made up of the hymns of peril and solace that the north sings to us, the last unbroken place in the world.

# 2.

Mid-November, 1973, two hundred miles northwest of Lake Superior, and it was already as cold as any cold I had experienced. They said it was only the beginning. It was, after all, only minus eighteen degrees Fahrenheit. The DC-3 was arriving out of the air, a boreal surprise, flinging up clouds of snow powder. I could see the pilots peering out of the slit eyes in the nose. I was going even farther north; to a village called North Spirit Rapids, a promising name.

I said, "That's a bush plane? It's as big as an oil tanker."

I was sitting on my bags with Nathan and Jeannie Nanokeesic and Elizabeth Peyton, and a charming youngish woman called Oldman Woman, an artist. She had come out to see us off. She was Elizabeth's friend. It was exhausting to meet all these new people. Watching the plane thunder at us in a storm of blown snow, I was nervous and thrilled and frightened.

A new snow had dusted all the spruce around the airstrip and now the sunlight was so bright that it was necessary to wear sunglasses.

Nathan said, "Have a doughnut. There's no inflight meals."

I said, "Thanks." The doughnuts were revoltingly sweet and frozen, and a raven sat up in a tree, watching us, first with one eye, then with the other eye, waiting for us to hurry onto the airplane and throw aside the doughnuts. It was the size of a turkey.

"How do you say airplane?"

Nathan got to his feet and grabbed his knapsack. "*Pimisewin.*" He shifted it up onto his back. "That actually means 'flight' in the abstract." He smiled, a big, amused smile. "Hurry. They won't stop long."

Oldman Woman had very long, wavy hair and a parka loaded with glossy fur. She waved to us.

"If you need something, Paulette, get hold of me. I'll send it up."

In every good tale there is adventure, in every adventure there is a conveyance of danger and magic, and here it came now. I watched, mesmerized, as the big World War II cargo plane sank down on the Sioux Lookout airstrip, its long head in the air and big doughnut tires galloping down the snowpacked strip. The DC-3 is a twin-engined aircraft, the kind the reader has seen in photographs flying the Berlin airlift, and more recently in a Ralph Lauren ad.

The large friendly pilots helped us load. Also going up as cargo were boxes and boxes of cheap FM transistor radios. There had never been any radio there before; now the villagers needed these FM things to catch the broadcasting like gill nets catch fish.

I thought I had brought all I needed to survive in a lonely cabin in the great north woods. I had a hurricane lamp, and scented kerosene, packages of caramels and *People of the Deer*, makeup and candles and an attractive tablecloth, pink cotton sheets, a mirror and matches and four or five blank notebooks. If I had been able to obtain a silver tea service and a twill ulster, I would have brought those too. We all have models on which we pattern ourselves, consciously or unconsciously. My models of choice had always been those intrepid Englishwomen who explored places in the world remote from themselves and their cultures, Lady Isabella Bird and Edith Durham, Freya Stark; ladies who stalked off into the Interior with hairpins and changes of sheets, cranky old maids with rare dictionaries and letters of credit. One could do worse. I was raised a southerner in the fifties, but Doris Day and Marilyn Monroe went right over my head.

We lifted off the Sioux Lookout airstrip like a rocket, tons of World War II metal vaulting into the blue boreal air shiny as a silver dollar, with both propellers spinning into sun-dogs, solar discs.

Elizabeth showed me where the seat belts were. The seats were webbing straps, and the seat belts were hard to tell from the seats.

I looked at my companions. I had just met them. They were wearing big northern parkas made of two layers. An inner layer of thick duffle wool, and an outer one of canvas or duck or something. Maybe Grenfell cloth. The hoods were roomy as shopping bags and rimmed with real fur. I had bought my parka in an Army surplus store. It felt like it was made of Saran Wrap, and the fake fur was the texture of a toilet brush.

I resolved to buy something authentic as soon as possible, and give this away to some needy person, or bury it.

I leaned over to Jeannie Nanokeesic and took some of the fur in my fingers.

"What is this?" I said.

She turned and looked at it too. She was alarmed.

"Did I spill something on myself?"

"I mean this fur."

"Oh. I don't know. *Wanjanagoosh*, maybe."

"Wanta-goose," I said. "What's a wanta-goose?"

Jeannie started to laugh. "Wan. Jan. A. Goosh. It's a fox."

The engines were earsplitting. There was no sound insulation.

I wrote *wanjanagoosh* in my notebook.

Out the window the Canadian Shield granites were tumbling into hills and distant blue cloud-shadows on the snowed-in forests. We were flying into the wilderness, beyond the rail lines and the highways and the mines and the timber cuttings. It was one of the last places on earth where the environment was undisturbed, was moving in its long, original cycles of weather and animal life and vegetation. Human beings had been here for thousands of years and had not left scars of their presence.

This is where I would live and animate the radio station, it would blossom into the native language, airborne voices in Cree, or Ojibway, whichever language it was. At the time I was not sure. Neither was my boss in the CBC. I would sit at night beside my roaring fire and write impressive letters to friends. I would eat roast duck, wearing a charming ensemble of parka and sealskin moccasins, toss the bones to my tame huskies, who would wag their tails and gaze at me with great, affectionate, yellow eyes. I would quickly learn whichever language it was, and wonderful new concepts concerning space and time would be revealed to me in the grammar. And if I couldn't grasp, really, these new, esoteric concepts of space and time, I could just say I did. Who was to know? Think of the advantages.

We were skimming through the upper air in a romantic-looking cargo plane, a red line running behind us across a superimposed map, like in the forties movies when a *Fairchild*, an *Anson*, a *China Clipper* sped across the continents to some far place, a place alien and seductive where the protagonist of the tale would be required to be resourceful and brave and clever. I always knew I was lucky about things like this.

"Now, listen," said Nathan.

Look, look, below us, obsidian glistenings where a river flowed into a lake, an unfrozen black gem of water!

"I have the feeling you're not listening to me."

"I am, I am!" I leaned over my seat toward him. The four of us were the only passengers and inside the cavernous interior of the DC-3 I felt like a BB in a boxcar.

"Life up here can be difficult. I suppose the CBC gave you some kind of orientation course."

"Not that I noticed. Maybe I was asleep or something."

Nathan Nanokeesic had a wonderfully expressive face. His eyes were black and round as coat buttons, he had a short, neat haircut and heavy eyebrows that went up and down. Jeannie was sitting beside me. They looked at each other. She was good-looking too, with a cascade of long, perfectly black hair and striking eyes. They were a handsome couple, and fluent in English, and helpful. I was glad they were friendly. North Spirit was their village; this strange land below us was their country.

"This is going to be like being parachuted into Outer Mongolia with chocolate bars and a phrase book," said Nathan. "The mail only comes in once a week. There's no telephone connection, only an HF."

"What's an HF?"

Jeannie stared at me for a beat.

She said, carefully, "High. Frequency. A radio-telephone. You hold up the microphone, speak into it. Say 'over.'" Jeannie had decided I was simple.

"Oh, what luck!" I said. "Just like a Somerset Maugham story. Did you ever read 'Rain?'"

Nathan said, "No, but this is nothing like it. I saw *North to Alaska* when I was out to college in Toronto. This is nothing like that, either."

"You know what, I looked all over for books about this part of the Canadian north before I came up, but I could hardly find anything. I got a Cree dictionary and an Ojibway dictionary. And then all I found was some anthropological tome about some shaking-tent magicians, or shamans, or conjurors, or whatever they call them."

He cleared his throat. "One way to understand people here is the legends. They're our literature."

"Okay. Where are some?"

"They're not written down. I'll tell them to you one of these days, if I can get a word in edgewise. In the meantime, you'd better find yourself a place to stay. There's a Department of the Environment weather station here. They have housing. Maybe you could get one in the single men's quarters."

"I want to move into a log cabin."

"There's a whole *section* of the village where white people live."

Jeannie said, in a strained, cheerful voice, "Yes! They have electricity and running water! You can find a room in one of *those* houses! Nice room! Hot water!"

Elizabeth Peyton said, in her English-Canadian, urban, gracious way, "I am afraid you'll find it hard. I'm living in a teacher's residence. You could stay with me temporarily. Me and my daughter."

"No," I said, stubbornly. Imagine Paulette Goddard, cheeky Métis maiden in *Canadian Wildfire*, ensconced among the ceramic ducks and gingham curtains! Formica! Tube-steel dining-room sets! Solitary confinement in Fort Appliance! "I can live in a cabin. I'm a country girl. I have plucked chickens with my bare hands."

Long pause.

"Well, I guess Mrs. Siannawap might be renting that place of hers below the hill."

Nathan looked as if he were about to bite himself in frustration.

"Good," I said. "Cutting wood can't be too hard." I looked out the frosted windows, down at the limitless forests of spruce and the rumpled, low hills. A great river was streaking the black forest with a vein of white. "What *burns*, exactly?"

Jeannie said, "In the summertime, nearly all of it burns."

Nathan said, "Never mind. Either you'll learn or you'll die."

What I never thought of at the time, of course, was how much effort it was going to take people like Nathan and Jeannie to keep me from freezing to death. The selfishness that is part and parcel of having glamorous adventures.

We came down quietly on the airstrip cut into the forest, at the far end of the village, the props threw up a snowstorm of white powder. It was like landing in an applause of snow.

The little cabin was in the main section of the village. There were evidently four parts, and the main part was around a bluff overlooking North Spirit Lake. My cabin was just down the hill, lined up with a lot of other little cabins at the edge of the lake.

It was made of logs about as big around as a one-pound coffee can, with small, paned windows. It was one big room with a tin stove in the middle. Stars would rise out of the forests' deep weaves, designs released into the night sky over my chimney. There was a stand of shelves, a counter against one wall, a shaky table and chair, and an iron bedstead. Just my speed. The sun would come up out of the spruce forest and set the world alight. It was like a movie set. *The Gold Rush.* I hadn't seen the radio station yet. First things first. First fire, then radio.

Nathan and Jeannie carried me and my baggage to the cabin on the sled behind their snowmobile. Dogs chased us. I hit them with my hurricane lamp, swinging it by the handle. The Nanokeesics left me with a stack of dry kindling, and a supply of green wood. I didn't know why there were two kinds of wood but assumed there was some logic to it. As for woodchopping, one simply applied a) ax to b) log and put the pieces in the stove and set fire to it.

"You begin with dry wood," said Jeannie. "First. Put in dry. Wood. I will come back first thing in the morning. Me, I will come back, okay? I'll bring hot water to thaw you out of your blankets."

Nevertheless.

Nevertheless, here I was, far from city lights, far from the roar of traffic and the imperative wails of sirens, the thunder of street-sweeping machines, far from urban manners and dispiriting little city apartments. I would sleep well. I would write poetry here, I would help start up the community volunteer radio station somehow, (no particular plans on exactly how) in the native language, do my bit for social justice in the world, and have adventures as well. Everybody in Toronto would be jealous. Especially my ex.

I placed my things around the shelves and on the plank counter. My mirror and books and a pottery dove from Mexico and a box of candles and the Ojibway Dictionary, written in 1875 and reprinted by Indian Affairs, Reverend Edward F. Wilson's *Dictionary of the Ojebway Tongue for Missionaries and Others Working Among the Ojebway Indians.* I was one of the Others. The Other Woman.

It was getting dark. People were walking by on evening errands, or charging past on snowmobiles that made snarling noises.

I went outside to apply a) ax to b) birch, and with my first blow the ax rebounded off the frozen green birch cylinder with a startlingly live sort of jump, as if the log section had been made of pressed tires. I hit it again. Half an hour later I was still out in front, beating on the log in earnest, and by this time everybody in the village of North Spirit Rapids, Kiiwatin Chebui according to Reverend Wilson, was sitting down to their supper. It was colder than anything I had ever experienced. A cold that pierced through everything I wore, especially the shrink-wrap parka and thin, city dress boots. I thought, why not take the log inside? It was still kind of warm in there.

In a manner of speaking it was warmer. My books were covered with frost. The sun was now gone, wouldn't be up for another sixteen hours. Not that it did any good; not that it had warmed anything.

Through the frosted windows I saw people walking down to the blue-white, snowpacked stretch of lake, and coming back with buckets of water. The lake was frozen thick enough to support airplanes, and there was a foot of snow on top of that; where were they getting the water? I left off hewing at the wood for a while and went outside and followed a path, a channel in the snow, to the shore, or where I thought the shore sort of was. With a foot or so of snow, I couldn't tell where the ground stopped and the lake started.

There I found a heap of snow mounded up and a long pole sticking out of it. I concluded the pole must be a marker of some sort. I pushed the snow aside and found a piece of cardboard. Weird. From the cabins all along the lake shore, the Spontaneously Created People gazed out at the newcomer, the idiot white woman messing about at Siannawap's water hole.

I asked myself, why are people heaping snow over a piece of cardboard and then marking it with a long pole? Beats me.

I supposed one hewed or chopped through the ice in some manner to get at the water, but was I standing over water? I'd look a damn fool whacking through snow to get to the dirt.

Kids passed by me, speaking in the Indian language, whichever one it was. It didn't matter, since I didn't speak it, but there was no doubt that people up here used the Indian language as a normal means of communication. Good thing I brought Reverend Wilson and that other Cree dictionary. Well, I guessed I had better stop staring at the children in their puffy-thick moccasins and beaded mitts, and pick up the cardboard and see what was under it.

A deep well in the ice. Black water suddenly splashed and gurgled, moved, as if somewhere out there in the fifty-mile stretch of North Spirit Lake, beneath the ice, something huge had turned over in the dark.

I looked down into the ice well and the water moved again. A star shone in the circle of dark water. The star moved too, quietly, wavering and silky in the deep dark. This was where people got their water of course. Now for the bucket.

When I came back with it, I realized the bucket was too big for the hole. I would have to have a dipper of some sort. Back to the cabin again. I scrambled around in my jumbled possessions and found the mug with Aries, my birth sign on it, in between the mirror and my makeup kit. It was nearly too dark to see. I lit a candle.

I went back out of the increasingly cold cabin and dipped up a bucket of cold, pure lake water. Can't get water like this in Toronto, I told myself. The Spontaneously Created People were sitting down to a warm, comfortable evening in their warm cabins.

Now to return to a) ax and b) birch. I went out and started hammering at it again, but once again the ax flew back up with such a powerful rebound that I began to think I would put my eye out, or be taken to the nursing station with a big square dent in my head the size of an ax butt.

I hit it with the grain, I hit it against the grain, I hit it on the sides and on the ends but it seemed merely to solidify it all the more, as if I were compacting it. I couldn't feel my feet. I took the wood inside to chop it.

That night everything came alive. I set the wood up on the floor and gave it a smash. The cabin had a springy, unsupported plywood floor and so the birch section leapt up in the air and sprang a couple of inches away. I hit it again and once again it jumped and bounded across the floor. I began to chase it around the cabin, bouncing and springing. Imagine trying to stab a watermelon while leaping about on a trampoline.

I finally trapped it in a corner and with a powerful overhead swing, knocked off a chip.

I laid the chip on five pieces of paper ripped out of a notebook and put this all in the stove and lit it. The paper burnt away and the chip came through the flames like Shadrach, Meshach, and Abednego. I burnt up an entire notebook, then went back to pursuing the birch. Then I had a drink of water.

Can't get water like this in Toronto. Then I unpacked all my blankets and my thin fashionable mountaineering sleeping bag with its ripstop nylon and made myself a bed that looked inviting except that it was so cold. I had broken my hurricane lamp on a dog's head, and so had to make do with candles.

I stuck all the dry kindling available in the stove along with half another notebook and lit that. It flamed up wonderfully and burnt away. It was ten at night. By this time my urban friends down in Toronto, lacking a sense of adventure, would be sitting in warm little city apartments having a drink. The same star that looked at me out of the water hole was looking through the window. Everything was alive.

I looked out my window. Next door the lamps were on and the chimney of my neighbors' log cabin poured out smoke, their windows glowed with light through a veil of frost. I was not going to give up and go to Nathan and Jeannie's house. Not tonight anyway. Tomorrow night.

By twelve midnight I had the birch section reduced to a kind of frazzled wood ball all decorated around with splinters. A tiny flame was wavering in the stove. I was never so tired in my life, or cold either. Everything inside the cabin glittered like an icy kaleidoscope and when I moved all the glitters followed me, sparkling. Everything was alive.

I put on my nightgown and my sweater and my cotton tights and two pairs of socks and my boots and parka and my woolen hat and mittens and I got underneath the covers. I would lie there until morning, and then the sun would come up, and then things would be better. Lots better. Somebody would rescue me. I'd apologize for the inconvenience and be humble. But first there was the matter of food.

It was like being pressed to death inside those blankets, *peine forte et dure.* My watch slowed down to infinitesimally slow time, as on the edge of a black hole where time slows down forever, and the space explorer pauses everlastingly at the end of her lifeline, drifting and unmoving and drifting.

At twelve-thirty I crawled out from under the blankets and lit all the candles I had; this seemed to keep the cabin at about minus twenty degrees Fahrenheit. Pretty soon it was quarter to one.

I couldn't bear to think of getting out from under the crushing weight of blankets again and rooting around in my boxes for some pancake mix or maybe some stone-hard cheese. Then to my great joy I discovered a caramel in my parka pocket. In order to get at it I had to push back the blankets, take off my mitten, and reach into the cold nylon, but I got it. Then I had to take off the other mitten to unwrap it.

All my friends in Toronto and all the Spontaneously Created People were asleep in their warm beds. The caramel was the consistency of flint. The silver paper glittered like frost and crackled. It was a delightful caramel. It was something to pass the time.

Time that had become glacial; geographical time. I had read that the beaches of Hudson Bay were rebounding by inches a year from the depressing glaciers, which seemed actually very fast. I mean it was positively speedy. I wasn't warm anywhere on my body. I supposed my guts were warm but they weren't doing my feet and hands any good.

Now a wind sprang up. The plastic tacked to the windward side of the logs on the exterior of the cabin rattled. The place was beginning to resemble a meat locker, a Siberian grave site with log tombs from 500 B.C. The alive water and the alive birch and the alive, gravid walls cracked and spoke in the wind. It was as if something were standing outside the walls of the cabin talking in low, sinister tones. As if It had walked a long way across North Spirit Lake, across the drifting, perfect, grainless snows of the lake and had some terrible message.

And really, something was making a nervy little sound outside the door. I listened with frozen white ears and I realized it was a meant sound. Nothing to do but open the door and offer it a caramel.

I shoved the plywood door open. Outside sat a puppy. A lifesaver, a bundle of canine warmth, a little package of something like 98.6 degrees. He was the color of a biscuit with black points, a ball of fuzz.

I said, "Hi, dog."

The husky pup whined and thrashed around; eager, appealing.

I said, "I could cook you, I guess, if I had a fire."

He said he didn't want to be cooked.

I said, "I bet you were one of those dogs that chased me on the sled all the way from the airstrip. You have an apparent hurricane-lamp dent in your head."

He never chased a sled in his entire life. Never.

I said, "I could take you under the covers and then we'd both be warm."

He thought that might be alright. The whole village was stark and unlit under the remote cosmic fires of the stars. I bent down and picked him up, and so spent my first night in a romantic cabin in the great north woods sleeping with a puppy, eating stray caramels.

So I fell asleep and dreamed. I was the heroine of a great dream. It was me and Amelia Earhart. We were flying a race across the Pole. Frost armoured my wings. Below me the last great forests of the earth shook out their raw silks in hunter green. Amelia was at my starboard side in some kind of plane, one of those old airplanes with the engines that look like cartridge belts, and she was catching me up. I was pushing my little *Spirit of St. Louis* for all it was worth. We were racing to St. Petersburg. Down there was a city of ice, and all the bureaucrats were frozen to their ledgers. I looked out my starboard window, and in her bright airplane Amelia raised her fair hand. She smiled and saluted and said, Fly on. Then she peeled off and down, with her courage streaming behind her like a flag, and I flew out of my dream alone.

Sometime before sunrise the elderly woman who lived next door walked into the cabin and sat down on one of the two rickety chairs. Later somebody told me that this woman and her grandson had sat up half the night, worried, watching for smoke from my chimney, which occasionally appeared.

"*Bojo!*" she said. It was a cheerful greeting, so I said "*Bojo!*" in turn.

She was dressed in a bright cotton skirt, and down jacket, a scarf, and layers of heavy cotton stockings under high-top moccasins.

I was lying in a pile of blankets in every piece of clothing I owned, with dirty charcoaled hands and chips scattered all over the floor, the water bucket frozen solid, clutching a stray pup. She sat there and looked at everything. She looked at all the details.

Then she said, "Tea?"

Tea? I could manage tea if I had some water.

Mrs. Mindemoya picked up my ax and jammed straight down on the water bucket. Water and ice flew up. I opened the Carnation condensed milk can all the way around the top, and chipped out frozen milk. Mrs. Mindemoya and I sat and smiled at each other and had a cup of tea.

Jeannie Nanokeesic came through the door as if propelled, stopped and looked around; her long hair was flying out over the *wanjanagoosh* trim of her parka hood.

"Ha," she said. She lit a cigarette. "You've been rescued by my great-aunt. I thought you'd be frozen. You. Here. Frozen."

"Not at all!" I said. "My neighbor and I were just having a cup of tea. Join us."

She looked around at the disastrous condition of the cabin. It looked as if wild hogs had been running loose in it all night, playing floor hockey with caramels.

She started to laugh.

"Okay, I'll have a cup of tea."

She sat down with it and picked out a bit of wood splinter, smoked her cigarette, and laughed some more.

"My mother-in-law was at my door at six this morning, telling me to get over here, that white woman is going to be dead in her blankets." She drank her tea. "You'll learn. I guess. You. Learn how. Soon."

And for the rest of the time in North Spirit Rapids, the elder Mrs. Mindemoya and I would have tea together nearly every morning. She pointed things out to me, said the word in Anishinabe-mo, I repeated the word after her.

A language that for all of its time had been unaltered by print sang around the cabin every morning; this is a dipper, this pole is an ice chisel, the word for water in the lake is different from the word for water in a bucket. This is the word for fire, and this the verb for *make a fire*. This is the word for friendship, and this for duty, and this for ignorance, and this for helping. I am bringing you a hot bannock, you will lend me your needle. This is a village of people and these the great, fixed stars that have something to do with a story so long, so complex, that only the very oldest people remember.

So, like a baby, I began to learn to walk and talk.

In the dark winter evenings, my cabin started to fill up with visitors. Nathan would say, "Now I am going to tell you a legend."

Then we were silent, attentive, and the stories unreeled themselves.

And the next morning I could say to Mrs. Mindemoya, *Kahyana*, and *Wimshoosh*, and *Wabusheshe*. The elderly woman nodded and smiled. That's correct, that's who inhabits this country.

So I began to learn to conduct myself as a Spontaneously Created Person, or at least as the guest of such people, and the great legend-cycles became real and walked through the winter with me. Everything was alive.

# 3.

The village was strung out into four parts. The main village on the hill and bluff, overlooking the lake was called Agamatin, Up on the Hill. There was another part along the bend of the rapids called Chebui Nayaushe, Ghost Point, and a third one strung out along the Severn River that I heard referred to as the River People, as in "she lives down there with the River People." The fourth area was below the Hill.

All parts of the village were connected by trails and paths, paths that wound in and out among the low hills, confusing, complicated short-cuts that bent a determined, bullheaded way into low ground. I carefully, cautiously, learned my way around the trails. What if I got off into the woods and froze? The temperature was dropping to forty below.

On Nathan's advice, I went to see the chief to introduce myself, as soon as I thawed myself the next morning at the radio station.

The band office (the office of the North Spirit band of Indian people) looked out into the clear air from the bluff, out over the lake. I clumped up the steps in my city boots, rather the worse for wear.

The chief sat in a tube-steel chair, looking at several topographical maps that were tacked to the wall. He smoked a large cigar. He was a tall, weathered-dark man with a hawk face and attentive eyes. Chief Joseph Makepeace.

There was a young man peeling the wrapper from a Kit-Kat bar. He had long hair and a bomber jacket.

I said, "Would you translate for me?"

Everybody wore their parkas and heavy high-topped moccasins stuffed with woolen socks. The fire in the wood stove thudded and sucked air.

"Yes. What do you want to say?"

I felt as if I were expected to make an important speech about the radio station, and how vital it was. But I suddenly felt very unimportant. Chief Makepeace was a man who had lived a long and challenging life. He regarded me with great calm.

I said, "Oh, nothing much."

The young man translated this with unexpected vigor. They both burst out laughing.

I said, "Wait, please say that I am happy to be here as your guest, and I'll try to do a good job at the radio station."

The chief listened, and nodded, and said something in return.

The young man said, "He says if you need anything, come to me."

And so I thanked him, and shook hands.

I decided not to scream for help until I was totally desperate.

The paths seemed to draw me along in my inadequate city dress boots, so fashionably formfitting that I could only get one pair of socks under them.

I found myself following them, and then appearing in unexpected places. A snowslide on the bluff, a chute of rocketing, screaming children on sleds and pieces of cardboard. At a clearing, with two small cabins and a tipi made of birch poles and orange plastic tarp; smoke billowed out of the tipi, and the smell of barbecueing meat.

I found myself at an empty community hall on the river, its front wall plastered with health notices and a church announcement about a collection for the starving children of Biafra.

I stumbled onto a tiny Pentecostal church with people singing in Ojibway inside, in the dim, late afternoon.

Tiny paths around the cabins, under the clotheslines, behind the woodpiles, were bright with child-laughter, stick tipis, play villages.

On the clotted topknots of the spruce, ravens sat and gazed down at the village, and at the dog-paths trotting importantly from a garbage can to a back door. The ravens had their own paths in the air. I stood under a tall spruce and looked up at two of them, curious. They looked down and said *bonk*. I always thought ravens said *kaw*. But they have a calm, reflective sound, *bonk*. They shake out their hard metallic feathers until there is a spiky ruff around their necks, and sing their bell-song.

They also look down at you with one eye, and then the other eye, and they say *yum.*

*First you stumble, then you freeze, then you are ours.*

The River People lived alongside the river. The Under the Hill People lived beside me. Ghost Point was to the west of the village. The white people lived at Agamatin, Up on the Hill.

The white people got their food from the Hudson's Bay Store, and from the weekly landing of the one scheduled airplane, and from other little airplanes that came and went. Some of the airplanes landed on skiis on a bay in front of the Blackhawk Store, and others landed half a mile from the village on the one stretch of flat ground. The airstrip could take airplanes on wheels. There they could land year around.

I walked around the village, trying to memorize the paths. They were confusing. There was a store called a Free Trader's Store on a bay. Blackhawk Store.

Nathan said, "Little planes land in front of the Blackhawk Store there on the bay. They land on skis. In the summertime, they land on pontoons."

"What's a pontoon?"

He smiled. My ignorance amused him. "A pontoon is a kind of giant shoe, a big silver rubber boot, that floats."

"Cool. Why are there little planes? Where do they go?"

"Out to trap lines, long distances away. They go visiting to the other villages."

"What other villages?"

"Long Dog, Summer Beaver, Ponask, Weagamow, Fort Hope, Lansdown House, Webequie, Caribou Lake, Fort Severn, Sachigo, Kasabonika, Muskrat Dam, East End, McDowell, Angling Lake, Wunnamin Lake, Sandy Lake, and Big Trout Lake. We're between Big Trout and Sandy."

"Jesus. All those? They aren't even on the map."

Nathan laughed and patted me on the head.

"Maybe it's a good thing. Don't worry about it."

The Anishinabek people got much of their food from the land. They came and went out of all four sections of the village on snowmobiles. They did their shopping out in the wilderness, out in Anishinabe-Aski,

they went out onto trails that led in all directions, spewing rooster-tails
of snow powder, pulling sleds behind them loaded with snowshoes, tied-
down boxes of canned goods and tea and sugar and milk, burlap bags
full of traps, laid alongside shovels and ice chisels and a folded canvas
tent. They went out with their mufflers and mitt-fringes flying, and they
came back with the boxes empty and a new load of whole caribou,
pieces of moose, frozen wads of fur that turned out to be martin, mink,
fisher, otter, beaver. These they turned into cash and they bought more
canned goods and went out again.

"What's that?" I asked a man. I pointed to a wad of fur.

He said, "You say, *Ohwehnin oohweh,* 'What is that?'"

So I did, after a fashion.

"Marten," he said. "*Ojig.*"

The Hill was the central place, the shopping place, the place of the
office of the chief, and the Anglican church building, and the day
school, and the teacher's residences, and the little building that housed
the devices and recording machines of the Upper Air Station. They
were a little station of ten men, two of them with families, enduring a
hardship post in a remote northern Indian village. Every morning
while I had a cup of hot tea with Mrs. Mindemoya, two men in
Department of the Environment parkas went out and released a weather balloon into the frigid air; it was long and draggy, with a bulging
head and an immense tail. As it rose up into the clear sky it developed
frost on its head, and the comet-like tail wandered out sideways, and
somehow it broadcast information to the men in the weather-station
building. Then everybody in Canada would know what the weather was
like up here in North Spirit Rapids.

On the Hill, the Canadian flag, with its red bars and red maple leaf,
flew from the Weather Station. The Hudson's Bay Company flew its
quartered flag with the red cross, stags, and beaver. The Anglican
church flew its flag, too: purple, with the Union Jack ensign. It was all
trim and proper on the Hill, very Royal Canadian Mounted Police, very
English-Canadian. The flags snapped and cracked in the wind, showing
their colors out over the vast whiteness of North Spirit Lake, the fields
of light and blazing snow, the distant rolling hills packed with the black-
green aggregate of spruce forests.

The rest of the village was log cabins, the Indian language, dances in log community halls, conversations between elders deep into the night by firelight.

But I wasn't in the village to make observations on culture or language. The day was brief and white, the sun rose on the southern horizon for a few hours and then left us for the dark reaches, one got up in the dark and the day flew past in a brief flash. I put my feet into wool socks and then the absurdly dressy boots, so that my legs suck up out of them like sticks. Then the parka. Thus attired, I made fire. Later I would package myself in a weighty bulk that would keep me earthbound in all the light-storms of winter brilliance, and appear at the radio station. My job.

The radio station was a three-room building. It had a studio room with an eight-pot console, two Revox reel-to-reel tape recorders, two mikes and two turntables. Outside the windows, children trudged up the Hill to school and people went past on snowmobiles with loads of wood.

The transmitter stood in the other room. It was an old one, the size of a refrigerator. It had two tubes in it. You turned it on, and when the tubes started glowing, you were ready to broadcast. Elizabeth Peyton told me they had tried to bring all of the equipment up in one shot on a Beechcraft, but they couldn't get the transmitter in the cargo door. So they hired a DC-3 cargo plane.

The young volunteers went in every morning and turned on the transmitter, and then the mikes, and began to broadcast. The one-watt FM transmitter sent out invisible airwaves, paths with words on them, for a mile radius, to all four sections of North Spirit.

They told jokes and stories, read announcements, played country-and-western music. They went home at noon to cut wood for their wives and mothers. They came back, eating sandwiches, and turned the mikes on again.

"Nancy Fiddler, come home. Your mother wants you. Tell your husband she wants to borrow the ax. Be careful of the ice. Come the way you came yesterday."

I came in every morning and wrote notes on the programs that were being offered by the volunteers. The volunteers were Bruce Sakakeep, who was short, with a very round face, a face that was always alight with a smile, a young man who found nearly everything funny. His rapid comments in Ojibway made the others fall about laughing. The tall guy was Eno Chapman, a studious young man with a pair of dreadnaught eyeglasses in thick black frames and a Prince Valiant haircut; he was thin and scholarly. At night he read thick tomes on history in English. George Nothing (an odd name, yes, but when the white men wrote down family names on the Treaty rolls, god alone knew how badly they translated the Anishinabek names) was terribly shy, until he got on the microphone.

I wondered how to expand the programs and get more volunteers. I made sure the air-check tape was running. I sat close to the oil stove and listened to the broadcasters speak in Ojibway.

Frost grew in thick crystals on the windows and, when the door opened, people walked into the little station in a cloud of steam, frigid outside air billowing around them. I was beginning to appreciate heat as a sort of *thing*. A *stuff*. I needed something to keep my feet warm. Charlie Morris, a volunteer member of the board of directors for the station, brought me a pair of high-top moccasins.

"My wife said you should borrow these. Be careful with them, though, she wants them back."

There was no pavement to abrade the soft caribou hide, or asphalt to grind it down, just deep, soft snow on which one padded, slogged, and which one fell into if one got off the path. The moccasins were wonderful, they were perfectly warm. I felt I had made an important stride ahead in northern living. I would struggle home from the radio station in blizzard-level winds, thinking of a nice supper of Spork and white bread and a boiled neck bone of moose (Yum! What an appetite I had! I could have eaten my husky pup, Animoosh, who was hoping against hope to be able to get in bed with me again, or at least get part of the moose neck bone). At night I struck fire out of the stubborn marble-like green birch cylinders with a light ax.

I went here and there with my notebook in my pocket. I wrote down, marten; *ojig*.

Jeannie met me on the path from my little cabin to the radio station. We were among spruce trees; spruce; *shingoob*.

I said, "If spruce is a *shingoob,* then what's a pine?"

Jeannie said, "*Shing-wauk.* When are you going to get more volunteers for the radio station?"

I said, "Gosh, I guess when they come in. We have some already."

"There's only three. And then the nurses come on and talk about the Four Food Groups in English. Then a pilot comes on and talks about how you should belt up when they take off and land — in English."

"The Four Food Groups!" I said. "What are they?"

"Moose, moose, fish, and pie."

"Do we need more?"

"Food groups?"

"Volunteers."

"Yes! This is an Indian radio station. That's why CBC put it in here. Go around, knock on doors. Tell people to come on and volunteer an hour."

"Well, I don't want to be pushy."

I was sure this was an impolite thing to do. I had observed the reticence and grace with which people treated one another. I didn't want to be a white oppressor. The Hudson's Bay Company was popularly known among young hip white folks in the cities to be an oppressor of native people, which had been ripping them off in the fur trade for three hundred years. Besides, I was having a better time writing things down. Oppress; *o-mudjje dodoowan.*

Jeannie said, "People are wondering why you're here. They keeping asking me, 'What is that white woman doing here?'"

I said, "Well, I guess I better, then." I paused. "Where do I get some moccasins made? Charlie Morris' wife lent me these. She's going to want them back."

"I don't know. Go around and look at the cabins, see who's got a fresh hide outside. Somebody will make you some." She smiled grimly, tossed her long, straight, blue-black hair out of the way and said, slowly, "Now. It is a good thing to get more volunteers. Good. Thing. You go around." She made a knocking motion. "Knock on doors. Or don't knock on doors. Indian people don't knock. Walk in. Say '*Bojo! Bojo!*'" Jeannie put her mitts around her mouth as if she were hollering. "Ask people."

"Maybe I can ask in Ojibway. I already learned the word for marten. *Ojig.*"

"No, no, no. A marten is a *wabusheshe.* Somebody just got mixed up about the English. An *ojig* is a fisher. Go. Go and ask people."

I met another person: Sarah Winnepetonga. She was tall and red-cheeked, with short, very black hair cut straight around and a pale skin.

Sarah was an open, enthusiastic person, cheerful and friendly. She was involved in some sort of project in the village, I wasn't sure what.

I said, "Could you help me go around and ask people to volunteer?"

"You'll never learn to meet people until you go by yourself. That's what I did when I went out to college. It was awful. People have to suffer to learn."

"Okay. But first, do you know where I can get a pair of moccasins?"

"Go see Elsie Half-A-Day. She lives down near the Pentecostal church. She's got an orange-tarp, smoking tipi. Maybe she'll make you some." Sarah whacked me on the back. "Good luck!"

Nathan saw me sitting in the radio station ante-room, in front of the oil stove, smoking and listening to one of the two volunteers broadcast in Ojibway. The short one.

He said, "Go quick, go see my sister Elsie Half-A-Day. She lives in Chebui Nayaushe. She's got a new moose hide, and I expect she'll make you a pair of moccasins."

When you find yourself in another culture, each contact with another human being is freighted with the unpredictable. One did not shop for boots in North Spirit. The first step was to discover a moose or caribou hide outside somebody's cabin. I found the path to Mrs. Nanokeesic's and the Half-A-Day house near the little Pentecostal church. I walked up to it uneasily, as if I were about to ambush and carry away the footgear instead of purchase it.

One of the cabins had a big moose hide stretched on a frame, and a woman who sort of looked like Nathan ripping the hair off it with a dull ax blade. Quilts made of bright squares hung on a clothesline, airing, and around the cabin were the tools of northern life. Axes, bucksaws, woodpiles, gas cans, stacks of burned-over logs, the smoking tipi made of orange plastic tarp, gill nets strung up to dry, empty ammunition boxes, several beaver hides on willow hoops, a marten on a form. These houses were not for the display of wealth; they meant business. Unless energy and a tall woodpile and stiff furs were wealth. Which it was.

Nathan's sister wore a bright head scarf, a down jacket and layers of brilliantly flowered calico skirts.

I said, "*Bojo.*"

The woman burst out laughing. She quieted down, then smiled, and said, "*Bojo.*"

A baby toddled out of the door with a can of Carnation milk in its hand, teetering, then poured the milk out onto the steps. A dog walked up and began drinking up the milk.

I said my first sentence in Ojibway: "*Animoosh miini-kweynaun jujusha-pu!*" The dog is drinking milk.

She said, "Yes, yes! The dog drinks the milk!" and laughed again. I wasn't sure what to do. Was I being funny? Did people laugh when they were embarrassed? Nothing to do but plunge on.

Nathan's sister said, "*Kin't'anishinabemo.*" You speak Ojibway, or, you speak as the Spontaneously Created People speak.

She laid down her ax head and went in the house. I followed her, happy and pleased with myself. An elder woman was inside, sitting by the window and doing beadwork on a piece of hide. This was Nathan's mother, Jemimah. She was working on squares of caribou skin devolving into the shape of feet. The hide was tanned a pale brown, the color of people. The woman's face was handsome, old, accomplished. She had been carved fine by experience and work, she was valuable and hard. The fire in the wood stove was a small domestic engine, radiant. It looked as if she were making people from the feet up, the Elder Woman of the World, stitching.

She looked up and said, "*Kin.*" You. "Ester *Mindemoya.*" My neighbor, Mrs. Mindemoya. "*Kiijikwae.*" Your friend, your neighbor.

I said, "Eyha." Yes.

I handed her a traced outline of my foot and, flushed with success, said, "Me want moccasin for little footsie."

The mother and daughter burst into startled laughter.

"Little footsie!"

"What is your name?"

"Paulette."

"Puan-ets."

"*Kawin.* Paul-ette."

"I understand. Puan-ets," said Elsie and this made them laugh all the more.

I left for home with a big wheel of new, hot bannock, and the promise of moccasins within a few days. Life looked much better; all you had to do to get along in a new culture was to endure your own ignorance, say stupid things, flush with misery and embarrassment and then rebound, stay cheerful, keep trying.

Jeannie walked into my cabin for a cup of tea and cried out, "Little footsie!"

I realized I was becoming the village idiot.

# 4.

Nathan chewed gum and drank a Coke and watched me write things down from my busted armchair in the radio station. They were using the Canadian flag for a curtain and the sun streamed through the bright red maple leaf. There was a picture of the prime minister over the console.

"How's the wood?" Nathan said.

"I'm murdering a log a night," I said. "I'm getting through."

"You got guts, I'll say that."

I said, "Hey, I'm a country girl." I was sort of lying. But my grandparents did have a wood stove. I used to carry wood *in,* at any rate.

Fire has its own technical devices, wood has its ways of resisting combustion. There was no skipping Step One. My cheap, cracked sheetmetal stove, which had been left in the cabin, was a frail shield against the cold. It was not airtight. Neither was the cabin. Snow must be kicked away from the door. Dry wood must be split into kindling, kindling from the size of matchsticks up to pieces the size of slim books of poetry, halved. Then larger pieces of dry wood, and only then the forbidding, metallic half-cylinders of green birch.

I was too anxious for the cabin to be warm. I was in a hurry to get up from the cold floor, where one had to kneel in front of the wood stove, the Goddess of Combustion; Agni, the Queen of Sheet Metal. The fire must be started and then fed. Fed slivers of dry wood, paper, cardboard. Then when it was burning enough to draw air, more dry wood added in increasing size. Soon it would make sucking noises at the grate, it began to breathe on its own, and I could sit back and see the processes of fire, its colors changing from orange-red to paler reds and blues. Jeannie could make a fire in her sleep, but I had to develop a deliberate patience. It is something our grandparents knew, great-grandparents. The lost art of domestic arson.

# 5.

Do you recall the scene in *The Gold Rush* where Charlie Chaplin is running in and out of the cabin, fleeing the clutches of Big Joe, the Engine of Destruction? Looking out my cabin window one evening I saw this sort of exercise or sport going on next door.

Evening was hard to tell from night, as they were both perfectly dark, but let us say evening was five o'clock by watch time. It was the other cabin, not Mrs. Mindemoya's place. It was the Wakwans' cabin.

The young man of the family was either drunk or had been sniffing gas or was having a bout of insane rage. I saw him run out the front door and holler things at the village. Then he ran back in and a young woman ran out. She hesitated, dancing up and down in anxiety in her black jacket and jeans, and then ran back in.

Then, out the back door, came Mrs. Wakwan in a hurry. She took up the ax and hurled it straight down into a snowbank. She did the same thing with the bucksaw. Then she covered them over and ran back in.

Whatever was going on, I didn't think the uproar would move into my cabin. Besides, I was busy with the grammar. I had obtained a sled-load of dry wood from Mrs. Mindemoya's son, Billy, and had banked the wood stove full of it, then set it afire with lighter fluid. I nearly blew myself up. But it was roaring. On top of this conflagration I had laid two split pieces of green birch. It was a going thing. I had a nice supper of Spork, Elsie's gift of fresh bannock, Coke, and canned peaches.

Reverend Wilson's *Dictionary of the Ojebway Tongue for Missionaries and Others Employed Among the Ojebway Indians* absorbed most of my nights. I guessed I was one of the Others so employed. But the good Reverend could never have imagined that there would someday be a Canadian crown corporation called the Canadian Broadcasting Corporation, or that it would establish an Office of Community Radio or a Northern Service and decide to expand services to even the most remote villages of Canada, or that in order to expand its service to the native peoples it would offer to set up community-run radio stations in the native language. Or that the CBC would have the audacity to send me, a southerner and a poet, to help one of these stations begin its life. *Shawan,* south. Shawnee? Were the Shawnee the "southerners"? Hmmm.

Reverend Wilson gave example sentences in every section; you were supposed to try and translate them, and then turn the page to see if you got it right.

"The second third person is not required of the active voice of the transitive verb animate, its place being supplied by the second third person singular of the passive voice, the order of the sentence becoming inverted. Thus, an Indian person never says, 'His father sees him,' but, 'He is seen by his father.'"

Well, I was glad to hear it. I was still at the "Him little dog drink-it milk" level, and was unprepared for two third persons, one of which I realized must be a fourth person.

The example sentences were doughty and full of rectitude.

*I did not see you at church last Sunday.*

*No, I did not go. I went to visit a friend at the Bay.*

What Bay was he talking about? Where? Where was this book written? When?

I puzzled over clues in the dictionary section. The coal-oil lamp shone yellow on the pages; from the roof dropped pieces of moss, melting out of its frozen state. The moss looked like curly buffalo hair.

There were no words for electric things, or highways or cars. There was a word for railroad train, "fire-sled," and a word for donkey. The donkeys were in the dictionary because they were in the Bible, and the minister must, simply must, tell the people how Jesus, Joseph, and Mary got to Egypt, and it wasn't on a fire-sled.

*But Sunday is not a day for visiting, it is God's day.*

*Piss up a rope, all of you!*

Teddy Wakwan had run out the back door and was now wildly declaiming at the entire village. His long hair flew around and he shook his fists. His eyes looked wild and mismatched. He was dressed only in a jean jacket and jeans. He would get cold pretty soon but in the meantime he was telling everybody to take a hike.

Indeed, he ran back into the house. Where are the guns? Here came Lila Wakwan running out the back door and this time she threw a rifle down into the snow and kicked more snow over it. There were the guns, or gun, *pashkeshigun*. The *gun* suffix applied to nouns having common daily handling. *Washtenigun*, lamp, *bakweshigun*, bread, kneaded.

I was learning how to speak; a language that had never been truncated by the shearing action of electronic media, or print in all its excesses, a language that had not been cut loose from its speaking, a language that invited poets and storytellers, and it was as thrilling to me as if I were an astronomer and something wildly new had opened up its remote icy blossom in my telescope. I would never again have this opportunity, I told myself. The radio station was doing perfectly well, I told myself. It would do even better if I could speak as well as, say, a two-year-old. The one-man riot next door sank into starry quietude.

A raven sat on the spruce above their house and said, *bonk*.

The nature of nouns; of things, objects. People always teach you the names of *things* when you are first learning another language out of school. This is a this, that is a that. Verbs are more difficult. *Things* are easily pointed to. Actions require frantic charades.

The Indo-European languages divided nouns into two great classes: feminine and masculine. English lost its grammatical gender in the Middle Ages, but grammatical gender remains in most of the Germanic, Slavic, and Romance language families.

Ojibway, in contrast, divides its nouns into *alive* things and *not-alive* things, animate and inanimate, and upon this distinction much of the grammar was formed. There were animate plurals and inanimate plurals. It would seem odd to us to speak of the parts of the body as inanimate; but they were. Mere appendages of the spirit, the workhorses that pushed the self on its way through snow and cold or into summer lakes. Fire was inanimate and spoken of with inanimate suffixes to the verb. Charcoal, ruined timbers, and charred foods were also inanimate.

But the animated things! The most marvelous things were alive.

Stars were alive.

Stones were alive.

Imagine.

Handkerchiefs were alive, and smoking pipes and corn and cakes and bread and money. Canoe ribs were alive, and a plank of wood, and trees in general were spoken of as personages. When the speaker told of seeing — *wabaun* — an inanimate thing, one verb ending was used; *ni wabundaun mukuk*; I see a box. If an animate thing was seen, the verb ending must change. *Ni wabumauh anak*; I see a star-personage.

Stars, stones, canoes, lamps, coins. All these things must be spoken of as Beings, as alive things. Their plurals were different from the plurals for dead things and their presence animated an entire sentence, for then the verb endings must change to accommodate their liveliness. It was an animated universe where, as in some magical film, like *Beauty and the Beast*, inanimate objects sprang up, took on life, sang and danced and spoke and made things happen. Some things became sinister; like ravens, they looked at you with one eye, and then the other eye. The bare, scored poplar trees outside were spoken of as beings, and so was a kettle with its dumpy legs and endlessly open mouth.

Verbs were enormous, charged and complex. Whole sentences could be made of one verb. The verbs needed prefixes to alert the hearer to the period of time, and the skills and abilities of speakers and spoken-to-ones. *Ki-nita-gepashin*; you are a skilled swimmer. Then the verbs could be shaded with plaintive, derogatory, and dubatative suffixes.

In one single verb, I could speak to the alive stars in a compassionate manner, or I could address the animate, lively teakettle in the dubatative voice, confiding that, although I was repeating what I had heard about Teddy Wakwan, I could not verify it as truth. I could talk quietly to the alive stone of the Canadian Shield in the derogatory, making light of my troubles.

The verb for "speak" took up half a page in the dictionary.

Kettles and stars and feathers and pipes and canoe-ribs and corn and bread came alive in Ojibway, and the verbs were the great, complex engines of the sentence, and the number of possible suffixes to the transitive verb, as it arrowed toward an animate thing-being, were endless.

When I opened the door to get more wood, my puppy rammed himself through the doorway and settled himself under the table. I let him stay. He kept my feet warm. I got into my sleeping bag and fell asleep with the Reverend, under the alive stars.

The next day Teddy Wakwan came to the radio station and rather shamefacedly sat down in one of the busted, donated tube-steel armchairs. He sat there and sat there. The two or three young volunteer broadcasters bustled around. They were teenagers with good English, kids returned from high school down south. They wore big bush boots, padded vests, jeans, parkas. They were delighted with this new thing, the community radio station. They set up shelves with donated records, kept logs, drew things on the walls with felt pens. NORTH SPIRIT RADIO LIVES, and so on. Bruce and Eno and Mike and George.

One of the volunteers, the tall one, said, "He wants to volunteer."

I said, "Great! I'll show him how to use the console." I looked over at the Engine of Destruction. He hid behind a tent of hair, a veritable lodge of hair, and fixed his eyes on the floor.

"No, it's okay. We'll show him. We know how."

The other volunteer, the short one, said, "He hardly speaks any English."

They were looking out for him. Maybe they'd convinced him to come to the station. Teddy's long, long hair fell in waterfalls around his face. Outside, snow was descending. It had warmed up enough to snow.

"He has a false eye. Is that okay?"

"No problem," I said. I glanced over, and then didn't glance over, at Teddy Wakwan. "A false eye? Like, glass?"

"Yeah. He lost an eye woodchopping one time. After that, he was sad."

I said, "Do you think being a volunteer broadcaster would make him happier?"

"You bet!" cried the tall and the short radio guys.

Teddy Wakwan sat down in front of the strange, complex console with its switches and mikes and dials. His eyes, both the real one and the glass one, lit up. The glass eye was animate, an animate noun, and must be spoken of as a living thing. He reached out a hard, scarred young hand toward the console, that live electrical complexity of the voice business, and carefully, tentatively turned the volume up on the monitor.

"*Ahi*," said the short one. "I do it. Watch me."

Teddy found himself banked in between the tall and short radio guys, and in half an hour, he bent toward a mike and said in Ojibway, in a terrified, low, shy voice that was only one millionth of a decibel above a whisper, "Good day, good day, Indian people, I am Teddy Wakwan broadcasting here in North Spirit Rapids and I'm going to play 'Put Another Log on The Fire' that is for our white-woman helper here, ha."

After that, he was always there.

Stones are alive.

# 6.

And so, beyond the world of electronic voices and imagery, appears the storyteller. Our perilous, dangerous gift of image hypnosis takes us into strange territory, on foot, and the storyteller is the guide. You surrender your right to argue, debate, object, demand evidence, ask for repetition, clarification. The storyteller is your guide, just ahead, appearing and disappearing in the veils of snow.

The storyteller is a person, a voice who has come from afar, and usually on foot. He or she has eaten strange foods, has been shipwrecked, has fought in wars, learned exotic languages, slipped out of walled cities in the dead of night. She has bribed her way past the guards, chipped through the stones of a cell, stood by the water well waiting for a messenger with vital intelligence.

The storyteller is one who has stayed home, fallen in love, made a fool of himself in public, lost a crop through impatience and a child in the hours of the dread night, he has helped to sandbag the levees in the spring floods, has been arrogant and selfish, generous and brave, married the princess and sold the cow for a handful of beans.

The storyteller speaks out of the unadministrated world of the mind, where great forces grind against one another like tectonic plates. The storyteller speaks out of the forces of the blue planet.

# 7.

Guests come in the cabin door. They enter like stage devils, surrounded by a cloud of fog. They take off their glasses and wipe them, place each fur-trimmed mitt in turn under the armpit of the opposite arm, and then draw their hands out, making it look as if they have small furry animals trapped under each armpit.

They pull up a chair or an overturned water bucket and unzip both layers of parka, light a cigarette, reach for a mug of tea.

The houses of the village sit half-buried in snow, hard and blue in the clear starlight. Beyond the village, the relentless, thick, short forest of spruce flows over the hills, crowding tight around the village, around the fifty-mile open stretch of North Spirit Lake. In the west, Arcturus is going down in a flash of stellar wreckage. The snow shifts, its top layer rushing through the village in a faint current.

The fire climbs the thermal ladder of the chimney toward the sky, spewing sparks.

Nathan says, "I will tell you how the world was made before I tell you about the son of Ayash.

"First created were the Thunderbirds. They were the beginning of all. They are the powers of the heavens, of the air.

"Second created were the frogs. In the spring they drum and drum like shamans. They are the creatures of land and water. They are amphibians. Mother earth is both land and water.

"Third created was us. Human beings, Anishinabek, spontaneously created, between heaven and earth. Between heaven and earth we live and we die, we come and we go. Third created."

Nathan brings the great, theatrical figures up out of nothing, with only his own voice. You are the central figure, you, the listener.

The legends are told only in wintertime, and yet so many of them begin with a still summer day, when the lake is perfectly calm and poplar pollen is describing the faint surface currents. It is always still, waiting, silent, the beginning of a new day. The earth has been just-created, and so have you.

You move across a lake of slightly disturbed dreams. Poplar cotton floats on the iron-smelling water and you approach the unknown land at the level of the beach.

You and I and the storyteller drift over a surface of still water. We are young, confused, on a quest, covered with black ashes from a great burning, afloat and adrift. We are afraid and thrilled at the same time.

The Stern Paddler puts us over against a cliff of red stone and there she is, painted in vermillion, with her long, forward-pointing horns, the supremely powerful Missepijou, Underwater Panther.

*She is the most powerful*, says Nathan. *She lives under the rapids. There is nothing like her. She is afraid only of the Thunderbirds.*

There is the chance that if you are resolute and courageous, she will come to your aid.

Be careful what you ask for.

But in the legends, you are perfectly strong, you were born in a good time.

The axis of the earth turned once on your arrival. You have been promised both silence and the art of noise. You move through the legend with some place to get to, some magical center, the treasure at the heart of life. The lake parts in front of you on your long drift down the story-road, it is like flying.

You are running through a burnt forest, chased by a rolling head whose sharp teeth chatter with greed and a wild eagerness to devour, but magical things happen: your hair comb becomes a forest, your water gourd becomes a river, alive, animate, protective.

You are plunged into the bottom of the sea by the Thunderbirds, but down there is a small lodge, and an old woman in it saying "Welcome." You are threatened by a frozen giant with legs like tree trunks, but the occult and dangerous fox that lives next to your heart leaps out of your furs and sinks her teeth into the ice-thing, and it melts.

You are wandering lost in the country of the sky, and Spider Woman spins her web and you drift back to earth on a lustrous, perilous thread.

Your cruel parent abandons you on a rocky island to die, but you are a royal being, your heart is pure, you have been given the gifts of courage and right-thinking, and the one who comes to your aid is Missepijou herself.

You dream of coming home in the universe to a place where you are honored and needed, coming home in the Universe with blood on your hands.

Third created, caught between the beings of the earth and the beings of the sky, stumbling, fearful, desperate to do the right thing and always drawn into temptation, contrite; always in movement.

The fire goes through frozen green birch. The legends manifest themselves in Nathan's memory, his voice, his skill at tracking down the story roads.

Chakabesh sets a snare for the sun, Wolverine is blinded once again and goes in search of the salt sea to wash his poor eyes, and the Giant Enormous Penis storms into a tipi full of portage brigands, howling, "I want somebody to help me kill my damned wife!"

The figures crowd around, called up by the human voice, by human memory. Kahyana, who seems to stand there by my books in all his shining furs, the rescuing hero. And there is the ice-maiden Blue Garters, and the silly Girls Who Married Stars, and goofy Grebe and his elegant brother Mang.

Mang is Loon, with his splendid necklace. He is the sort of man I always thought of as an officer in the Coldstream Guards — cool, handsome, spendthrift, aristocratic, gazing down with a cynical smile at the young women crowding around him, young ladies in pearls and crêpe de Chine.

The fire warms them into existence, or maybe it is this fire in the wood stove of our skulls, the combustion of the imagination, that draws them to us out of the cold. Grebe, Mang's brother Shingebish, stands there by the water bucket, envious and furious. He has messy hair and big flat feet and no color, no girlfriends, no reputation, and someday he will drive a red-hot flint spearhead down his brother's throat but not now. We haven't got to that part of the story yet.

Nathan says, "All these stories are related, they say, but I don't know how, really." He drinks his scalding-hot tea. The fire bursts with hot spruce knots.

I say, "Do you have constellations that are named for the legend people?"

Mrs. Mindemoya says something, and Nathan translates.

"She says the North Star is Nemetahamun, the Bow Paddler. She doesn't know anything more about it."

"I see."

Mrs. Mindemoya bends over to Sarah Winnepetonga and says something more.

Sarah translates, "She says, have you got your moccasins for your little footsie?"

Everyone in the cabin screams with laughter, including me, although I am actually *trying* to scream with laughter and only halfway succeeding. But, really, here I am, in my romantic cabin in the north woods, in a charming ensemble of shrink-wrap nylon parka and new caribouskin boots, tossing scraps of Spork to my tame husky, who gazes at me with affectionate blue eyes, and we are safe in the arms of winter.

# 8.

Two months later I was in the radio station when the short volunteer radio kid came in, out of breath.

He said, "There's been a terrible thing. A terrible thing has happened in Fort Severn. Some people were killed."

I said, "What? My goodness, this is a thing called 'news.'" At last I had something to teach. "There are certain ways you handle or announce this sort of thing." I lit up a cigarette confidently, reached for a pad of paper and a pen. "First, we ascertain the very facts of the matter. This is called *hard* news."

"No, wait," said Bruce. Teddy Wakwan stood behind the glass, out in the ante-room, staring in with a frightened expression.

"Wait what? What happened?" I was in a takeover mood. The village people wanted me to do something — well, this was what I was qualified for.

"What happened was, a man got drunk at a party, real drunk, and he went out and got a shotgun and came back and killed a man and also he hit a twelve-year-old girl and blew her jaw away."

I said, "Oh."

The tall volunteer, Eno, said, "The elders are going to take care of this. We just leave the radio station. Except Teddy. He'll fix the mikes for them and everything."

Sarah Winnepetonga was living in a little tiny house behind the Free Trader's Store. I decided to go over there and listen to the radio and wait this thing out.

The elders at last came into the radio station. They had avoided this whiteman's gimcrack for months, and now here they were.

I listened at Sarah's house, as the solemn voices in Ojibway spoke on and on. They prayed for the soul of Billy Bluecoat, and for the recovery of the young girl. They sang "Amazing Grace" in Ojibway. They prayed again, this time for the mental health of the man who did the shooting. They sang "Abide with Me" in Ojibway and prayed for the mothers and fathers of everyone concerned.

This went on all day.

This was how the Anishinabek handled hard news.

The world was turning toward the spring of the year, and the Bow Paddler Star, the North Star, swung its constellation around its head like a bolo.

# 9.

The community entertained itself without television. This meant that they had to produce their own fun and relaxation, single-handed, every evening, or not.

The log community hall down on the River was packed with people, cheek-to-cheek; they stood back from the dance floor. Twenty people flung themselves into the complicated figures of the Oyster Dip and the Texas Star.

It was hot. I took off my parka and sweater and fanned myself with a potato-chip packet. There was only one light bulb in the hall. Normally, there were two light bulbs at one end of the hall. However, the record player and speakers which were blasting out "Ste. Anne's Reel" were also plugged into the same socket. To increase the speed of the record, the operator reached up and unscrewed one light bulb. This poured more electricity into the record player and so it spun faster. To slow it down, one re-screwed Light Bulb II.

Teenagers ran in and out of the door. The girls clung together in dark clots, dressed in navy blue and black and dark-brown parkas, blue jeans and high-top moccasins. They whispered desperately to one another, looked up out of their conferences at one boy or another boy across the room, bent down to continue whispering. Then one of them would burst into tears, rush outside in a wild foaming of steam from the minus forty degree Fahrenheit outside air. Two or three girls rushed outside after the sobbing one, then they all rushed back in. The River People's community hall was surrounded by trees and high snowbanks. There was a glazed trail to the entrance, and the enchanting music came drifting through the forest as one approached, inviting, seductive.

Young girls were supposed to be very, very, very shy. Ostentatiously shy, shy in a public, demonstrative way. Some cultures bind women's feet, others put enormous neck-rings on them to weigh them down, others require high heels and tight skirts, but in some way, all over the world, young women must display dependence, helplessness. In this north, physically disabling any person would be to invite disaster. So the young women must be seen to be cripplingly shy.

The men dancers flew about confidently, flinging their partners with gay abandon. The women danced in a shy, helpless shuffle, head down, hair falling in a veil around their faces. The music boomed, teenagers rushed outside to whisper, the walls of the community hall were lined with smiling, laughing faces.

Everybody must dance, including the white woman. She must go out and bumble through the measures of the dance.

I found myself grabbed by the hand and pulled out into the dimly lit dance floor, thinking, What if this place caught fire?

And, Must I act shy too?

Elizabeth Peyton was there, talking with Nathan and Jeannie. Her daughter was with Nathan's sister, asleep on the floor on a pile of coats with the other Spontaneously Created Children. Jeannie's cousin was there, a young girl named Celeste, who was so shy and properly passive she had to be dragged out to the floor by two grown men. I guess she won the Shy contest.

In all folk tales, fiddle music is the invention of the Devil. You cannot not dance, and so I was pulled, shyly, into the maelstrom of the Texas Star, longing to demonstrate my jig-step.

I had learned the Texas Star in high school, forgot it, remembered it again. Journeys to far places call upon all our resources, including square-dance steps learned in high school, jig-steps your mother taught you.

Everybody had to dance. Nobody was left out: elderly women in their brilliantly colored headscarves, creaky with arthritis, were pulled out of the crowd by the men dancers and thrown into the whirlpool. Around the dance floor in the allemande, the men nearly carried the women dancers off their feet. In the Virginia Reel, your partner flung you down the alleyway of dancers like a hockey puck.

I rushed outside to breathe. The air felt wonderfully, refreshingly cool. Back inside for another set; teenage girls were snatched "reluctantly" from their places against the wall, pulled "hesitantly" into the sets, danced "shyly" around the circles, "allowing" themselves to be pulled like toboggans through the serpentine Oyster Dip, and when the set was over, rushed off the dance floor with "relief." They must demonstrate their desirable shyness, their imperviousness to the need to show off, their deep self-containment that was so self-contained that they had no inner pressure to be seen or looked at. Where else to demonstrate this but at a dance?

The men demonstrated their strength and vitality by dancing every set, flinging the women nearly off their feet, and choosing women to be flung.

Also, dancing was fun.

It was exhausting, exhilarating, fiery. I couldn't resist, and during the fiddle break on "Hen And Chickens," sprang into my best jig-step, demonstrating my lack of feminine self-containment.

Mrs. Mindemoya was pulled from her seat beside the sleeping children, but carefully. She was danced through the measures with solicitude and vigilance by the man who had custody of her through the set, and returned alive. Elizabeth Peyton was selected, chosen, drawn out and thrown wildly through the allemande. Nathan and Jeannie, Sarah Winnepetonga, and perhaps every member of the community on the River, plus visitors, ended up moving through the precision steps of the dance. No one must ever be left out: it is rude and ill-mannered. The Ojibway have the social graces of royalty.

They had these dances at least once a week, and when the word went around, I put on my parka, laid my books aside, and walked the half-mile to the River, down a long, sloping trail. From a distance, through the spruce trees, I could hear "Ste. Anne's Reel," fast and entrancing, and hear the door open and shut, open and shut, as teenagers rushed in and out on their endless quest for gossip and complications, and I couldn't wait to get there.

Sometimes I just walked, listening to the rhythm of life in the village. It seemed so isolated, so removed from any other town or place. It was a principality of independence, busy and occupied with the energy it takes to live in the fierce cold. Men and women rose up in the mornings, started their fires, began to boil water. Then there was wood to cut, a trip to the Bay or the Free Trader's. The children trudged down paths to the school, the weather balloon lifted into the sky, trailing its long tail and sparkling.

Why was North Spirit here, at this place, and not at the entrance of the Pipestone River, ten miles away? Because the Hudson's Bay Company, the Company of Gentlemen Adventurers Trading Into Hudson's Bay, had discovered, two hundred years ago, that this was the gathering-place of the Anishinabek every spring. They came together and re-invented the concept, "village."

"It was on a high hill," Nathan said. "With a good breeze to blow away the mosquitoes and blackflies. There was a rapids, and there one could get fish. So the Bay men set up a post here."

Two hundred years went past, and every spring, still, the Spontaneously Created People met here at North Spirit Rapids. They brought their winter furs, and traded them for needles, axes, kettles, red-wool leggins, shot, gun-powder, ulu-knives (which were Inuit women's knives but were also popular with Indian women), sled-runners, powder-bottles, vermillion paint, bright silver earrings, and bottles of beads.

Then Canada, in 1907, still a Dominion of the King, sent men in suits. With papers.

When the Treaty was signed with His Majesty, more men in suits came, to take the children away to school in boarding schools.

That was a bad idea. Nobody liked it.

Not even the missionaries. Not even the most theologically correct missionaries. The noise of children hiding their sobbing under rough blankets was too much even for the most well-meaning heart.

So in the mid-fifties Indian Affairs began to construct a day school.

Nathan said, "And then, people stopped going out to the trap line anymore. Nobody could go and leave their kids in the day school, could they? It's not a *boarding* school. So most people run trap lines within a day's journey, or just take their kids out of school. Then the kids fall behind. There's a few jobs, like at the Hudson's Bay Store and in the band office, but people have to depend more and more on welfare payments of some kind if they want to keep their kids in school. The more they keep the kids in school, the less the kids will ever know about trapping. I don't know if it's a good thing or not. I guess some-day people will make up their minds what to do."

The children came laughing and running out of the school at around three, darkness came soon after, smoke rose from chimneys, and I walked home, my hood around my ears, my fingers painful with cold and my hair frozen to the fake fur of my parka by my condensed breath.

And because the Hudson's Bay post was here, and then the day school, there was a place for white-people's constructs to go. There was a place to put them. So the Department of the Environment needed an upper-air weather station in northern Ontario, and here was a place to put it. Then the Department of Transportation and Communication carved out an airstrip to supply constructs other departments had constructed. Large things that needed to be heated and lit kept flying up on tax dollars.

There was also a place up on the hill called Saagaatey, which means "the sun just shining out of a cloud". It was the young men's lodge. This was a construct out of the thoughts of the Anishinabek.

The young men must have a lodge, a place to hang out, gang up, sleep when they run away from home, a place to get away from parents and women. It was very long, like a boxcar, made of plywood, and it had a wood stove and the friendly litter of bachelor life.

They showed movies there occasionally.

These movies were terrible cheap things made in the Philippines, about vampires or space terrors. The young men (all of the young radio guys were members of this young-men's club or gang) had subscribed to some sort of movie club in Winnipeg, which sent up one movie a week with Ace Lawson on the DC-3, and they put it on, no matter what it was. They charged a dollar entrance fee and so subsidized their rock band. The rock band was two guitars and speakers as big as Buicks.

I went and pushed my way into the crowd and sat down on a hard bench. The chief, Joseph Makepeace, was sitting next to me.

He said, "Eh, *Bojo*, sit down."

We sat there, side by side, in our parkas.

The movie was roaring through desperately improbable situations. The projector clattered, cigarette smoke rose up in wavering columns, kids screamed and pinched one another, people pushed past our knees where we sat on backless benches to buy hamburgers and strawberry tarts in the back, where Nathan's mother and sister, Elsie Half-A-Day and the elder Mrs. Nanokeesic, were cooking them on a Coleman gas stove and selling them. The teenagers whispered and rushed outside to have intense conversations with each other.

This movie was about Space Things. The mother ship wavered on a piano wire against a background of painted stars. Inside the mother ship, a woman dressed in something like glittery car upholstery rushed around and around a console made of PVC piping and old airplane dials. She was being chased by a space thing that the movie people had knocked together out of a scuba-diving suit and a rubber squid.

"Is everything okay in the cabin?" said Chief Makepeace. "It's okay?"

"Very good," I said. "I am okay. Fine. Mrs. Mindemoya helps me."

"Yes," he said. "My sister."

I said, "Oh."

He laughed, turned back to the screen, which was a white sheet noisy with screams.

He said, "Some man will come on the radio tonight and speak. He used to be a chief. *Ogemakan-bun.*"

I said, "Oh, good! We need volunteers. It's wonderful if the elders come and speak."

He stared at the space thing as it was shot out the mother-ship cargo door, and turned into fire-extinguisher foam. The car-upholstery woman then flung herself into the arms of the hero, who was trying to drive the spaceship somewhere more pleasant against all odds.

Around us was a sibilant, buzzing whisper; the children, I realized, were translating for their parents and the elder people. How would one translate these things? Outer space, alien, crash-test dummy, the Undead, hyperspace.

I said, "The thing will die out there, I guess."

The chief said, "Yes, yes. Yes." He smoked. A teenager smashed past us, clutching a hamburger. He was looking for words in English. "A man will come on the radio tonight." He looked at the screen a moment and gave up. He looked down at my new high-top moccasins, beaded in yellow and blue and white, pointed and said, in Anishinabek, "What's that?"

I said, "My little footsie."

"Hahahahaha! Good! Good." He sighed. "Keep trying."

# 10.

That night the man who used to be a chief came on the radio. I sat in Sarah Winnepetonga's little house, a storage room, really, that she had made pleasant with calico curtains and an oil stove, banked high with insulating snow. It was near the shore, and so it was surrounded by the thin scrawling of diamond-willow bushes. We listened.

I said, "What's he saying?"

Sarah bent her head and listened intently to the little FM transistor. She looked disapproving and unusually reticent. "He's just giving advice to people."

I said, "What's his name?"

"Nimrod Kanakakeesic. He used to be a chief here."

"Kana ka-what?"

"Keesic. Shhhh."

Sarah was the daughter of the north's first Indian Indian Agent. Before her father, all the Indian Agents had, of course, been white men. She told me that her great-grandfather had been the man who signed the Treaty with the Canadian Government.

"With the King, really," she said. "That document was signed with the English King. Not Canada."

I didn't know why this was important.

Sarah tossed her hair out of her eyes and said, "Well, you know, you should learn this, and I hope I can explain it. Um, because the Province of Ontario is trying to say that we have to obey the game laws, like white hunters down south do. That we can't hunt moose out of season, and we can't use gill nets. We have to go fishing with hooks. We can't use moose or caribou meat or fish to make school lunches for the kids, and we can't sell any meat at a restaurant or to each other. And those white hunters are a thousand miles south of here, but we have to act like we're them, down in their little fields and those woods. Like we would have to go without meat for a whole nine months or whatever it is, just hunt in the fall! And for school lunches, they fly them up here from I don't know where! Toronto or somewhere!"

Her eyes were black and furious and her red cheeks were flushed. Sarah was freshly outraged by the mere fact of recounting it.

I said, "You've got to be joking."

"I'm not!" She paused, staring out her window at the bay and the corner of the Blackhawk Free Trader's Store. "Our position, well, I mean the position of the native organizations, is that we signed that agreement with the King, back then, and not with the Province of Ontario, so they can't apply their game laws to us."

I said, "I guess it's a long fight."

"Oh, it just goes on and on and on."

"Could take years."

"They're so *slow*! And my mother is wanting me to come home. They're arranging a marriage for me." Sarah was troubled. "I got a degree in child care just to come here and do this project."

"What project?"

"Oh, they're building a day-care center, but they're slow *too*! They ran into permafrost this fall. I wonder if I ought to get married. But I don't think I'm ready, really."

"To who?" I said, interested.

"I get so carried away about things. I bet I'd argue with my husband all the time."

"Yes. Sometimes I think the same thing. About myself I mean."

"Listen a minute."

Nimrod Kanakakeesic's voice could only be described as beautiful. It was deep and rich, it carried its own reverb and its own double timbre. He sounded like two people double-voicing, it was that textured.

His voice sprang out of the radio on some long, complex speech, flowing in airwaves to Agamatin, and the River, and Under the Hill, and Ghost Point, called Chebui Nayaushe. It was hypnotic.

I said, "He has a beautiful voice. Can we get this guy to come on air regularly? Like, get him a show or something?"

Sarah laid out a hand of solitaire on her little table.

"Well, I don't know, Puanets," she said. She was suddenly reticent. She flipped up a jack, laid it back down, a queen of diamonds. She had the confidence and the perfect English of somebody whose father was the first Indian Indian Agent in the north. Whose grandfather was an Anglican Minister, one of the first native ministers, and whose great-grandfather signed the Treaty. Whose family tradition was public responsibility, probity, rectitude. "Although, I don't know what the people here would want."

"Why not?"

"He's a man who . . . well, people are frightened of him." She paused. "Well, they say he's a shaman."

I decided to let it go. The queens and kings and jacks were laid down one after the other, Nimrod's voice moved on through untranslated assertions, and the people of the village listened, and agreed, or did not agree.

None of my business, I thought.

# *11.*

I got a letter from my ex.

I went to the post-office window in the Hudson's Bay Store and it was handed to me, and then I was jostled out of the way. It was Family Allowance Day, and so the store was packed.

I received a letter from my ex and also a package of books from Oldman Woman, the artist. She had offered; so I took her up on it, and sure enough a package of books arrived. Grey Owl, Farley Mowat. Also this letter.

I sat down to read it on the steps of the store, overlooking the fifty-mile stretch of North Spirit Lake.

I read about all his political activities in Toronto, and how he and his new girlfriend were investing their money in an old house, which they were renovating, and which they would re-sell, and more important political organizational fights, and how we should be friends, and when I came down to Toronto he would like to go out and we could have a serious talk and analyze our former relationship in the light of something-or-other.

He didn't ask anything about my life, of course. I felt like pouting, or indulging myself in a good short-term pout.

Far across the lake, I saw a snowmobile approaching, pulling a sled.

It was arriving out of that world where I wanted so badly to visit; the world outside the village. I was neither a biologist nor an anthropologist, I had no profession that would take me out into the land on trips of discovery. I was not independently wealthy like Lady Isabella Bird; I was here to animate a community radio station. Without that task, I would not be in the north at all.

I watched the traveler arrive, the long sled churning up snow powder, wavering in the atmospheric distortions caused by a bright sun on fields of snow. The islands in the lake, ten or fifteen or thirty miles distant, seemed to lift themselves slightly above the level of the snow and float, shimmering. They were spiky with the topknots of spruce, the shores laced with the thin wire-work of diamond willow and stunted ash bushes. Like a merchant at some ancient post spreading his wares for the customer, the land laid out its white silks. The traveler would have stories to tell.

He was coming out of the stretches of the original world. I sat and looked and thought how keen and sharp the north was, with its violent temperatures, its calm, unmoving stretches of snowed lakes. One can still hear the sound of the bone flutes that I think everybody remembers in their hearts.

I wished I could find some of the old Hudson's Bay post journals. Some of them were from the late 1600s. Those men came to this country in the old time. Sometimes they still heard the flutes. Sometimes they wrote about what they heard. They wrote their reports but in secret they were high on the glamour and ferocity of the boreal world.

The traveler was coming out of the other world of the forest and the hard northern earth. Coming out of the maps I had stared at for so long down at the chief's office. This person was emerging out of the real land, out of the geophysical symbols of a hard climate; out of the little spikes of marsh symbols, out of the altitude lines and across the blue lines of rivers, now frozen like flint. Out of all those books about Indians, libraries and libraries full. Out of the anthropological reports, and the old photographs and the stiff wording of treaties, the "His Mark for Missinaibi, a cross for Walks Like A Wolf Howling." I wanted to go out there, but I was a poet and a radio person, not a biologist. My job was to stay here and flounder about in technology.

The traveler spun his machine and his loaded sled to the left when he approached the bluff, to move up the less-steep trail at Under the Hill, where the river came out through rapids to boil under the ice of the lake.

I got up off the steps.

Some other time.

# 12.

"Come with us, we're going to Burnt Island. You need dry wood."

Jeannie paused briefly at the door to my cabin, looking around to see that I hadn't set fire to myself or eaten the pup. I jumped up and ran for my parka.

My transistor radio sat on my windowsill, soaking up the sun and talking. It was speaking Ojibway. Each pane of glass was charmingly frosted at the corners. It was a blue day, full of early, new sun. The station was now filling up all its hours with volunteers and it had become a language-net, spun out over the village, and it captured people's attention as they worked, their listening minds, as if these minds were deep fish. The radio station was using animate positive transitive verbs in the dubatative mood and the mysterious Fourth Person.

"Dress warm," she said. "We'll be gone all day. Wear old stuff, we're going to the place where there's a lot of burnt wood."

All day out in the forests!

I began the process of dressing warm.

"*Kaowin!*" she said. "No. Don't put gloves on under your mitts. It just makes your hands colder."

I had been lent some caribou-hide mitts. Now that I had learned they were animate nouns they seemed to have personalities, charged with life. The brilliant day poured its buttery light through my small windows, my cracked tin stove sat back on its legs, tilted toward the back, like a duck, mostly cold.

I had gotten used to temperatures going up and down, up and down, in a wood-stove rhythm.

I said, "I dunno, Jeannie, I get to writing in my notebooks and it just goes out."

"Well, pay attention to it." She patted me on the back. "It will be better."

She tore at the starter cord. Snowmobiles (and generators and canoe motors and many things) are started with a starter cord. You take hold of it and give it a rip and this kicks the engine into life sometimes. Sometimes people stand there and rip away at it all day. Sometimes it comes away in their hand. Sometimes people standing close behind the person jerking at the starter cord stand too close, and the person who is starting the machine jerks back with a powerful, desperate snatch and hits the person standing behind, and then they take that person to the nursing station on a sled.

"Stand away," said Jeannie. "My brother-in-law, Emasiah, he broke a man's jaw like that one time."

"Emasiah, the big man that runs the airstrip?"

"Yes. He's Sarah's brother."

"How is he your brother-in-law if he's Sarah's brother?"

"He married Nathan's sister, the other one, not the one that helped make your moccasins. Can't you tell? Emasiah's wife looks just like Nathan and Elsie."

"Oh."

"And your door is half-open. You must shut. Door."

"It won't shut."

Jeannie took a deep breath and ripped at the starter cord again.

"Shovel. Snow. Away. You don't have shovel? Take a tin can. Scrape it away."

I got an empty soup can and scraped away the incrementing mound of snow from the doorsill of my cabin. It met the warm (sometimes) air of my cabin and froze, and then people walked in, and kicked more snow on top of that, which froze; it was as if the snow creeping in were a life-form, a growing thing in crystalline structures that fed on cold.

At the Nanokeesic house, the radio said in Ojibway, "Jeannie Nanokeesic and the white woman are going to the burnt forest today."

I said, "Is this a public event or what?"

"He saw us out the window of the radio station when we passed, and he saw my old blue parka. New word, Puanets. *Weesahkudah* is a burnt forest."

We left the village in a convoy of four machines. Nathan's brother and his wife came with us, and several other cousins. Snow flew as we crossed the lake, we rode in a cloud of powder. It was only about minus twenty-five degrees Fahrenheit. The first machine, a large, powerful one, broke trail. The snow was new and light as swansdown.

I looked back when we were far out on the lake. The buildings of the Hill — the church, the metal dome of the weather station, the school — looked lonesome and dramatic.

After six miles we came out into the forest. The machines ground and heaved. I sat behind Jeannie with my head bent, hair frosting to the fake fur of my parka. Sometimes I couldn't see my feet for the snow, and we were like a boat half submerged. On some ridges there were small pines, the last of the pines. They had tiny thick cones, looking as if they had been boiled.

We went through thick colonies of black spruce, and the limbs reached down and whipped us, we slid over a stretch of bog, a frozen flat surface with small dead spruce in it. A flat plate of snow like a skating rink.

"Beaver," said Jeannie. "A beaver did this. There's a live lodge here somewhere. See the poplar?"

Chewed poplar stumps, pointy heads thrusting up out of the snow. They looked like a small group of pointy-head people, short and alien.

I said, "Can we go see the beaver?"

Jeannie said, "You'd have to wait until spring."

I was disappointed. I thought they'd be sliding down the banks and snow chutes like children, and if we waited long enough, we'd see them.

"No, no, no," said Jeannie. "They stay in their lodges like smart little beaver. If they go out, they go underwater. Under the ice."

I still thought maybe we could look down the lodge-hole, but we were plunging on into the country of winter, toward an island of black sticks.

Burnt Island was a spiky granite turtle-back sticking up out of the white lake, a strange giant head just appearing from under six feet of ice and snowpack, some enormous being standing asleep in the deep lake, with a hairdo of black spikes.

The island had burnt over very thoroughly years ago, and its stick-like forest was a source of dry wood for the entire village.

When we arrived, Nathan immediately got off his machine and put on his alive snowshoes. He whacked down two standing black sticks, busted them up, and started an inanimate fire. It burnt down through the snow until it was a roaring firepit. One of the other young people that had come out with us started a pot of tea in the alive kettle-being and we began the day's work.

Nathan lent me a pair of snowshoes.

The snowshoes grinned up at me, animate and sly.

"Now listen," he said. "These are long and thin for forest work. Always wear moccasins with these, they are handmade, they're Anishinabe snowshoes."

The alive snowshoes smirked as Nathan showed me how to tie down my toes. Black thin shadows like stripes fell on us and the snowshoes whispered to each other. I teetered backwards on them, and then luckily teetered sideways before they tipped me over into the snow, just before I smashed the delicate, hand-shaved birch frames and just before I ripped out the extremely thin sinew webbing. I pitched straight over sideways, disappearing into the two-foot surf of new snow. The snowshoes tittered.

I said, "This is complicated."

Everybody else was flying around light as elves, walking on their four-foot-long webs on the surface of the engulfing snow like water-spiders. The fine webbing of the snowshoes sifted the snow through itself like a flour sifter so that as they walked, a fine spray of powder flew up in front of their moccasins.

"Yes, it's complicated," laughed Nathan. He was sawing down a black tree-trunk. "We're just a simple folk, living close to the earth, utilizing the socio-economic resources of our aboriginal territory in a variety of tasks."

I teetered carefully off as the animate snowshoes, the *ahgimak*, tried to pitch me into the snow again. I said, "It's a known fact that a degree in sociology rots your brain."

Axes bit into the burnt trunks, spraying fine grains of charcoal. I thought, *fire, fire, good dry wood and fire.* We were covered with charcoal smears, we smelled like woodsmoke, there was a light sizzle of delight and fun over the day's work. We became thirsty as we sawed and chopped and loaded, so one of the young men cut a hole through the lake ice with a chisel, and I poured ice water down my throat from a tin cup. It was wonderful.

We ate Spork and bread and dried meat, drank tea, went back to work. The snowshoes settled down and ceased pitching me into the powder.

Nathan found wolf tracks at the shore, and in the snow they looked big as cow tracks.

"He was just here," said Nathan. "Just before us. Look. He took a shit. That's says, 'I was here.'"

I sang, "'Thanks for the memories . . . '"

Jeannie pointed to the tracks and said, "*Maeengan! Maeengan!*" in a strenuous manner. Wolf. I never forgot it.

The good noontime wore out, and then it was afternoon. I found myself suddenly very tired. In deep cold, the body uses up enormous amounts of energy staying warm, keeping the interior temperature at its proper level, and I had figured out how to work the bucksaw. Delighted with this new skill, I had bucksawed on and on, and then in one moment, I was empty of energy. I thought, time to quit.

The sun was pouring itself out of the sky in red waves as we headed home. It was the darkest time of the year; it was perhaps four-thirty. Suddenly, as if it had been dropped down a well, the temperature plunged. It just bucketed downwards in a steady fall that left me alarmed, shocked. The wind created by the machines tore at my face.

We were heading back on the trail we had made coming out, so I expected we would make better time, but I realized my interior temperature was dropping too. I bent down and hid behind Nathan's back. The sleds were now full of blackened logs, and they wove from side to side, slowing us down.

Stars came out. I began to gasp for breath. Not long, I told myself, not long. This terrible cold and this evaporation, this hemorrhage of strength had happened so suddenly.

I couldn't move my hands. The village was far away. We were out in the alive forest and there were no roads, no telephones, no 911, no radio contact, we were in the aboriginal uncut forests, far past the northern limit of instant help. It was the time of year when we most need fire and light and take great risks to get these things.

I thought, what if something happened and we were caught out here? The cold was setting in, inanimate, the line of the northwest horizon was now barely red with sunset and the stars were appearing. It was like being ejected into outer space. Chief Makepeace had understood perfectly well what was happening to the alien-thing when it was shot out of the spacecraft. I was the alien, caught in the wrong world, feeling as if I were made of cracking plastic scuba suits and rubber squids.

I was the one thing out of place, unprepared. The snowshoes were laid along the running boards, looking like folded dragonfly wings. The blue fires of the cosmos sprang out of the black sky in their jewelled patterns, warming nothing.

As we lifted over the big humps of snow of the lake-bank, and pushed out onto North Spirit Lake again for the final stretch home, a snowmachine tipped over in the soft powder and wrenched loose the sled hitch. Tall black poles like jackstraws tumbled down and then sank into the snow.

It took all of us to get the machine upright again and the sled re-hitched and re-loaded. We had to jimmy the machine around into a position where the tracks could grip. I was frosted with a gleaming coat of snow like confectioner's sugar. I looked all crusty-white and sparkling in the last sunset light.

I waded by main force back to Nathan's machine. It is exhausting to walk in thigh-deep new snow. Big exciting orange rays were shooting out of the last sunlight into interstellar spaces. The air was fresh with the smell of spruce and hard to breathe. My muffler, wound across my mouth, was so caked with frozen breath that it was board-hard.

Nathan was panting, wiping his hair out of his eyes with his heavily beaded mitts.

"Damn these goddamn machines," he said. "I wish we'd kept our dogs."

I was in pain by this time. I thought, if we lose another machine one more time, I'm done for.

"She's about to die," said Jeannie. "The CBC will arrest us if we lose her." Jeannie was panting with effort, lifting two blackened thin trees onto a sled.

"I'm alright," I said. "I'm a country girl." I stumbled stiffly over and grasped at a charcoaled tree trunk.

"Yes," said Jeannie. "South country. You probably burnt palm trees down there. Heave!"

It was now simply a straight shot across the white fields of the lake, toward the village. In the distance, on the bluff, I could see all the electrical lights of the weather station and the white residences shining.

I bent down behind Nathan and endured the rest of the trip as cold fell around us like a clear material, a state of being, a vague, invisible, sinister threat. These temperatures would make one hard and inanimate in a short time; this was inhuman. This is what one lived with. These were the Ice Ages, every evening of the winter. The deep snow flowed past us in its surf-like rush, on and on, and it seemed we were sitting in one place on a loud machine while the plates and fields of white tore past us backwards.

I was almost unable to get off the machine as we pulled up in front of the Nanokeesics' house. We all tried to get into the door at the same time.

Jeannie loaded their big Fisher stove with dry wood and set it afire. We stood around warming out backsides like a covey of quail.

Someone made tea, lit the Coleman, and the panes of the windows became reflective mirrors against the black night. The hot, scented air drew itself about us.

Dry wood made life so easy, a fire so easy to start. It caught fire so quickly and burnt so very hot, and there was so little of it. We had brought it back at a high cost of energy and endurance, and not without some risk. I loved the black, grainy pieces. Pre-burnt dry wood became a new object of affection in my life. I thought about it the way I used to think about paychecks, or birthday gifts. My hands flushed brilliant red, recovering from the cold.

Jeannie and Nathan were starting to argue with one another over who hadn't emptied the slop pail. They began to glare at one another, and soon they would precipitate into battle.

"Look at your hands," said Nathan's brother. "They're the color of a bandanna. They should do that when you're out *in* the cold. Not when you get back and warm up."

I said, "I know." They were, indeed, bright red now, and puffed. I made my right hand talk to my left.

"Ever seen cold like this before?" said my right hand to my left.

"No. Awful. How come she bring us here?" said my left hand. They began to laugh.

My right hand said, "Tell her either she buys us a good pair of mitts with fur or we'll creep up on her tonight and slap her face."

Even Jeannie was laughing. Nathan began to smile.

"Let's just slap her face right now!" said my left hand, and it crept up in sneaky finger-walkings to my collar and slapped my cheek.

"We want mitts!" it cried.

Nathan said, "Tell them we'll go to Elsie again. I know she's got another new moose hide."

"There's a generous fellow!" cried my right hand. "Get that man some tea!"

Even though we were tired, we somehow recovered and sat up late playing cards by Coleman lamp. The electricity went off at ten, when the school generator shut down. I thought, Elsie's husband is a good hunter, and I was grateful for it.

# 13.

It took two bush planes and one jet to get me back to the Toronto airport.

I had originally come to Canada with a draft dodger in the late sixties. He left me for a beautiful redhead from Saskatchewan and we were all supposed to have intelligent conversations about it, in the manner of the time, but the upshot was that the breakup of this young partnership had left me by myself in a strange city. I expected someone soon to make me non-single again, but I was in unknown territory.

Strange cities are hard on country girls.

Luckily, I was plucky and charming and strenuously cheerful, and I began to free-lance radio documentaries for the CBC. It was almost like a regular job but not as boring.

There is an observation chain, like the food chain. Instead of who eats who, or what, this chain is concerned with who gets to observe who, and come to conclusions about their behaviour, and do analyses, and arrive at judgments, and then broadcast these judgments. These observations arrive most often on television; ubiquitous, banal, inaccurate as often as not, but impressive. This is what I found out by becoming a radio reporter. It was engaging work but it worked at contraries to poetry, or storytelling, and I had found myself failing at it when I was first offered the chance to go to North Spirit.

Human beings are at the top of the food chain; we eat nearly everything and are not, save for the depraved appetites of a few grizzlies and mountain lions, eaten. And so there is an observation chain.

At the bottom of the observation chain are the "exotic" peoples of the world, who don't have access to media. They are the observed. No Anishinabe or Inuit or rural folks come to our cities, walk into our apartments or houses with our bentwood rockers, our antiques, our plants in bathrooms, observe, and return home to write about our weird, isolated lifestyles.

I wish they would.

I stayed with friends who made suppers of eggplant and trifle. I found it odd, if perfectly digestible, food. We were all still young enough to name our cars. They were so astounded that a) there were native people living in villages, square dancing, and eating caribou they had shot themselves, and b) I was living with these people, that they didn't even ask any questions.

It was December. I didn't have the money to go home to my own people in Missouri, but I wrapped packages and sent them home for Christmas. Meanwhile I tried to make myself amenable and listened to the gospel singing next door at the Apostolic Temple of the Holy Ghost.

My ex had gone to Vancouver with his new person. I got out my ragged poetry manuscript and tried to think in poetry. It was impossible to do.

I finally caught a bus and stayed with friends out on a farm and enjoyed myself with snow and horses. And there I met a country boy; he was engaged in the occupation of finding lost people. Search and rescue. He had a very large dog which was expert in finding lost people, and so Sergeant Preston and I had a marvellous week together, and I felt better about my ex being in Vancouver with his new person.

But I couldn't wait to go back north. It had happened, the thing they always warn you about. The Call of The North.

# *14.*

Returning to North Spirit, I stayed for two days in Sioux Lookout, waiting for a plane. It was too cold to fly; planes are grounded when the temperature drops to minus forty-five degrees Fahrenheit. I stayed with Oldman Woman, whose name in Ojibway was Akewence, waiting for a flight, for the weather to warm up.

Sioux Lookout was a compact, busy small town, surrounded by forests and lakes. Because it had no industry, it was good-looking, with a classic train station designed with the pointed roof and the long windows. Planes generally went in and out all day long. There were northern outfitting stores.

I went into the main one and looked at parkas. There were ones made of down, overlaid with heavy poplin, with real wolf-fur trim. They were four hundred dollars. I was being paid steadily for the first time in my life — something poets deeply appreciate — but I wasn't being paid that much. However, they said I could buy it on time, and I walked out in a dark-brown, canvas-shelled down parka with white-and-grey wolf trim. I felt like I was ready for fifty below or a direct hit, whichever came first.

Oldman Woman had a tiny apartment near the train tracks, and I could hear the train come in twice a day; once east, once west. It arrived in a cloud of steam, with passengers on their way to Winnipeg or Toronto, the people in the coach cars staring out, looking as if they had spent the night in a duck press, the people in the sleeping cars reading magazines with the aid of their overhead compartment lights.

Oldman Woman had paint-smeared jeans and an easel set up in the north-window light. I yawned and read and watched her lay on tight designs in acrylics. It was crushingly cold.

I said, "Sometimes people call you Akewence."

"That's Oldman Woman in Ojibway. Really, it should be Akewence-equae, but they just say Akewence."

"I'd hate to tell you what they call me."

"I heard." She laughed. "Let's change the subject. They're going to set up a new organization," she said. "Run by Indian people. Radio stations and a newspaper. They want my, *ahi*, nephew to work on it."

"Here?" I looked up from my scabrous manuscript. *Ahi* was the Ojibway word for "uh." I was on the verge of a good encircling metaphor. *Flying Lesson*, I wrote.

"I guess. Hmmmm. Where's my cobalt? I guess. It's supposed to cover the, um, north. I don't know if I like this."

"What?"

"All this ocher."

"Don't ask me." *These are the wings of the airplane.*

"I didn't. We, ah, sort of got a newsletter going already, a small newsletter. Then we tried to make it into a newspaper." She laughed. "It was really fun. We put in all the babies that were born every month, and then for recipes, we made up drinks. I mean, alcoholic drinks. I made up one called 'Pikanjikum Sunset.' Cranberry juice and vodka. The elders on the board of directors had, a, like, you know, *fit*."

I started laughing. A Pikanjikum Sunset! The name of that village is pronounced Pii-*kan*-jee-kum. I learned it by ear before I ever saw it spelled, so therefore was not subject to the confusion most white people fell into. Newcomers seeing it spelled usually pronounced it something like pickin' chicken. Nevertheless, I could see how the elders would be offended. Alcohol was enough of a problem without a native newspaper presenting recipes for candy-sweet drinks with seductive names.

"What about news? Like, hard news."

"Well, we ended up with *gossip*. I mean, they need a professional to get it really started. Haven't you had some journalism?"

"Oh sure, lots." Well, not really lots. I did documentaries for CBC; not exactly hard news, but at least I'd been on air and I knew some of the rules. "But actually, I prefer gossip."

"Speaking of which," she said. "I think Jeannie and Nathan are going to get a divorce."

"Oh-oh."

"You'll have to visit my reserve some day. It's only, like, um, thirty miles from here. We're more southern Ojibway down here. Like the Minnesota people. Different."

"Different how?" *They have leading edges and cut the air like a pie-knife through a fine meringue.*

"We speak differently. This green is all I can get. I wish I had a catalog . . . . Hmmmm. They're Anglican. Up there. Catholics came here. Came this way, I mean. I think . . . ummm . . . ."

"Yes?"

"French and Catholics came down this way. Hudson's Bay Company and English and the Anglicans went north. Different influence."

*This is the altimeter which tells us of the earth, where we owe a life, despite the aviation of souls.*

"What am I speaking up there?" I said. "I can't figure out if it's Cree or Ojibway."

"Northern Ojibway. Just speak like they speak." She wiped her brush on her jeans. "Then if you ever live down here, you can learn to speak *properly.*"

"Wait till I tell Nathan you said that."

Oldman Woman s-t-r-o-k-e-d on a slow, long brushstroke in cobalt, sinking into the pure sensation of undiluted color waving upwards through fields of ocher.

"Don't carry tales," she said.

*Claimed by our bodies like baggage, we, the earth-people, descend again.*

I walked down the main street of Sioux Lookout with Elizabeth Peyton to see the new Wawatay radio and newspaper offices. They actually had three rooms all to themselves, over the post office. That is, we started to walk down the street to look at them. We got one block and realized we couldn't make it any further.

It was so cold we couldn't breathe.

The entire town was covered in a fog of microscopic ice crystals, and the sun had a wild, dangerous ring around it.

Elizabeth had come north originally with the Department of Communications, but now she was working for the new organization,

Wawatay. She was doing Wawatay's funding paperwork. The board of directors was to be made up of elders. She was renting a house in town.

I said, "What's going on? I can't even walk a block."

"Neither can I. Let's go back into the house."

Listening to the radio, CBC out of Thunder Bay, we found that it was sixty degrees below zero Fahrenheit.

The plane to North Spirit Rapids didn't attempt to fly until it was up to thirty-five degrees below. One had to wait. Patiently. One had to learn patience. So I loaded my bags nearly every day and drove in a borrowed car to the airport, writhing with impatience.

"Hello, Skinny," said Ace Lawson, the pilot. He was lounging around the prefab building at the Sioux Lookout airstrip. "God, if I wasn't married I'd take you out for a drink of whiskey. Maybe a bucket."

"Are we flying?"

"Get aboard, child, it's only twenty-five below. I don't know what you're doing up here in the north all by yourself, but you seem to be surviving."

"I'm doing all right."

"Look after yourself."

Then Ace put on his earphones, whistling, and we flew north.

# 15.

Once, at sunset, at about six o'clock in the evening, I sat at the console and looked out across the hills. The short rays were illuminating a light ground-blow. I felt suddenly and inexplicably wonderful. This was a beautiful place. I was lucky to be here. I was lucky that people were being generous and helpful to me, making a pair of caribou mitts for me, showing me how to cut wood.

The wind whispered some strange, urgent psalm. The sunset placed heavy glows inside the moving currents of snow 'til opals and pearls were flying past. The station was not on air; so I put on the headphones and a donated record: Beethoven's Ninth, the big, triumphant main theme, and watched the evening lamps come on all over the village. The cabins seemed like ships in the night, sailing steadily without moving. Electric lights flashed on Up on the Hill, the music rose in choral triumphs.

I pushed a button to record the section of music I wanted so I could do this again. It was a moment of privacy and peace and comfort, and I needed moments like this.

I didn't get what I expected. I never do. I cannot make machines do what I want them to do. I never learn. It's a new world every morning. What I hit wasn't *record* but *play*, and it was Nimrod Kanakakeesic's magical, seductive voice at top volume in my earphones, superimposed over Beethoven's Ninth.

I had never heard a sound mix like it in my life. It was the voice of the shaman and the music of the spheres, it was electrifying, terrifying, and the wind moved tidal waves of glowing sunset ground-blow past the windows. I couldn't get the machine turned off. I felt like the Sorcerer's Apprentice. I cried, "Good God!"

It was like being lifted out of my seat by the hair of my head. Nimrod's voice roared on, deep and heavy with meaning, rich as meat, full of some undefinable menace. It was a sinister, sexual, thrilling voice. I banged at the STOP button, and then I realized I was hitting the button on the wrong recorder.

I jerked off the headphones but the big monitors were on, speakers the size of foot lockers. The music rose to glory. Nimrod, the mighty hunter before the Lord, poured out his voice of cosmic whispers at a thousand decibels and the main theme of the Ninth surged on to greater and greater heights and the door of the studio flew open and Nathan rushed up and jammed his finger down on the correct STOP button, and, to my horror, flipped both the OFF switches on the microphones.

"What are you *doing?*"

"I don't know, I got Kanakakeesic by mistake, I was just listening to some music and . . . "

Nathan said, "You were broadcasting. You left the mikes on, and the transmitter is on. People thought Nimrod was coming out of *nowhere.*"

I said, "Yikes."

The station was off the air between four and seven, but people left their FM radios on anyway.

Nathan said, "The elders say this radio station makes them uneasy and no wonder." He sat down, his parka still dusted with snow. "There's enough trouble about this radio station without weird broadcasts when it's supposed to be off the air."

"I don't know why I came in here," I said. "Except it was warm, and I wanted to listen to some music."

"It's alright." Nathan was still breathing hard. He must have heard the strange broadcast, bolted out of his and Jeannie's house, ripped the starter cord half out of its sleeve on his snowmobile, and come across the Hill at top speed. I thought of how it must have sounded. There they were, eating caribou-and-macaroni soup with their little boy, peacefully watching the flames in the grate of their wood stove, when the shaman's voice blasted out of the FM radio at top volume, accompanied by enormous, expanding orchestral music.

Nathan calmed down.

He said, "I was always scared to death of the old people, you know. Indians are raised to respect and fear their elders. They know things, they know how to survive and how to live. Then I went out to college and decided they were all kind of stone age or something. Now I've come back to the village, they all seemed to have smartened up considerably."

"What are they saying about the station?"

"This is a small community and, like my father says, speech can be as powerful as a high-powered rifle. I guess we need a course in gun safety, so to speak. Speech is powerful enough as it is. The radio amplifies it. And this is not a two-way. It goes one way. You can't answer back." He dug in his parka pocket for a cigarette. "Who recorded Nimrod Kanakakeesic?"

"I don't know, really."

Nathan nodded.

"Never mind. New word for you."

I got my tattered little notebook out of my parka pocket, and a pen, and opened the pages. *"Djeeshakan.* That means a radio. It's also very close to the word for shaman."

# 16.

The shaman touches forces. They are not necessarily benevolent. Neither is the shaman. He is bound in winter snows and then breaks the chains like a Houdini. He is a masculine force, a master of flight and fury, he is like a lawyer or a pistol, and will serve any end. You are the end, and if you are not benevolent, then neither is he.

Perhaps you want a shaman for power or prestige. Neither one of these is benevolent. Either is expensive. You don't get these things without paying. Perhaps you thought you could go and sit at the feet of a shaman and learn wonderful secret tricks to amaze your friends.

But there is always a price and the tricks backfire with regularity and you find you have paid several thousand dollars for a spirit voice that will not stop talking and natters on and on and on about the unfairness of the present administration, about the observation chain, about city tribes, and nothing will turn the voice off, and then you must go back and pay another thousand dollars for the shaman to shut it up.

Who knows. Who knows what you will get. Who knows what the price will be. Be careful. A twin-engined airplane flies out of a thick fog and rains parts down on a village, the master of flight sits in his snow temples and the Underwater Panther rolls over in her sleep, crushing stone, sending the ice slabs flying.

# *17.*

We had turned past the solstice, the days became longer with amazing rapidity, there was a change in the air. This was the sudden movement of seasons, they blow forward in a rolling charge, like a canoe caught in a rapid current, flying out of a calm lake and into the rush of changes.

There was to be a meeting at the school about something, I was not sure what.

The teachers had urged everyone to come; they especially wanted the elders to come.

I had learned very quickly that the elders of North Spirit were important people, addressed with a respect which manifested itself in silence and shyness in their presence. One was to avoid using "I" when speaking to an elder. Try to avoid sentences using *'nin*, "I." It made things complicated. "One is going to the Hudson's Bay Store."

The elders are respected because they have lived through experiences, and, by training and culture, are supposed to have reflected on these experiences.

Experience can only take place through time. Time ages us, and so old people are expected to become wise elders. A hard job. Experience and time give us hard hands, calluses, bodies heavy with childbearing.

I supposed one should have both kinds: experience working in the world and the data from books and from elders that help us live through it. Data can be accumulated in minutes. Experience happens over the years. Sometimes we do not know what our experiences mean, even, for years. Like now; it took me years to decide to write this book.

It is easier and more comfortable to read about David Thompson's journey to the Pacific than to have gone on that journey.

If we sit down in a library to read about it, we are in a place where the lights and temperature are controlled, and comfortable. We are in control. We are not suddenly going to have experiences coming at us out of left field; unpredictable, chaotic. We are not going to be tipped out of our chair into a foaming rapids, the librarian will not suddenly begin speaking an aboriginal language or fire at us with a muzzle loader from behind her desk.

This is what makes a Spontaneously Created Person. The Great Spirit did not make these people out of accumulated data. They were made out of experience, which flies into our lives spontaneously, and reflection, which happens late at night, the fire from the wood stove grate throwing spider light over the walls.

I sat in the Nanokeesics' comfortable house and watched Jeannie rolling Sarah's short hair on little plastic rollers the size of cigars. The fire had burnt low and nobody cared. I suddenly noticed Jeannie's cousin, Celeste, sitting shyly in a corner, smoking and saying nothing.

I said, "I liked it straight."

Sarah said, "Yeah, but everybody thinks I'm Chinese or something!" She seemed upset. Sarah's emotions were always close to the surface, making her seem vulnerable and helplessly honest.

Jeannie said, "I keep my hair as long as I can. The old people say, long hair means long life."

Jeannie had great respect for the elders, even though there were elders she didn't personally like. She finished with Sarah's hair, blow-drying it (the Nanokeesics' house even had electricity! They robbed it from the nearby school generator, with a long extension cord) and brushing it out. It had been cut in a bowl-cut and so it sprang up and the curls all conflicted. They kept on about elders. Sarah was distressed.

"The elder women have just smashed this whole idea of a day-care center," she said. "They say no preschool kids are coming to that day-care center. And they built that whole new building! And I went and got a degree! In child care!"

Sarah's nose got red. She was about to cry. Her red nose stood out startlingly against her pale skin.

"Yeah, well, why should they?" said Jeannie. Jeannie was tough as saddle leather. I think Sarah always seemed a bit weepy and too sincere and idealistic to Jeannie. Jeannie was raised on a trap line. Nobody ever cut Jeannie any slack, why was Sarah getting all wet about this? "I remember crossing that lake on foot when I was five years old." She pointed with her lower lip toward where the lake was, its general direction. "In a snowstorm. I remember begging and begging Chief Makepeace to carry me. And he said, 'No, you have to walk.' It did me good."

"But it would have taught the kids things they needed to *know* before going to school!" said Sarah. "They would have been fed a nice breakfast!"

"Then you'd have to take them out of the cradleboard to teach them things they'd need to know before they got to the day-care center," said Jeannie. "I didn't learn to read until I was eleven."

And besides, the elder women were the grandmothers, and if the young women wanted to be free to go to the fishnets, or run around, or hang around the Hudson's Bay Store and gossip, they could just leave the kids with their grandmothers, the respected elder women, who had the knowledge that comes from experience.

"They need to be around their grandmothers, if their moms want to go play broomball all day," said Jeannie.

"But it took six months to build that day-care center," said Sarah. She blew her nose. "Indian Affairs had a complete plan."

"They always have a complete plan," said Jeannie. "Except one thing; they never ask the elder women. Never. It's like the elder women don't exist. Piss on Indian Affairs."

We packaged ourselves in parkas and tall moccasins and trudged off on the school road. Celeste drifting along behind us, silent as a mummy.

I am still not sure what the meeting was about. It was about the school-children. It was about the teachers teaching things that ought to have been taught by elders. It was the clash of cultures, ideas, ideals. It may have been about survival, the continuation of a struggle that began on this continent in 1519, when Hernán Cortés first moored his ship in the mouth of a tropical river far to the south of the boreal forest and the land of the Spontaneously Created People.

Everybody came and sat on the floor of the main hall, and the teachers faced the crowd from behind tables pushed together.

The teachers were embattled. They were white men and women who lived in comfortable housing with running water and electricity in the school compound on the Hill, facing parents who lived very different lives.

One elder woman stood up and said ———

"What's she saying?" I asked Jeannie. We were sitting on the floor in the back, in our parkas.

"She's saying the school ought to be shut down. She says, 'What are these kids learning?'"

A teacher said, "They have to learn hygiene, and there has to be some kind of health education. They aren't getting these things at home. At home, they just go home and work, they carry water and cut wood, they don't have time to do homework. So we have to do it all here in school."

This infuriated the Indian women.

Another elder woman stood up, with a young teenager by her side to translate. I looked; it was Nathan's mother, Mrs. Nanokeesic, who had made my high tops, and the boy was Nathan's younger brother.

Mrs. Nanokeesic gave them a blast. Her high-pitched, rapid, nearly shouting voice drowned out the teenager.

"My mother says they learn plenty. My mother says, the kids have to learn to work hard, they don't live in a city and so we work hard here. You white women live easy lives and you're going back to the city someday. We don't. Go back . . . she says . . . go . . . " He was starting to fumble, losing himself in that chasm between English and Ojibway, in the rapid stream of his mother's speech. "You have our children all day, the law says we have to give them to you. We don't know what you're teaching them. She says, why don't you teach something good, for all those hours the children are in school? She says . . . my mother says, what's wrong with teaching to repair snowmobiles? Is everything important . . . the Kings of England? What is wrong with to teach the . . . she says teaching about . . . about . . . *ahi, nimama . . .*"

He asked her to repeat herself. He was diffident, respectful.

"My mother says you shouldn't be teaching about the things of washing ourselves and all that. That's none of your business, she says."

The principal said, "Would it be acceptable if some of the elder women came to the school and helped us figure out what to teach in some of the hours?"

Beside me, Jeannie cried out, "Yes! Yes!"

I said, "Drag 'em across the lake in a snowstorm, that'll teach the little shits how to survive."

"Stop joking," said Jeannie.

Sarah said, "Well, I lived in the village most of my life but I can do as much as most people."

"Hmm," said Jeannie, a true trap-line baby.

I looked at the teachers. They were preparing the children to survive in a world where, inevitably, the powers that would affect their lives were white bureaucrats, the English language, Indo-European culture, and life that lay beyond the world of word-of-mouth. Information that would come at them in an avalanche of print. Like this book, for instance. Like the adventures of Beryl Markham and Isak Dinesen.

The Anishinabek women knew that the children would rarely succeed in that world, as that world sees success, and that the children must learn, by experience and by example, the old virtues of courage and patience and endurance. They must become physically strong and psychologically resilient.

When experience is devalued, elders lose their value.

The things we can learn in school are limited to data. On the other hand, that's not entirely true. We learn to sit still for hours and hours, and live in our heads the greater part of the day. We learn to force our eyesight to move along strict lines from left to right, instead of taking things in at a glance. We learn to keep our hands in our laps, or around a pencil. We learn how to organize our thoughts, we learn all the past that can be communicated in print, worlds open up in books. Our teachers tell us that the world is not a island on the back of a turtle, but a globe. Our teachers say, "Look people in the eye." We believe everything they tell us.

We learn things from other adults; we hear them tell stories of human failures. Or rather, more importantly, we *overhear* these things. We sit respectfully on the edge of adult conversation, with our big ears, and these words are not addressed to us, or at us, as admonitions, lectures, nattering instructions, chidings. We sit in our childlike private space and listen, avidly.

We hear admiration or disapproval in the voices of people we love the most. Their human smell and their hard, muscled hands are beloved and valuable. Along with laps and sips of forbidden coffee we learn what to value, what to risk. We learn the musical structures, the accents of speech, the sequences of rhythms, that we will carry the rest of our lives. These were my thoughts. I took notes, and later lost them. Maybe I started a fire with them. The dog ate them.

The teachers wanted to impart some of the better things of our culture: the literature, the music. The paintings. The great achievements. And why not? I have always loved foreign literature. I got a degree in it.

The elders knew that the myths and legends of the Cree and the Ojibway contained a world. That in those legends one is always young and strong; that we are always poised at the edge of a great adventure, that we were orphaned and abandoned by evil stepparents, that we carry some great secret of our royal birth inside us, we are rescued by enormous and dangerous forces that nevertheless look kindly on us. In the legends, we choose fearlessly between right and wrong, we are welcomed by sinister strangers, given magic knives, animal totems come to our aid. The elders knew they must somehow communicate to the young about the spirits of the things that are alive, and that despite their admonitions, the alive things, the stars and pipes and handkerchiefs and kettles and stones and canoe-ribs and money and corn and cakes and bread and driftwood and fishnets, had to introduce themselves to the children on their own time. That the children had to learn that learning by experience was learning.

Several elder women sighed and said they would come to the school and talk to the children in Anishinabe every day, if they could get somebody to look after the babies.

# 18.

I seemed to have little work or responsibility compared to the women living around me in North Spirit. I was childless, single, living in the shadow of Mrs. Mindemoya's care and daily cups of tea, borrowed bucksaws, advice given by gestures and single words.

I could see women all around me engaged in an endless round of work. Here, it was ladylike and feminine to be able to cut wood, haul water, rip the short hairs from a caribou hide with a dull ax blade, take an ax to a haunch of frozen moose, whip a beaver hide onto a willow hoop, make the willow hoop. I stopped and watched in astonishment as Jeannie's mother laid a new hide over a spruce stump and began to strip it of flesh and tissue with a piece of caribou thighbone that had been split down to a sharp edge.

I had never felt that being ladylike was much fun; on the other hand, it seemed to be a state that promised comforts. Having delicate hands, a law degree, a social-worker's position and a husband to help provide things like children, a house, a car, paid utility bills, and a future always seemed a bit of a trap, but if it was a trap, it was a gilded one.

My ex-boyfriend, He of Brief Duration, was even now down in a comfortable city preparing to endow my replacement with just those advantages. Elizabeth Peyton, a ladylike person if there ever was one, had just gone south to visit with, and enchant, a CBC man with a large old house in Toronto and a Mercedes. If he didn't marry her he was crazy.

But here I was in another world: a village of seven hundred and fifty Ojibway people, who spontaneously created their comforts from the living wilderness. These women walked up to heavy objects and picked them up; they didn't look around, hesitantly, to see who would come and help them. They looked for handles and then grabbed hold. They took up very cold things and very hot things with heavy mitts. They pitched accurate billies of wood at dogs and ran them off from their stretched beaver hides. They used their bodies as leverage, they started up cranky machines.

When the snow-fields over the lake had begun to go gray and patchy, Sarah Winnepetonga arrived at my door and said to pack up.

"You're coming with us to spring camp, Paulette. I'm going with my brother, Emasiah, and his family." She smiled happily. "I know you'll like it."

I jumped up.

"What do I bring?"

"Warm stuff, and snowshoes, and rubber boots . . . be *comfortable.* That's the trick. Don't *stint.*"

I packed my paisley-print sheets and a lawn nightgown and my book light, and makeup and hair rollers and all my wool socks and mitts and high-top moccasins.

I packed all this and put it on my back and walked down to the Blackhawk Store, to a tiny airplane that would fly Sarah and me into the wilderness fifty miles away, and I was pleased and scared with the tight, chilly, thrilled feeling of moving into a new world.

Lucy's gill nets were strung across an open rapids; wild, thundering ropes of white water. From the edges of this open water the ice was melting back; it was spring. It was not melting back evenly, but in rays and faults and loose slabs. I could hear the rapids from half a mile away.

We went from their spring-camp cabin toward the open rapids by snowmobile, pulling an aluminum boat behind us on the ice. Lucy and the girls rode in the boat. They were out on their daily task, laughing hysterically as the lightweight boat banged along, swinging from one side to the other. It sprayed grainy, wet snow, and chips of ice.

I had no idea how we were supposed to get past the belt of collapsing ice around the edge of the open water. I trusted them all completely, however. They were all still alive, weren't they? This was the women's daily job, wasn't it? The women and young girls went out every day to fishnets, they brought back the big, taut bodies of the leopard-spotted jackfish, or pike, the predators of the underwater world. They came home with whitefish, with the repellent suckers that were usually thrown to the ravens.

The air was different now; there was the smell of water in the boreal air, free radicals of loosened $H_2O$, the damp smell of a northern spring when temperatures rise high enough to set free frozen juices, the saps and melts and trickles and drips. The world smelt of caribou moss and birch buds.

Alongside us on the shore the quick little bodies of spruce and *minahik* rattled by like the pales of a picket fence. The long stretches of the lake were a storm of white light. It went on forever and forever. This landscape never ended. It simply jumped a short stretch of the Atlantic and then rolled on through Scandinavia and Russia and China and Siberia and then it leapt the Bering Strait and came around again.

All through it the circumpolar peoples cut their moccasin boots in slightly distinctive patterns, harnessed their dogs in fans or pairs, spoke respectfully of the Bear, told long, complicated jokes and then said, *Oh, I can't translate it, it's too funny*, drew pike and trout out of gill nets or struck them with tridents, hunted caribou and moose and knew many, many words for ice, for love, for awe.

I was terrified of ice, actually. I guess I was in awe of it. Where I grew up in the southern United States, we were taught never to go out on any ice under any circumstances. It was rarely thick enough to hold even the weight of a child. I had an ice phobia, which I was apparently about to get over by becoming habituated to repeated demonstrations of falling through either the ice or the phobia, whichever came first.

My tongue clave to the roof of my mouth as Emasiah untied the boat, and then Lucy and her big husband and daughters and Sarah all stood around it, grasping the gunwales. I realized they were going to run toward the water and leap in it, like a lot of merry elves, and I was expected to go with them.

I ran up and got ahold too.

"Now!" said Emasiah cheerfully. "We run, and at the last minute, everybody jumps in!"

Last minute? This was the women's daily work of collecting fish from the nets. Just another day's food-gathering, ho-hum. What if I missed my grip, what if my cold, slick hands skinnied off the gunwale? There was no rewriting this script. We were out of radio contact with anybody who could provide help, we were fifty miles from the nearest village, and, if I fell in, well, I would just turn into a stiff white thing.

So; it was all for one and one for all, and this is how we get supper. So to hell with it, let's go.

Lucy yelled, "*Asha!*" Now! And we all began to run with the sixteen-foot boat across the collapsing ice shelf, banging and shrieking across glare ice as bald and white as an eyeball, stumbling on slick moccasin bottoms, faster and yet faster, the aluminum keel crashing, until a) we were going as fast as we could and b) the ice began to go to pieces beneath us in collapsing, tipping slabs.

Lucy was yelling *poswundan!* Get aboard! All six people leapt into the boat agile as deer, Wabuus fell to the bottom, I tumbled in on top of her, Emasiah threw his two hundred and fifty pounds in the stern, the increased weight in the boat sped our advance and in the midst of crushed chunks and spraying needles of candle ice we shot out into open water.

While I was recovering from this, Lucy and Emasiah and Sarah grabbed paddles and fought the heavily loaded boat through the water.

At the point where the Severn River ran into the lake, where the rapids were, Lucy had strung her gill net between two spruce poles, one at each side of the open water. We paddled up alongside the ice and Lucy began to lean perilously far over the side, drawing up the net.

It froze on contact with the air. There were yards and yards of light, spiderweb net, frosty aquamarine crinolines, sparkling with tiny ices. Fish came up through the dark green water. They arrived in our hands like regal gifts. Pike, jawed like crocodiles, and whitefish in pure silver, the color and luminosity of a new moon at the rise.

I laughed, feeling a little crazed with fear and delight.

"*Gitche*" I said. A lot.

Lucy laughed and nodded. "*Eyha. Gitche.*"

We were a boatful of people in big, loose parkas and wet caribou boots, hair flying, ripping the big, slick fish out of the nets barehanded while Emasiah kept the boat in position with a hand-carved paddle. I was near the bow, and pushed up my parka sleeves to try to untangle a great pike. He was a gem of green and gold, with a long snout and clever wolf teeth, the tiger, the shark of the north. It took me a long time. But I got him. There is a hunter in us, male or female, that walks through the long ice ages by clans and on foot, carrying nets and spears, and this person reappears in us and fills out our parkas and discovers all the joy of a boatload of pike writhing and dying at our feet, and says, *We are going to eat this tonight and more tomorrow if we can and we will say thanks for being alive and for these things not being alive; that's how it is.*

That night I unpacked my expensive decorator cotton sheets in a dark paisley print and made myself a bed with a recently purchased Woods Five-Star down sleeping bag by the fire. It was a serious northern sleeping bag, not some goofy designer invention in ripstop nylon that melted on contact with a wood stove. Lucy was boiling the pike in a big pot. The whitefish, the size of oven mitts, had faded to a resigned pewter color and Leonard was frying two of them in lard on the edge of the stove, humming. Emasiah was stripping a snowshoe hare of its fur. The cabin smelled of fresh spruce logs, wood smoke, food.

"Look what I found," said Sarah. She walked in the door of the cabin with pieces of a rusting concertina. "I found it at the lakeshore. There was an old camp there."

She sat down and we picked over it; there were bits of decorative metal, velvet, rust, and damp.

"That must have been the Makepeaces' old camp," said Emasiah. "A baby died there many years ago."

"How come?" I said.

"They got caught in a long breakup," he said. He was a large, kindly, thoughtful man, over six feet, more than two hundred pounds, with hands like baseball mitts. He dwarfed the wooden ammunition box he was sitting on. Rabbit fur foamed up around his feet and his youngest daughter patiently picked up the pieces and twisted them between her finger and thumb into strands. Wabuus was unwinding some brass wire from my snowshoes, where I had repaired a split. She was going to string the wire up between two spruce trees outside and attach another string to the little FM transistor radio to see if she could pick up the radio station in North Spirit. "They couldn't get out with the canoes because it was freezing and unfreezing, and they couldn't get out with the dog sleds either. The baby starved. It is a heart-breaking story. They almost all starved."

We ate fried whitefish and snowshoe hare boiled with oatmeal and bannock and boiled pike and then we had tea with a lot of sugar and milk. My interior hunter faded away politely, without an objection, and she went on her way down the trails of the Ice Ages, fierce and lean.

Orion lifted his blue gems into the south-east and sparkled through the wavery panes of the cabin window. I clipped my tiny book light on a spy novel, but I wasn't interested in the print, I was interested in the silences. People breathed in exhausted sleep, the fire tinked and crisped frozen birchbark.

Sarah told me that Orion's belt is Oda-ka-daun, the Stern Paddler. She said there was some reason the three bright stars we see as a belt were called a Stern Paddler, but she had never heard why, exactly. Somebody must know. He must be in a canoe up there, but where the rest of the canoe lay, and who was in it, she had never heard. It was the only Indian constellation she knew, but now her curiosity was aroused and she made a note to herself in her journal.

I fell asleep with my book on my stomach, and fell into a nighttime cough. I dimly realized Emasiah had gotten up and laid another blanket over me. His enormous, caring presence allowed me to fall into a deep sleep; the silence of dreams fell over the little cabin, over journals and spy novels and busy minds. The huntress and the child float upwards into the night sky, at the very beginnings of humanity, on a distant sea at the edge of the glaciers, plunging their canoe into a dark riptide full of long, predatory, green-and-gold fish.

# *19.*

That spring I flew on an old, beautifully restored Norseman to a place called Muskrat Dam. I went with the chief and several councillors. I forget what the trip was about but it was a chance to go someplace. I was surprised to see pines; tall pines. We went to the Winnepetonga house, and there I met Sarah's father, the Anglican minister who had been, for years, the Indian Agent for the area. He was a confident, welcoming man. His daughters, Sarah's sisters, set out sandwiches and tea for everyone, made conversation, took me walking around the village while Chief Makepeace and Father Winnepetonga and the North Spirit councillors went into a deep conversation in Ojibway. I don't know what it was about. However, I had the feeling that the world was in good hands. One doesn't have that feeling very often. One must treasure it when it arrives.

When we took off from Muskrat Dam, the exhaust manifolds shot out shafts of fire backwards, a woman came running up, waving, with a large section of caribou haunch she wanted to send back to North Spirit with us, for her sister. It was dusk when we took off on the grainy snow, the skis rattling. It got darker and darker as the Norseman ground through the air. There were no seats, as such; there were hard wooden benches along the sides. We must reach North Spirit before dark, for there were no lights at the airstrip. I noticed the chief and councillors watching uneasily out the windows as the sun sank. I was still luxuriating in the feeling that everything was taken care of, I didn't have to make things right, arrange things, meet expectations or deadlines or strangers.

Chief Makepeace reached over and buckled my seat belt and pulled it tight. We edged home at the deep corners of dark. Emasiah set out smoke pots on the unlit airstrip for us. I rode back across the long forests sitting on top of a case of Carnation, the milk of human kindness, borne up by the darkening but friendly air.

That March a plane went down in Sachigo Lake, killing a young woman and injuring the pilot. He lost both hands in the long, cold night, waiting for rescue.

I listened as the HF radios all over the north talked to one another, frantic, searching for the plane.

It occurred to me that these planes went down and people died. When the full news of the crash reached North Spirit, by word-of-mouth, by people calling in to the nursing station HF radio, which was the best radio in the village, I saw a young nurse burst into tears, seized by hoarse sobs.

A woman came back from the hospital with twins.

Life was close; both birth and death and the ordinary graces of the day.

Little girls came to visit me nearly every evening, small and officious, setting themselves down at my table with Crayolas and felt pens. One day I came back to find my entire cabin labeled. I suppose at their lessons in school that day they had been taught English vocabulary by printing labels and sticking them on things. My door said DOOR, the window said WINDOW, the table said TABLE and my pottery dove from Mexico said TURKEY.

Men from the Indian Affairs Adult Education Department came and asked people what sort of education programs they wanted. Once again, I sat in the back of the hall at the school and watched.

People told them they needed a bakery, and a snowmobile-repair shop. Or, at least, somebody trained to repair snowmobiles.

Then the bureaucrats from Indian Affairs told the people what they would get; a typing course for the young women.

I thought, why did they come and ask?

One of the men was so drunk he fell asleep on his table in front of the crowd.

At the Hudson's Bay Store, I stood and looked at the things for sale. I paused at the rack of rifles, the hanging complications of Conibear traps, leghold traps; the racks of clothes — T-shirts, canvas jackets, rubber boots, one or two brightly colored dresses and a rack of skirts. I suddenly longed for the world of consumer goods. I wanted to *buy* something — anything. A skillet or a frying pan or a plastic hair thingie. Ice cream, a pizza, a book. You have no idea how you would miss this activity if you stopped doing it. I wanted to buy something with one of my North Spirit dollars — Canadian bills worn so thin the image was barely visible. Nathan had told me how the bills simply circulated around the village, from hand to hand, until they disintegrated. I looked at a rack of socks and rock tapes. These things came up from the far south, on airplanes, flying north, following a sort of grid of expectation, habit, trade.

Maybe I wanted to go south myself.

The radio station was pouring out voices now, every slot was filled, it told people the time, elders went there to pray during emergencies, and I felt I had been of some use.

# 20.

Most white people, at some time in their lives, would like to think they have an Indian name existing somewhere in the universe, a sort of authentic title of the self, our inside nature-self with a label.

One hopes one would conduct oneself well, and get a good name. One thinks of the great names of history: Missinaibi, Red Sky, Changing Feather, who was Tecumseh's right-hand warrior; Sacajawea, Matonabee, Wovoka, Almighty Voice, Crazy Horse, Dull Knife, Black Wolf; how did they get those names, what did they mean? Names like Thigh, and Hump. Vision quests, maybe.

In late April of 1974, on a day when it was actually above the freezing mark, I was sitting in Jeannie and Nathan's house. Nathan was helping me with word-lists. Jeannie was being provoked by their son, Solomon. It was early morning and Jeannie was still in her nightgown and housecoat. Like most three-year-old boys, Solomon was fascinated with what lay under women's dresses. He was snatching up her hem and peering.

Nathan said, "Insects. Spring's coming, you'd better learn some words for insects. Now, there's . . ."

"Stop that!" yelled Jeannie. "I'll stuff you back up in there!"

Nathan said, "Like Wimshoosh. It means a water spider. But you know, also, Wimshoosh is a character in a long, funny legend. It's about an old shaman and his son-in-law . . ."

"Quit!" yelled Jeannie. She grabbed up her birth-control pills from between the salt and pepper and thrust them at Solomon. "Here, take one; you'll disappear."

"Why would a shaman get that name?" I asked. I was thinking of the busyness of water spiders, their magical ability to skate on top of the water.

Nathan broke into a smile and tried not to laugh. He coughed and excused himself. "Actually, it's the larvae of the water spider. They swim on top of the water, they have all these arms . . . Wimshoosh had a magic canoe, magically propelled. . . . " He burst out into a short laugh. "I have to tell you . . . that's what they call you, you know."

"Really?"

"Yeah. That and . . . em, well, 'Sioux.'"

"Sioux?? Like in Dakota? Like in Sitting Bull?"

"Right. It's because of your English name." He was now laughing outright. "There's no *L* in Ojibway, so 'Paul-ette' becomes 'Puan-ette.' A *puan* is a Sioux."

"Why are you laughing, Nathan?"

"You'd just have to know the language! It's too complicated!!" He fell into frank, outright laughter.

Jeannie said, "I'm taking this child outside. Maybe he'd be interested in a roast duck." She swept Solomon outside in her nightclothes. I heard her talking to her father; he must have just walked up outside. "Look, it's Jom-jom, with a duck for you!"

It was no longer snowmobile weather. It was time to walk everywhere. In rubber boots.

"What about this Sioux business?" I said.

This touched my vanity. I can be very vain. I wanted to be thought of as a vague but charming poet with a name like Gazes At Dawn Sky, or Snow Bunting Flying, one of those verb names that had become fashionable with movie-makers, something starring Kris Kristofferson, maybe.

"It's just that *puan* means something like, oh, 'weird foreigner.' And *ette* becomes *ess*, that's a diminutive suffix that implies something kind of messy and worn-out. Ha ha ha! Shabby Little Sioux! Oh, sorry, excuse me." He got up and laughed himself out, poured himself a dipper of cold water and sat down again, coughing.

But he saved my wounded ego by explaining that people just liked to pun, to play on words, and really, my Indian name was Wimshoosh, Water Spider. (Or larva?) I liked it lots better, even though it implied I was running around the village on fast-forward, a water-spider larva or full-grown insect, skimming over the surface, desperately busy but never getting to the depths.

I laughed grimly along with Nathan. It was okay, I could take it.

"Hey! Stop languaging, you two!" called Jeannie. "Come out! Come on out here!"

The geese were coming.

We flung down our books and ran outside. Long strings of geese were floating in the brilliant heavens. They were like banners, celebratory and jubilant, as if they were pulling spring behind them on a windy rope, and after they passed in their thousands with these salvos of honks, spring would simply come and settle down on us in a brassy glow.

"Look, look, they're here!"

Jeannie stood out in her long robes with her black hair flying, holding Solomon. "Look, over there, there's the Weh-wehs, you can see how white they are!"

Suddenly the entire village was outdoors, people standing in the open and shading their eyes. The sky was filled with Canadas going north-west, crossing through streams of snow geese going straight north. It was like an aerial traffic jam. Old ladies were shouting, men stopped their three-wheelers, the Anglican minister rushed outside with his finger marking his lessons, Mrs. Mindemoya stood craning upwards, tugging at her head scarf. Lucy rushed out clutching a baby, Emasiah ducked out of the airstrip shack with the crackle of pilots' voices behind him on the radio, the men in the weather station left their ticker-tape data machines, the Hudson's Bay manager came out the storeroom door in his white apron, at the radio station the radio guys took off their headphones and ran out, Elsie Half-A-Day left off her woodchopping, Mrs. Nanokeesic put down her beading, the Free Trader looked up from repairing a canoe motor, the Chief arose from his consultations, and I rushed out onto the hard snow in my socks.

It seemed they would never finish flying overhead, there was no end to them, *nika* singular and *nikawak*, animate plural, streaming in all their animate plurality northwards to the shores of Hudson Bay, a triumphant parade, the Arctic Air Force.

Then we sat outside by an outside fire and ate roast duck. It was brought over by Jeannie's father. I remembered my fantasies, that I would eat roast duck and toss the bones to my tame husky. Animoosh lay on his stomach several yards back, whacking his tail on the ground.

"No," said Jeannie. "Don't throw duck bones to the dogs."

"I guess you want to know why," said Nathan.

"Here comes Sarah," said Jeannie. She waved. "Come have some duck!"

"It's inevitable," I said.

Nathan said, "I'll tell you one of these days. It's a legend. About the Son of Ayash. How his father was turned into a white duck that sailed away on the lake. But another time."

I said, "Nathan, who are the important people in this village? The people who really count?"

He stared lakewards, his round black eyes in a deep pondering.

"Well, the really important person is the feast-master."

"Okay."

"The person who arranges for ceremonial feasts in honor of somebody. To honor an elder or . . . somebody important. They arrange the food, and the time, and . . . they also distribute things. If there's a surplus of something, they arrange for it to be distributed to people who need it."

"I see. So who is it?"

"Well, here in North Spirit, I guess it's my mother. Jemimah Nanokeesic. She was the one who told Jeannie to come and check on you, that first night you spent in your cabin, there."

I had been looked after from the moment I had arrived.

I said, "Okay."

Nathan said, "She liked it, that you moved in that place by yourself."

I said, "I'm honored."

And she had sat and beaded her beads as I came up the path to ask for a pair of high-top moccasins, listened to my clumsy first sentence in Ojibway. The dog is drinking milk; *Animoosh jujushabu minikwakan*. A woman of respect and honor, unknown to the outsider. Quiet. Diffident. The feast-master and distribution-master of the village.

So spring came.

# 21.

I decided to leave North Spirit Rapids in mid-June, as my contract had run out, and, although my superior at CBC's office of Community Radio said they could extend the contract, I needed to go back south and attend to my poetry manuscript.

I was also tired. I needed grocery stores. I had a desperate desire for an indoor toilet. I was overwhelmed with greed for work-free heat. I wanted to see a Hollywood movie. I longed to walk on a floor with a rug on it. I wanted smoke-free electric lights, and running water that filled up a tub with hot water and didn't have to be carried in by the bucket, and an interior temperature that stayed the same all the time, and, generally, I was tired.

> *These are the struts. They hold the wings to the fuselage, they correspond to the arms of angels that you see in ancient paintings, held out in surprise or warning . . .*

Before I left, Nathan said, "What's happening, Puanets, is that we're incorporating this radio station into an organization called Wawatay Communications. What the chiefs of this area really wanted wasn't a community FM radio station, but portable high-frequency radios for the people out on the trap lines. But it sort of came in a package — the community radio station and the trap-line radios too."

"Oh, I see," I said. It was deflating.

"Oh, but your work here was very valuable! The people appreciate the radio station!"

I said. "And they also appreciate the trap-line radios."

"Yes. They save lives. With a high-frequency radio out on the trap line, if something happens, they can get a plane or a helicopter in. In the old days, you suffered, or you died. There were a lot of cases of starvation in the old days, too, when people were caught by breakup."

I said, "Yes, I heard a story about Chief Makepeace, out at the camp where the Winnepetongas go."

He nodded, thinking. "That's right. That's right. And someday I'll tell you what happened to my family."

I said, "Okay."

"So, maybe in a year or so when we get organized, I think we'd like to ask you to come and work for us. We might start up a newspaper. I'm supposed to manage this organization." He bit his lip. He looked worried. It was the first time I had ever seen Nathan look unsure of himself. "I'll figure it out. Anyway, you know, maybe you'd like to help start up the newspaper."

"Well, maybe so." Actually, I was thinking of trying to settle down with Sergeant Preston. He was going to meet me at the airport. Now, wasn't that a commitment? And help me find a farmhouse to live in, in the country, and I would write a whole *book*, not just poems.

But it made me feel good. So, I wasn't a total loss.

# 22.

There was to be a little ceremony of some kind at the radio station. Jeannie came and got me.

We walked through high, lustrous grasses, silver and green with new growth. Cotton grass flooded the low area by the river with snowy heads of light fiber.

Light streamed through the windows of the radio shack. It was warm in there, even with the oil stove on low.

Chief Makepeace was there, and Mrs. Nanokeesic, and Elizabeth Peyton, and Sarah and Nathan and the radio guys and several other elders.

Chief Makepeace said they would now pray and give thanks to the Great Spirit for this radio station, and how it helped the village, and for this new technology, the trap-line radios, because they are going to help the people, and for the white women that came up and helped out.

I bowed my head. Chief Makepeace prayed for a long time in Ojibway.

Children rushed by the door, chasing a dog.

"And now the gifts," said the Chief.

Gifts were handed around; to Elizabeth, and the radio guys. Mrs. Nanokeesic smiled and handed me a beautiful beaded bag.

"That's because you came to help us and worked so hard," said Nathan. "My mother wishes to give you this."

Nobody is ever left out.

# 23.

I boarded the DC-3 with Ace Lawson and his copilot, a new young fellow named Charlie. To get back down to Sioux Lookout, I flew with them on a long leg, all the way up to Fort Severn on the Hudson Bay coast, across to Wabuk Point, Winisk, and then finally down to Sioux Lookout. It was the pretty little town I had begun this journey from, on the northern rail line, only one hundred and fifty miles north of the Minnesota border. A journey I had started ten months and several lifetimes and three personalities ago.

Before we left, as I was standing out in the prop-wash holding my knapsack and a cardboard box full of underwear, Emasiah said, "You're going to fly over the Hudson Bay coast! It's all bog there! But look, look to see if you can see a big tall rock, standing up out of the bogs there on the coast! They say a shaman put it there! Watch for it!"

He waved goodbye.

It was a difficult flight; I was the only passenger in the empty spaces of the DC-3. They had a load of apples and bread. We hit air pocket after air pocket over a land gone wildly green; there were limes, mints, hunters, kelleys, flush with spring. Tall thunderheads skated across the sky on flat bottoms, exchanging thunderbolts. We passed the limit of granite hills and then we were over the Hudson Bay lowlands, marked with the descending layers of string bogs.

We struck so many air pockets that the apples came loose from their boxes and started cannonading down the aisle, shooting down like missiles, *thwack! thwack!* Fruit wars! The loaves of bread crept out of their container and came humping and tumbling down between the seats. I got up in the navigator's bunk to get away from the apple-cannonballs and clung to the bulkheads. Ace Lawson tried to drink a cup of coffee and during one terrible drop of two hundred feet or so, the coffee came out of the Styrofoam cup in a solid mass and struck him in the face.

"Well, then, now, you're going home down south," Ace yelled. "Bet you'll be back." He wiped coffee from his face. "Goddamnit, Charlie, I told you to hand me a cup of coffee, not throw it in my goddamned face."

"I can't predict these goddamn air pockets," said Charlie.

"Nah," I yelled. "Maybe not. I guess it's time to settle down."

A loaf of bread came slapping down the aisle. White bread, Dominion brand, determined to reach the flight deck. We rose up and were slammed down again.

"Settle down my ass," said Ace. "Settling down is for house plants. You don't strike me as a begonia or anything."

Actually, I sort of resented this. I was entranced by adventure and travel, and at the same time I would have liked for somebody to recognize that, inside, I was a very sensitive, tender, frail poetess.

"Begonias don't have any fun," I said.

"I guess not, there now, eh?" said Ace. "Damn little. They're starting up that Wawatay Communications thing, eh?"

"Right. Is this plane going to stay in the air?"

"Yes, it is, Skinny. These are Pratt and Whitney radial engines, it's the best-balanced airplane ever built. There's never, in all history, been a structural failure of a DC-3. That Wawatay Communications thing, that's their trap-line radios and a newspaper, isn't it? Going to be a newspaper in Indian?"

"That's what they're planning."

"That's what I mean."

"Mean what?"

"I reckon we'll see you back up here."

I said, "How do I know?" I picked up a MacIntosh and flung it back down the aisle. We landed briefly at Fort Severn; I peered out the sweaty windows, trying to see Swampy Cree people. This was a Swampy Cree village, a people I had never met, a language I had never heard. It was like landing in a completely different country. It was very flat, a long flat plain of sand bordered with spruce, with roofs and a tall church steeple. The sand plain came to a halt and became a bank that plunged straight down a one hundred-foot drop into Hudson Bay.

On the way back we flew over North Spirit again, and then Pikanjikum, and Poplar Hill, and Fort MacPherson, and Cat Lake, and then finally, down to Sioux Lookout.

I never did see the shaman stone.

# 24.

I spent two years in the south of Ontario, in apple country. I lived in a rented farmhouse and decided I would write something. I lived mostly on my savings, and drove a Volkswagen bug that was completely submerged when the township snow plow came by with its white surf of thrown snow. I had to go dig it out. This was only one of many distractions from writing, most of them far more entertaining than the writing itself. In return for a nominal rent I looked after a horse and three cows. The grain bin was in the shed, and the horse had discovered how to get out of the barnyard and into the door of the shed. The shed was attached to the house, and when I heard loud clumping sounds and snorts, I had to jump up from my desk and go back him out.

I felt I should write something about my experiences in the north, something in prose, and bought an electric typewriter, laid out a stack of clean paper, and gazed out the window where I could see my neighbor, the eighty-year-old Mr. Risk, going out to throw hay to his cattle.

But the stack of paper did not diminish and the ribbon on the typewriter rarely needed to be changed. It was easier and far less work to write a few poems by hand. I acquired a dog to go on walks with me. It was far more enjoyable to go on walks with him through the valley. The relationship with Sergeant Preston had not gone well, and therefore it was unhappy and interesting and time-consuming. He was a good man who had chosen the wrong, non-domestic person.

I thought perhaps I should write down some of the legends I had heard in North Spirit, but in cold print, with the pale light of a watered-green Ontario spring coming through the window, they seemed to have lost their magic. They were like the whitefish pulled up from the depths in a gill net, at first they shone silver and then they turned a dull aluminum color, drained of life.

The legends were always a series of episodes, one after the other. Like all ancient epics, they were another way of comprehending human life, and chance, and fate. A way we have not only lost, but of which we have lost all knowledge. Often they used what we recognize as literary devices: information conveyed through dialogue rather than direct narrative, flashbacks, exposition, various devices to heighten suspense. But all told, they seemed, on paper, to be rambling and disconnected, one event following another, held together by the forward impulse of the main character through a world of challenges and obstacles. Heroes, tricksters, foolish or wise young women, animals in their thick furs and their fixed characteristics — the lazy but powerful lynx, the goofy rabbit, the malevolent skunk, the regal moose, and, my favorite, mink. Mink, who is shamelessly self-interested, a trouble-making Iago, the clever personal-injury lawyer. All of them were propelled into the world of action by these immutable aspects of their inner selves. There was no character development as we knew it and the elements of style were those of the storyteller who took upon himself or herself the task of the story.

It lay in the hands of the storyteller to evoke these great forces that ground against one another: the Thunder Beings who were in continual war with the Underwater Panther, the serpentine Missepijou. Or to evoke laughter at the antics of Chakabesh or Wisekejac. Tales of the great powers have remained intact among the northern people and in the south we only recognize them occasionally, in symbols, perhaps. The national flag of Mexico depicts an eagle devouring a snake, sky forces and earth forces in eternal conflict.

But we are urbanized now, and these forces seem remote. We are in control of the environment. The stories seem odd. I tried again and again to write them down, and again and again found something far more interesting to do. The voice of the storyteller was missing, as well as a knowledgeable audience and the dim light of the fire that allowed the teller and the listeners to sink back into the imagination.

There was an old man named Ayash, he had a wife and a son. The old man decided that his wife was growing older and his son nearly grown, so he took a second wife who was very young and quite pretty. Before long she had a baby, and so she considered herself much above the first wife. Ayash and his new young wife began to mistreat the first wife. She had to do all the hard work and the new young wife did very little.

One day the new young wife decided to get rid of the first wife and her son. She went to her snares and found she had caught a partridge. She held the partridge between her thighs so that it scratched her. That night in front of the fire, she pulled up her dress and said, "Ayash, my husband, look what your son has done to me."

So the son of Ayash was driven out into the world.

He is known only as "the son of Ayash," and his mother is known only as "the first wife," or "the mother." The legend is told in great detail; the struggles of the partridge, the glossy hair of the young, new wife. And in all this detail, the son of Ayash is hurled precipitately out into the world, young and untried, abandoned to die on a rocky island. The legend creates, according to the skill of the storyteller and the general knowledge of northern life among the members of the audience, a scene which every Anishinabe is familiar with and looks forward to, a scene which can bring tears to the hearers.

The son of Ayash was sent out of the canoe by his father to collect sea-gull eggs on a rocky island. The father watches his son wade to shore, and then turns and paddles away. When the young man saw his father paddling away, saw the canoe get smaller and smaller in the distance, he knew he had been left to die.

He sat down on the shore beneath tall boulders and began to cry. He sobbed his heart out. In the midst of these wet, noisy sobs and the screaming of the gulls, he thought he heard a deep, whispering voice. "Why are you crying, my grandson?"

He turned around but there wasn't anyone there. Three times the deep, other-worldly voice said, "Why are you crying, my grandson?"

And the third time he turned quickly, at just the right moment, and he saw the terrible Missepijou starting down at him from behind the boulders, with her enormous horns and her serpentine body.

"Because my father has left me here to die."

"You will not die. I will help you. You must take heart, have courage. Sit on my back and take hold of my horns, and I will carry you to shore."

He overcame his fear of the great being, sat upon her back and grasped her horns.

She said, "But if you see the Thunder Beings, tap my horns, and warn me, because they will kill me."

They roar off through the water, Missepijou half-submerged, and as they surf through the cold water, the son of Ayash sees a dark cloud on the horizon. But they are still far from shore, and he thinks, I won't warn her just yet. Not just yet.

In the old days, Nathan had told me, it would take four days to tell the legend of the son of Ayash. How he didn't warn his benefactor in time, how she was struck by a thunderbolt and died, leaving a drop of blood on his hand, how the young man was plunged into Kitche-gum-mink, and drifted down into the darkly transparent depths, his hair drifting out around him. How he floated down to the bottom of the great water to discover the lodge of the tiny woman who lives at the bottom of the water world. He resurfaces again, and in his journey across the face of the earth he encounters the man with the poisoned leg, and the women with teeth in their vaginas, monsters, and dangers. He seemed, on paper, unfamiliar and episodic, robbed of his audience of knowledgeable listeners who had heard all their lives about Missepijou and the little old woman who lives at the bottom of the sea with her cauldron of good meat that never empties.

It was difficult for urban listeners to understand that these forces were at one time both world forces and inner forces. That the inner aspects of the characters were separated off and manifest as natural forces. That when the son of Ayash was plunged into the deep waters, he had been dropped into his own inner realms, that the little wise woman at the bottom of the sea was both inside and outside, true and not true.

And, besides, the horse had got out of the barnyard and had squeezed himself into the shed again. This was far more engaging than typing. It would be an entire week or more before I sat down to the disagreeable chore of thinking up stuff and typing it out.

# 25.

Since I had published a book of poetry several years ago, and was apparently a full-time writer (little did they know), I was asked to come to a creative writing class at a community college in Toronto and tell one of the native legends. I knew this boded ill, but thought I would plunge on, especially since I would be paid for it.

I knew these would be creative writing students who had been taught that episodic narratives were not a good thing; they had been told this was "mindless action." They had been instructed to evoke inner conflict in their characters and to describe complex psychological reasons for decisions made by these characters.

So I decided not to tell the story of the son of Ayash, that is, what I knew of it. It was the tale of a vision quest, and that was also hard to explain. What I knew of vision quests.

I would tell something light and amusing. The mini-legend of the Giant Enormous Penis. Humor, that's the trick. Make them laugh.

I drove down to Toronto on a rainy March day, found the parking lot, and then the classroom, and laid out my notes.

I said, consider this.

There was, at one time, a Giant Enormous Penis whose wife, a normal person, had to tow him around on a sled. And it was in early spring, when there was a crust on the snow. He was a terrible martinet, and was always shouting at his unfortunate wife, "Be careful how you pull me along! Don't go that way, go the other way! Look, stupid, I'm coming unlaced!" And so on.

They were passing along the banks of a little creek, when the towline "slipped" out of her hand, and the Giant Enormous Penis, yelling and shouting all the way, slipped and slid on the hard crust of the snow all the way down into the creek.

Crash! He broke through the candling ice, sinking lower and lower into the freezing water.

"Come back here!" he yelled. "Come back here and haul me out!"

His wife just kept on to wherever it was she was going. To visit her sister, perhaps. She would say, "Gee, I don't know, it just slipped out of my hand."

The students stared at me and then at one another. This crude tale was an Indian legend? I rushed on, I remembered that the people of North Spirit had started to giggle even before the storyteller reached the part about the boulders. The teller was expected to invent new twists, more clever insults, to do voices, drop significant pauses. However, not here. I hurried. Maybe they'd like the part about the portage brigands.

The Giant Enormous Penis crashed around among the boulders, yelling. The boulders in the creek began to laugh and make fun of the Giant Enormous Penis. I have forgotten all they said, but it was lacerating.

He struggled out of the laces of the load on the *djaban* and floundered his way onto the creek bank, soaked and furious.

"She did that on purpose!!" he screamed at the world. He floundered and flopped his way back down the trail until he came to the portage into a lake which lay open; it was inviting and shining with open water. He saw, just to one side of the portage trail, a tipi of portage brigands.

The storyteller explains that there were thieves, murderers, and generally repellent bands of criminals who lived within sight of the portage trails. When people came along who looked fairly defenseless, they would rush out and rob and kill them.

The portage brigands were lying about at their ease, waiting for victims. They had sticky hair and moccasins made of raw hides put together with big stitches because no normal woman would live with them. They smoked and drank anything they could get from the Free Traders and told horrible jokes that were boring except that they concerned murdered people, and then they would all bray with crude, honking laughter.

"Well, well, well," said one. "Look what's coming down the trail!"

"Oh my, isn't he just the cutest thing," said another.

"Let's rush out and kill him," said a third.

"Forget it," said the first. "He's coming this way. Let him walk in here, I'm too lazy to get up."

The Giant Enormous Penis hailed the tipi of portage brigands and joyfully floundered toward it.

"Hey! Hey!" he yelled. "Hey, you guys, I want somebody to help me kill my wife!" Just what the Giant Enormous Penis wanted: sadists, homicidal maniacs to help him kill his neglectful wife.

The students in the creative writing class shifted and writhed in their seats as the Giant Enormous Penis thundered off down the trail shouting for revenge. In North Spirit, by this time, people are falling out of their chairs with laughter. They are weeping with laughter.

On the other hand, in this classroom of writing students, there is silence and even hostility. Clearly the Giant Enormous Penis is an abusive husband, and killing one's wife is not a matter of laughter. The television and the newspapers are full of horrifying stories of wife-murder. This isn't funny. Not at all. In addition, the prospect of native people as criminals is also not funny. The percentage of the prison population made up of native people is far too high, another fact obtained from the media. I am talking to media children, whose life experience is extremely narrow and whose fund of accumulated data is extremely large.

I flounder, grin, give little laughs to indicate to them that this is "funny." There are a few uncomfortable heh-hehs. I forge on.

And so the Giant Enormous Penis tumbles into the messy tipi of the portage brigands and (I hurry, I am rushing to be done with this) then they cut him all up in little pieces, and so the storyteller says, "And that's the way it is with men, now. Some have big ones and some have little ones, like all those pieces they cut him up into, but nobody ever was as giant as that one again."

The men and women in the cabin are in seizures of laughter, each man and each woman thinking to themselves that's me alright, and the storyteller's reward is the high feeling of full-out laughter. In the classroom, I hurriedly slap together my notes and thank everybody and get out of there, walking through the blue undifferentiated, shadowless light of fluorescents.

Well, so much for that. Ethnocentricism bedevils us in many disguises. It is only after we become, or try to become, citizens of the world that we give up some of our ethnocentricism, which is why we travel, and live among other people.

I was tired of my occasional peckings at the typewriter and bored with driving myself to it. I had a grim stupid novel with lots of amateur character development that needed to be used as fire-starter. Sergeant Preston and I were clearly not meant for each other. So after two years of living on my savings and boring myself to tears on the rare occasions when I sat down to the desk, Nathan called.

He said that Wawatay Communications had obtained funding for a bilingual English–Ojibway newspaper, and would I come up north and help out?

I said I was packing already.

For storytellers all over the world, this is how life is; a constant series of journeys down the roads of plot and narrative and alarming incidents, improper conduct, failure to yield; always looking, always curious, and only occasionally sitting down in peace and silence to arrange events into a coherent whole.

# 26.

It was good to arrive in Sioux Lookout and strike out across town to find Nathan and Oldman Woman, to walk in on them in the offices of the new enterprise: a bilingual newspaper, a monthly journal of news and stories. There was a sense of excitement in the air.

I found a small cabin six miles outside Sioux Lookout and unpacked myself. The lakeshore was only twenty or so yards away, it sloped down to the water in long plates of dark stone. The cabin yard was bordered by spruce and birch and lake. The water made a continuous small chopping sound outside the north-facing windows.

Sioux Lookout is a complex knot of communications and transportation. Wawatay had established its offices there to take advantage of the availability of these things; typewriters could be repaired in Dryden, not too far away, and the organization was on that grid of communications which was imperative for its functioning. The Canadian transcontinental passenger train came through, in the seventies, twice a day; one eastbound, the other westbound. The engines squirted billows of steam out from between the wheels and trucks and the undercarriage, there was a crashing of couplers and the conductor in his big blue dreadnought overcoat yelling *booooooooaaaaaaarrrrd* ! There was a movie theater and outfitting stores, fried chicken stands, grocery stores, and offices for most of the bureaucracies: Indian Affairs, the Ministry of Natural Resources, Community and Social Services. There were two hospitals.

To the north of us were twenty-five or thirty villages of native people, most of them at the end of a bush-plane flight, some on gravelled roads near Sioux Lookout.

Obtaining news and stories for the newspaper meant travel. Over the next year I became accustomed to flight in small planes, some of them sleek and well-maintained like the fourteen-seater Navajos, others overworked and shaky little kites with pinholed pontoons and the copilot's seat torn out to make room for more cargo. I became accustomed to landing on small airstrips of three thousand five hundred feet, bulldozed out of the spruce forest and sticky as flypaper with clay deposits. I was in search of stories.

# 27.

It was a magical thing to be up in the complex, turbulent atmospheres of spring over Anishinabe-Aski. I was not yet afraid of flying on bush planes. Building towers of thunderheads were sailing up out of the west like the great ships of the Hudson's Bay Company in the last century, and the century before that. Ships top-heavy with sail, clouds of sail, bearing beads and mirrors and gunflints and Grenfell cloth and duffle cloth and red wool for leggins, bales of blankets, fish-hooks and kettles, ice-chisel heads, big axes and little hatchets, needles, awls, buttons, and peaveys. Then they sailed away for England with furs. Furs. More furs. The Company of Gentlemen Adventurers Trading out of Hudson's Bay became old and tradition-proud. While the cartographers modernized the spelling of the great Bay, reducing it to Hudson Bay, the Company kept the apostrophe *s*. Hudson's Bay Company, Here Before Christ.

We were heading to the James Bay coast, where those ships had arrived from England, and the Bay men had set up posts on islands in the mouths of rivers. The coastal Crees called the English "sail-around-behind-the-islands people."

Generations of Scotsmen had come to the New World straight through the Hudson Straits, never knew southern Canada existed; didn't care. These posts, which became villages, were built as early as 1680. From the coastal forts, the Bay men spread inland, setting up small sub-posts at Indian spring gathering places, like North Spirit Rapids. They came with knee britches, silver buckles, ponderous Tower-of-London muskets. Generations of Crees had traded with them, arriving in the spring, middlemen, men called Captains, hard bargainers, great orators whose speeches were often preserved in the journals of the post factors. *Give us good goods, I say. The young men have worked hard this winter, they wish to look fine, with red leggins and gun cases in red wool. Do not put your thumb in the measure. Give us good goods.*

If we wanted to sell the newspaper to the Cree people of the coasts of Hudson and James Bays, we had to get news from there. People like to read about themselves, or at least other people who are somewhat like them, or, failing that, disasters and weird facts.

This was *Wawatay News'* first assignment journey into another area, and I was anxiously thinking of angles, something to make the trip worthwhile.

"All I know about Swampies is that they all wear, um, you know, hip waders," said Oldman Woman. "They're born in them. They come out in the delivery room in hip waders. They live with those tides coming in and out." She had a sketch pad and pencils; always an optimist. I carried my poetry manuscript. I was optimistic too.

The land sank on the way north-east. The hills of the Canadian Shield subsided, went underground, and were covered with flat bog-land. The reflection of the occasional sun chased us like a brilliant, shining, rolling head across the wetlands.

It was a four-hour flight to the coast, through rags of disappearing clouds and rain. Here, I thought, was a truly remote village. Free of bureaucracies, far from the image-generation of televisions and radios, from railroads and towns. Perhaps there are mysterious coastal secrets here. The long trading relationship between the Swampy Cree and the Company of Gentlemen Adventurers shaped the Cree political focus. When they looked outside their own culture with imagination's telescope, they aimed it toward England, not Toronto or Montreal.

As we came down from an altitude of eight-thousand feet toward the coast, I could see far out on the water of James Bay, where the clouds were breaking and reforming, pouring sun down onto the gunmetal water, an occasional flat plate of unstable summer pack ice drifting toward Akimiski Island.

We disembarked onto a sandy airstrip that made gritty, wet sounds as we walked on it. Oldman Woman looked around at the two Cree men standing by the airstrip shack, suddenly uneasy among a strange tribe. We trudged off onto the main road to the village as if we were stepping on a new carpet in an unknown house.

# 28.

Oldman Woman and I sat in the band office of the village of Henley House, down by the shore, trying to appear professional, pens poised over our notebooks. All around us the walls were covered with plans. Perfect plans. Drawings on architect's paper of plans for housing, water, electricity, and my god, an old-folks home! Clearly we must concentrate and do a thorough job here.

It was a very quiet place. One would think with all these plans up on the walls, there would be people bustling around, rattling papers, dropping tools, that there would be sawing noises and gunning motors and the *beep beep beep* of earth-moving equipment backing up. But it was very still. A steady, whispery drizzle pattered on the windows and the roof.

The chief was a thin, elderly man.

His young translator was full of purposes and plans.

The first thing about doing interviews is to appear professional and competent; you will take this person's speech in hand, carefully, like a pilot, and do something to it that will make it take off gracefully into the atmosphere. Even if you are completely at a loss. Never *appear* to be at a loss. If you do, your interviewee panics, thinking of his/her words in a jumble in print, and then *everybody* panics.

"Indian Affairs has a complete plan for this village," the translator said.

Outside in the office, I could hear a woman arguing with the band clerk, loudly, in Cree.

I said, "Why are the houses so close together in a grid?"

"So Indian Affairs can get water and electricity to each house. All the teachers' houses have running water and electricity, why shouldn't the native people?"

I said, "That is very true." I shifted my pack off my lap. I was wet and sticky. I could hardly believe it. This place was a bureaucrat's dream, a whole village of people to be planned for, controlled, set up in little dollhouses.

Oldman Woman said, "Well, we were thinking about trapping news. . . . "

"We have very few trappers anymore. The school has a program to teach the young people about the land."

I thought, but it's all around you!

"What do the kids do? Are there square dances?"

"We have a recreation program for the young people."

I said, "You mean Indian Affairs has a new whole village completely planned out and activities and everything?"

The young translator nodded.

"Including a senior citizens' home for when our elders need to be taken care of. Of course, the recreation programs are funded by the Ministry of Community and Social Services, and Health and Welfare will contribute to the senior citizens' home. The Ontario Provincial Police have started their native constable program, and so we now have two native constables. This all will make a good story for your newspaper. It's an Indian newspaper?"

"Yes," said Oldman Woman. "Um, I think we'd . . . well, we would like to . . . um. Is there anything happening? Are there any events here we can report on? Dances or fishing or . . . "

"Well . . . " the translator considered for a moment. "There's a diphtheria epidemic."

I said, "*Diphtheria*??"

Wonderful. My first trip back to the remote north and I'm in the middle of an epidemic I don't even know how to spell.

"They are giving the children immunization down at the school. But this isn't the only important thing in our community." He waved his hand toward the charts, maps, graphs and blueprints on the wall. "We are one of the first completely planned communities in the north."

Oldman Woman said, "What is that, *ahi*, lady arguing about out in the front office?"

The chief listened to the translation of the question and said, "She wants to build a cabin a half-mile outside the village. We can't allow this. We can't allow people to just go off and build a cabin anywhere they want."

So I took out my notebook and sat in the band office for nearly an hour, writing furiously, trying to get all the names of the plans straight. And when they were to be "implemented," and how the "implementation" was to "impact" the community.

I looked out the window at the jumping, quick, animated waves of James Bay. There was a dock with a lot of canoes tied up, bonking against one another.

I said, "How do people make a living here?"

The chief said, "Well, most people are on some kind of government transfer payment. Social services and so on. And when they build the rest of the houses, there will be carpentry jobs and so on with Indian Affairs."

I said, "How come she can't build outside the village?"

"Because all the houses have to be where we can bring electricity and water to them."

"What if she doesn't want any?"

"The chief says she will. People go build far off and then afterwards they want electricity."

Probably so, knowing human nature.

"Where's the energy coming from for all this?"

"Indian Affairs will bring up a larger generator, and the fuel for that will come up on the summer barges."

And, of course, the weirdo who wanted to build a cabin away from all this would be regarded as a dangerous heretic who didn't know what was a good thing, away from all the dust and oil and flickering blue TV lights.


The school was new, clean, modern. The designers — probably young architects with red suspenders and laddered haircuts down in Toronto on lucrative Department of Indian Affairs contracts — had designed for a lot of plate glass, which was mostly broken. Can't keep teenage men in recreation programs twenty-four hours a day unless you chain them to something.

The gym was heated and briskly lit with fluorescents. We were immediately tangled up in a line of parents holding squirming children, people wearing hip waders and rainproof jackets, in dark blues and grays and browns. The fluorescents made everybody weird-colored.

They were moving toward the tables in the gym where nurses were stabbing fine needles into children's arms.

"Here honey, hold still. Yes, a family went out to Winnipeg and contracted it. They brought it back. We notified Winnipeg. Oh now now now. There! That hurt, didn't it? Yes, it's on the national news. My, what a great pair of lungs!"

The nurse's hair was all in a frazzle from the humidity and many hours of sitting and inoculating thrashing children. Her ears must have hurt. And this was on the national news! This was serious big-time reporter stuff. It was depressing.

Oldman Woman took pictures, half-kneeling to get at the lap-level of the children and the nurse. I thought, we have to get out as soon as possible and phone in this story. Just last week we had practiced phoning in things. It was difficult to do; one had to think at the same time.

"Hello, darling," said the nurse. Her jeans and sweatshirt were wrinkled and spotty. She reached out for another child. "Now now now. Diphtheria is airborne, not water-borne. We're running out of serum. The chief was talked into this completely planned community by Indian Affairs guys, and so everybody's packed up together within thirty feet of one another. There! Hurt like hell, didn't it. My, what a great pair of lungs!"

We shouldered our gear and walked back through the hard sand streets in a light summer drizzle, back toward the band office. A television's blue light blared out of a small window in one of the boxy Indian Affairs prefabs.

I said, "Are they getting television reception all the way up here?"

"Search me," said Oldman Woman. It was very flat. There were no views, as such; the houses were so tightly packed all you could see was houses.

They must have had fun down in Toronto or wherever it was they made up the plans for Henley House. It would have been like building a dollhouse, with little pictures on the walls and unwalked-on carpets that would never get worn; little figures of Mommy and Daddy and Johnny and Suzie (no grandmother or grandfather, of course) could be moved about at will.

At the edge of Henley House, the forest came up and stopped in a exact line. The ditches between all the houses were filled with water, and tin cans, and used Pampers, and plastic bags, and socks, and in one I saw a dead kitten. The houses themselves were the ordinary Indian Affairs-built prefabs, but jammed so tightly together, cheek to jowl, that they seemed awash in their grid of drainage ditches. In the summer there would be no shade, dust would roll in billows down the streets, and in the winter the wind would come cracking through. There were simply no spaces or buildings — none — for public activity. No snowmobile repair shops, no sawmill, no restaurant or coffee shop, not even a public square. Okay, a public square is a totally European idea but if you're going to jam people up in a village, you've got to have some kind of gathering place.

It was like a bedroom community with no urban center, a barracks in the middle of nowhere. It looked like it had been built over a weekend at an oil strike.

Oldman Woman said, "I wonder if they have a restaurant in their complete plans? If that translator had given us any more bullshit I would have killed him and eaten him."

I said, "Here's a headline. HENLEY HOUSE YOUTH WATCH TELEVISION."

"How about, HENLEY HOUSE PEOPLE PLANNED FOR."

# 29.

We finally managed to talk with the Hudson's Bay Company manager.

The Hudson's Bay manager (they weren't called "factors" any more) told me there was hardly any fur of any kind coming out of Henley House.

He was a young man from the Orkneys. The HBC had been recruiting kids from the Orkneys for three hundred years.

"No' verra mooch," he said. "There used to be. 'Twas a gued post here. A gret dill of fur. But that was before the dey-school. Now the kids heav to be in school all dey, and wh' are the perrents goin to due? Gang awa' and doomp them on the teachers? And wi' the anti-fur folk, you know, the prices are doon. That's my theory of the loss of fur harvest. But I'm na expeart."

News here would be news about what was being done to people, for people. They themselves would generate no news, no activities or events. The only thing to write about was what was being done to them. But people never really do *nothing*. They always do something. You just might not like what it is that they *do* do.

A man came weaving through the drizzle at us and, when Oldman Woman approached him, he fell over into a ditch. When he struggled up out of the water he was talking furiously to himself, and so we fled.

I said, "We *have* to find people to talk to."

"Sorry. We've apparently landed in Margaritaville, or maybe it's the, um, Planet of the Pod People."

"Then all we're going to have to report on is this cussed plan business, and it hasn't even happened yet."

Akewence waved her delicate hand at the rain, and the situation, and the coast, and the ditch man, who was even now still stumbling in our direction.

"*You* go find somebody. There, get a kid shot. Take a picture of those kids."

I said, "You do it. You talk Cree to them and get them to give you big happy grins."

"Hand it over."

She grabbed the camera and walked up to the three little children playing in the ditch water. She knelt down on one knee and raised the camera.

"Hey, *bojo! Bahpin!*"

A little girl looked up and said, "Fuck you."

So we went on.

We found a mud room on the outside of an abandoned old teachers' residence and sat there and ate Hot Rods and potato chips and watched the rain come down in glistening streaks like ephemeral sky-jewelry, stringing beads along the edge of the roof. I didn't know why these teachers' residences were abandoned. They looked perfectly good to me.

We were invited to stay at a teachers' residence. The teachers we stayed with were a young couple from Winnipeg. He was an urban Indian, a Saulteaux from the city. She was a white woman, anxious to be part of the north but confused about what part, what north.

I asked him, "What do people eat?"

He said, "Store food. White flour, white rice, Vienna sausages, Spork, Popsicles and oatmeal. That's what you can buy on family allowance. Welfare food."

I said, "You guys are exaggerating."

"We're not. If somebody goes out and gets a caribou, it's cut up and all over the village in five minutes. The guys don't come in with meat very often." He tapped his fingers on the new, unscarred kitchen table. "What if something were to happen? What if the government ran out of money or there were a depression or something? Governments don't make money out of nothing. The kids can't *do* anything, they're losing all the old skills. Which would be okay if they didn't live here. But they *do* live here; they're not going to all move to Winnipeg, are they? And we're supposed to urge them to get high school degrees, college degrees. And they can't even repair a snowmobile, or fire a gun, and they don't know their way around the land. And it's getting to where they can't speak Cree anymore. That's what gets me."

That night I sat up late, unable to sleep, as usual. I was reading a historical romance. *The Game of Kings*. All that crazy, unplanned buckling of swashes.

I looked out the window over the houses laid out in exact squares. I thought, people from Toronto are planning this village, but nobody in Toronto would want to live in a place like this. They couldn't do this to farmers, or little city neighborhoods. No. Down there, there would be resistance from farmers and little neighborhoods. The residents of Toronto Islands had fought for years to keep their tiny eccentric village from being plowed under the big scraper-blades of Plans. But the people of Henley House were remote, far away, and so the planners put out contracts and the chief and band council were convinced and the great paper machines ground down.

I wrote down some notes. None of which would serve for a newspaper story.

Somewhere back in the lines of history the Cree people had been in possession of places of public celebration, places of mystery, story roads. They had harvested the gifts of the land, bought, sold and traded. They exchanged songs and rituals and services. They had arrived at the post in the spring with mink and marten and beaver, there had been days of grand speeches, dancing, arranging of marriages, and then the hard bargaining. They had acted as middlemen between the English and the Ojibway. Even the missionaries and the Hudson's Bay Company had not managed to eradicate their way of life and their language, but somehow this benevolent bureaucracy was managing to do just that.

I listened to the noise of the slow, reluctant tides of the great Bays perishing repeatedly on the shore, setting the few canoes to knocking.

# 30.

At about midnight, the door downstairs flew open with a bang.
Suddenly the teachers' house was filled with shouting, lights,
breaking crockery.

Something happening at last!

Oldman Woman jumped up from her bed and ran to the window
and looked out. It was still light. A police van was streaking across the
sunset village toward us.

Yells and shouts from downstairs.

I said, "Are they anywhere near my cameras down there?"

"You think I'm going to . . . you know . . . go down there and *look?*"

The air rang with violent emotions and fright. BANG!! a dish hit the
wall. There was yelling in Cree and then a switching in mid-sentence to
English; unimaginative swearing. "You asshole!!" I could hear the young
Saulteaux man saying soothing things.

I crept out in my nightgown and peered over the bannister. There
was a young man flinging himself about, being dangerous, but it didn't
look as if he had a gun. The native constables were both big men with
braids falling down their backs from under their caps. They smelled of
rain and wet wool and coffee.

There was more screaming and imprecations as they jerked the
young, drunk man out of the kitchen and threw him in the van.

I crept downstairs.

The teacher and his wife were sweeping up broken shards of dishes.

"It was just a drunk kid. He gets drunk once in a while and goes looking for trouble, usually at the teachers' residences."

The woman said, "It's envy or something. We have these nice places
and the community people don't. It'll be better after everybody has
electricity and running water."

"No, it won't," said the constable. He had come back in. "These kids don't have anything to do but watch TV." He looked at me. "They order televisions here, and VCRs, and people get videos mailed in. A lot of the videos are soft porn. Lots of violence."

I said, "You have a jail here?"

The constable laughed. "Yes. We have a jail." He and his partner took up cups of coffee and started laughing. "But we don't have any jail *doors*. Well, yes we do. The doors for the detention cell got shipped up yesterday but they're not installed yet."

They laughed; exhausted, discouraged, sad.

# 31.

I said, "Now where?"

There was a canoe going down on the Sand River to the next village south, a place called Sand Rivermouth. Oldman Woman found this opportunity by hanging around the dock, talking to people, writing down words in Cree while rain dripped off her turquoise and silver bracelets.

At the band office, I tried to call David on the high-frequency radio telephone.

"David, David, we're off into the northern coastal forests here any minute. You heard about the diphtheria? Over."

Squawk squawk squawk garble garble flutter bzzzzt bzzzt Akewence, over."

"You're fading, talk to you from Fort Albany, over."

"Why bzzzzt Albany, over?"

"The serum is there. The serum is there. Going by way of Sand Rivermouth. Sand Rivermouth. By canoe. By canoe. Out. *Miweh.*"

The translator and chief sat and listened. They talked together for a moment.

"The chief says he hopes you have seen something of the new plans we have for our people. He says he remembers twenty-five years ago, at the long portage between the Attiwapiskat and the Ogoki, seven people starved to death during a bad break-up. He doesn't ever want that to happen again."

I paused a long pause.

I said, "Who were the people?"

The chief listened, and then said, "My mother, my two younger brothers, a family from Ogoki."

I said, "I understand."

Would I have taken the new planned village too?

As we stowed our backpacks and camera bags aboard the twenty-four-foot freight canoe, a man walked up to Oldman Woman.

"*Eyha*," he said by way of beginning a conversation in Ojibway. "*Kin Wawatay kint'anoki na?*" Do you work for Wawatay?

"Hey. He's speaking Ojibway," said Oldman Woman. She listened. "He's from Fort Hope, and he has something for the paper. Cool. Somebody's *giving* us something." The small, elderly man handed her a paper. "He says if they ever try to do this to Fort Hope, he'd like to offer this."

A suggestion from a village person, at last! I rolled it up and put it in my camera case. I was now in possession of the secret scroll, handed down by a respected elder, the ancient document that held all the answers.

The secret of this secret document is not its suggestions; these are ordinary, commonsense ideas that anybody with the IQ of a hockey score should be able to grasp. What is secret and extraordinary about it is its method of arriving here, in hand. It is a suggestion actually forwarded by an *elder*, given from one Ojibway to another. Apparently, the people in the architectural professions in Toronto find these documents rare and nearly impossible to come by. This is the answer. This is how you come into possession of these shadowy scrolls whose existence is only hinted at in the halls of planning offices in the cities.

Here it is.

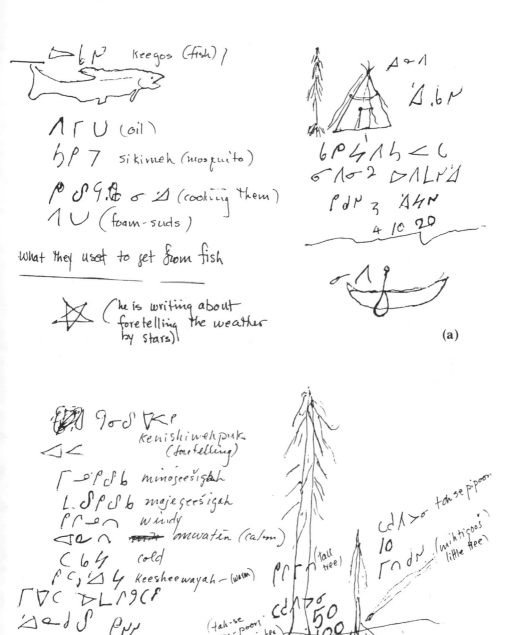

ᐅᐸᑭᕒ keegos (fish) /

ᐱᕒ U (oil)
ᔤᑭ 7 sikimeh (mosquito)
ᕒ ᐁᕊᖈ.ᕗ ᓂ ᐱ (cooking them)
ᐱ U (foam-suds)

What they used to get from fish

_____

(he is writing about foretelling the weather by stars)

(a)

ᐁᐢᑊᕂ ᐅᕒᕒ

ᐁ 9ᓂᕊᐟ ᐸᖈᕒᐱ
kenishiwehpuk
(fortelling)
⊲<

ᕒᓂᐱᕊᕀᑊ minoseesigah
L.ᕊᐱᕊᑊ majegeesigah
ᕒᕒᓂᐣ windy
⊲ᓂᐣ mwatin (calm)
ᐸ ᕀᖾ cold
ᕒᕓᐱᕀᖾ keesheewayah — (warm)
ᕒᐁᕐ ᐅᖈᕒᐱᕐᑊᕒ
ᐱᓂᐊᕊᐱ ᕒᕒᕒ

(tall tree)

(tah-se poon
Tii-poon every winter)

ᕐᐱᐸᕊ
50
100

10

ᕐᓂᐊᕒ (mihtigoos
little tree)

ᕀᐱᐸᕊ tahse pipoon

(b)

(a) Before Indian people used to live 10–20 feet from lakes or rivers, now they live too far inland — in villages — and the dust is not good for them.

(b) Years ago Indian people had no chemicals in their food or alcohol, and they grew up well and lived long, 50–100 years old, like a tree well-grounded in moss. Now they are shorter, stop growing, and are like small trees with no root system; alcohol and TV and canned food.

# 32.

We were cast down the dark alluvial currents of the Sand River, floating musically downstream. Mr. Whitesky had loaded his vessel with a rifle and nets, a box of shells, a tow sack of supplies.

"I'll live on a river!" I shouted at Oldman Woman. The little gasoline engine was noisy. "In a houseboat!"

It was a heavy, dark river, the banks were covered with tamarack and poplar. The sun shone. We ate cheese sandwiches, threw things overboard to see them float away.

"What would you do in the winter?"

"The Caribbean!"

It was very pleasant, if a bit windy. Mr. Whitesky sat in the stern and operated the tiller, the little twelve-horse-power kicker purring nicely. I could have spent a week or so on the river, eating cheese sandwiches and smoked fish, if there were any smoked fish to be had.

"*Ki-wi-miijim, na?*" I asked Mr. Whitesky in Ojibway if he would like some of my cheese sandwich.

"*Moya.*" He said no in Cree.

"I understand that!" I yelled at Oldman Woman. "He said no. *Moya.* That's Cree for no."

Oldman Woman put her slim hands around her mouth and shouted, "*Miijim! Miijim! Nemegoose!*" She wanted food, and specifically fish. "I hate cheese."

Mr. Whitesky was amused at our antics. He was a stout man of about fifty, very broad across the shoulders, in rain gear and hip waders. He bent over to pat his 30-30 rifle.

"*Atik. Atik,*" he said, and pointed a finger and made a shooting noise, and then put up a hand to shade his eyes and looked ostentatiously along both banks.

"He's looking for caribou," said Oldman Woman.

I said, "Hey, even I can figure that out. I never get credit from certain unnamed persons as to how well I can really speak the indigenous language."

"He's speaking Cree," said Oldman Woman.

"Going *bang bang* and gazing at the shore isn't Cree, Akewence."

We floated down the Sand River, arguing comfortably with one another and hoping we might see a caribou. I forgot all about the diphtheria and the totally planned village.

Suddenly Mr. Whitesky shouted and pointed.

"*Atik, na?*" I said. "Caribou? Yes? No?"

"*Moya atik. Pashkesigun!*" No caribou, a gun?

"What?"

"Look, look," said Oldman Woman. "Look at that!"

We were passing through a series of high clay banks, and I looked where they were pointing on the gray-blue slides of the bluffs. There, where a small spruce clung to the teal-colored soil, was a long thing sticking out, long and black and rusted, and there was the slimmest remnant of a trigger guard and heavy plating where the flintlock mechanism had eroded into a lump.

I said, "My god, it's a flintlock! It's an old flintlock rifle!"

We were moving downstream, farther and farther away from this artifact. Someone had dropped it in an old channel of the river, a birchbark canoe had overturned, they had all swum for their lives, the rifle sinking and sinking, the baby in the cradleboard, the *tikinagan*, floating downstream. . . . I watched as the eroding barrel burnt dark with history and acid soils disappeared around the bend.

"Can we go back?"

No. He was looking for caribou. Some other time. But there never was another time. Maybe somebody else, two hundred years ago said, some other time, we'll go back and get it. And it became an enchanted gun, reappearing every hundred years . . . maybe someone had lain in ambush for an enemy, had fired out of the green, new-leafed tamaracks, but his rival (in love?) had fired back, killing him. Bones and gun drifted to the bottom of the river, the gun took on magic.

Oldman Woman said, "He says, 'Some other time.'"

I forgot about being a hard-nosed hard-news reporter. The paper came out only once a month. It wasn't like we had daily deadlines. We drifted down the Sand River, stayed over at a trapping camp, where the dark moss roof of the cabin was polka-dotted with new lime-green poplar leaves. Passed through the little five-cabin trapping community of Sand Rivermouth, and went on. We ended up in a village called Kasechewan, took photos of two young women wringing out a wet moose hide with two sticks, slept in a schoolhouse, all the time promising to pay people. We'll pay you when we get back. No problem. We spread debt all the way down the Sand River like princesses throwing out coins.

We found an elder woman who was smoking fish, and came away with rich-smelling golden fillets. At least we had enough cash on us to pay her. She had a smoking tent with racks and racks of good trout. She wrapped them in a brown paper bag. What we had just done, according to the Ministry of Natural Resources, was illegal. The elder woman was not supposed to sell her fish or game; she was not even supposed to use her gill nets to obtain them. We three criminals bid each other good-day and we went off with two days' supply of protein.

In my notes I wrote "Diphtheria" means "a piece of leather" in Greek. I discovered this fact in a school dictionary, in the little day school in Kasechewan. A false membrane forms in the throat and air passages, it is spread through the air, by people coughing and sneezing.

We got a flight out of Kasechewan to Fort Albany, a matter of leaping up into the air for fifteen minutes, drifting down again through light, cottony cloud-rags, bumping onto the sand airstrip of Fort Albany, on the island at the mouth of the river, right at the edge of the houses.

"I know some people here," said Oldman Woman.

The Hudson's Bay post was, as usual, on an island at the mouth of a great river. This post had been here since the late 1600s. There was also a Catholic school, a church, and a convent on the mainland. The Oblates. Fort Albany also had a sawmill, several stores, a good fur harvest. There were poplar and tamarack throughout the village on the island and the mainland both, all around the Catholic school and residences.

"You can find us a place to stay?"

"I can find *me* a place to . . . um, it's an old school chum . . . I bet you could stay at the convent across the bridge, over on the mainland." Akewence drifted off down a path, in search of an old school chum, her silver bracelets and earrings winking in the foggy light.

I got photographs of the boxes of diphtheria serum, packed in dry ice, being loaded aboard the plane I'd just left. They were smoking, and the men handled them as if the disease itself were in there and could burst out and grab them by the throat any minute.

# *33.*

The Sisters of Charity were accommodating. They had an efficient, clean, little convent; it sat near the big Catholic school. Everything was gray and weathered, in this outpost of the Faith. The fathers, the Oblates of the Order of Mary Immaculate, lived in another, grayer building behind the school.

There was a telephone in the little parlor. I could call the newspaper, they said. One small nun in particular was interested and helpful.

"Oh yes, we're all concerned about the diphtheria. My goodness! At Henley House. They've got a lot of new building going on up there, don't they?"

I said that they did.

"I hope it all works out."

The little parlor was very neat and clean. Our Lady gazed down from the walls. It was strange to be back into a *parlor*, with its dainty furniture, doilies, the smell of lemon oil, and runners on the floor. I could actually dial the number of the newspaper and listen to their telephone ring.

"Tokyo?" Tokyo Rose was a high-school journalism student working for us part-time.

"Right here."

"Ready?"

"*Asha, asha.*" Yes, already.

"Dateline capital F Fort capital A Albany paragraph capital D Diphtheria has struck capital H Henley capital H House comma a small village on the capital H Hudson capital B Bay coast comma a disease that has rarely been seen in capital C Canada since the capital S Second capital W World capital W War period. Capital N nurses have managed to immunize most children of capital H Henley capital H House since the first two cases were discovered comma but they are running out of

serum period capital F fresh serum is being rushed from capital T
Toronto. . . ."

The small nun, Sister Joseph, brought me a tiny cup of tea on a delicate cup and saucer, and a spare, pleasant little cookie.

"Having a good time?" asked Tokyo. "You guys having to rough it?"

I said, "Tokyo, you won't believe this, but I have just been handed a
cup of capital T Tea in bone china with a darling little capital C Cookie.
A nun cookie."

"How was Henley House?"

"They have it all planned out. Except for diphtheria and juvenile
delinquency."

Sister Joseph was a small nun with great round brown eyes. I knew it
was she who baked the cookies. She looked like her own cookies. She
anxiously enquired if I would like to see the convent library. I said I
would. I said I would also be grateful for a place to sleep.

No problem.

Sister Joseph was young, and intense, and had something rather
intense to say to me.

"In your newspaper, why don't you write about how the anti-fur people are destroying people's lives here?"

I said, "Well, it's an Indian newspaper, and it's read by native people,
and they already know it, I think."

"They're destroying these people's only source of income! It's dreadful to watch these young people grow up with no purpose, no training
. . . it's cruel. It's cruel to raise generation after generation on welfare."

"Sister, I know it," I said. "Nothing can be done. The anti-fur people
are people of importance. They're movie stars. They get listened to.
Indian people don't get listened to." In fact, the young people of
Henley House were probably watching some of these movie stars on
video at just this very moment, utterly, blissfully ignorant of the activities of the glittering star-people.

"If they would come up here and see what people's lives are like. . . . "

"I don't think they will."

Because they were afraid of outdoor toilets and strange languages
and they wouldn't be on their own turf. They'd be on somebody else's
turf.

This was turning into a very upsetting trip. I felt deeply the utter *voicelessness* of community people, of village people. Voiceless. At least, at one time, the native people had had something to exchange, or to withhold, a bargaining position. They had been masters of the fur trade. How dare Indian Affairs design a village without consulting all the elders?

The worst of it is our conviction that we are well-meaning. That we can pour down goodness and rightness from the top. *We* are maple syrup. The rest of the population is a stack of pancakes.

I saw the best minds of my generation destroyed by maple syrup. Little Sister Joseph clasped her hands together and bethought herself of cookies, of dead beaver, of Christ's poor, and nun journeys through the north and through life in general; women who devoted their lives to the principle of the feminine divinity.

"Would you like to see our albums?"

# 34.

I sat up in the convent library until two o'clock in the morning. I looked through albums of old yellowed photographs, taken when the first nuns had come up to Fort Albany in the twenties, swathed in warm furs, standing beside dog teams, waving cheerfully at the camera.

Intrepid women; journeying overland from Sault Ste. Marie, camping out on the way, wondering if they would live when the temperature began to plummet, until mercury froze at the bottom of the thermometer to such hardness it could have been shot out of a gun without losing its shape.

They were alive with the love of Mother Mary and the sacrifices of Christ. They had taught, acted as nurses, helpmeets, cooks, and bottle washers. They had pressed the catechism of the Church relentlessly on young minds.

They arrived at Hudson's Bay Company posts where the three hundred-year relationship between the Cree and the traders held firm. They watched it disappear. I turned to the Xeroxed copies of the post journals.

I read through copies of the Albany post journals, dating back to 1743, written by the infamous Orkneyman Joseph Ibister; day after day of trade reported, of wind and weather, village gossip.

Ibister ran a tight ship; there were rules against strong drink and keeping native women as concubines. He enforced the rules with a cat-o'-nine-tails. According to a second report, the only exception was him, and he snatched, kidnapped, and seized the daughter of the Cree captain.

This was astonishing. I read on.

Ibister lived here, at Fort Albany, and sent Joseph Lamb up to run the little post of Henley House. So Henley House, as a village, and the HBC post, were two hundred years old.

Lamb took his superior's example and began living with a native woman himself. This so enraged the Cree captain, Woudbee, that he and his sons, Sheannap and ———— who? I couldn't read the handwriting — ——— rose up and massacred *massacred* ? ———— every man in the post!

Well, I thought. This is something.

It was an argument over women. The mellow lamplight from the reading lamp illuminated the Xeroxed, spidery handwriting. It was the report to the board of governors. The white men on the Henley House post had kidnapped the wives of several important men in the band, and the men of the tribe had slaughtered the post factor and clerks.

I suddenly liked the people of Henley House. This is how self-right-eousness, in which I was indulging myself, can make one delight in murder, even historical murder.

I slapped the Xeroxed pages shut, had another nun cookie, and went to bed. I sat up in bed and made notes.

I stopped making notes. I realized that for a year or more I had been living with a culture that did not have any mechanism or any desire to impose ideas on other people. The native people did not debate beliefs or ideas; they were not debatable. One never argued with someone else's convictions, except in the mildest way. Perhaps it was because these electrical disturbances inside our skulls, inside our hearts, are thought of as advice or invisible gifts from our guardian spirits, the spirits for whose presence one suffers in a vision quest.

For a whole year, in North Spirit Rapids, the incessant noise of propaganda and the pressure on society to think this way or that, had been absent. It was as if a great machine had stopped. All the advertising, with its accomplished, subtle urging, all the political messages, the debating and the arguing over politics, offhand disparagement of how this group thought, or those people thought, this line or that line; it was gone. No noise.

I put down my notebook and smoked. Mother Superior will have a fit when she smells this room. At least the nuns actually came up here, gliding in their furs over the white, glistening fields of experience, risking death and frostbite.

The poetry manuscript was untouched, full of half-completed poems.

I gazed out the window. It was two-thirty and the sun was rising again. It went down only three hours ago, then it had been sunset for another hour. I had read and thought right through the night, what there was of it. Purely gray dawn, beaded in drizzles. An ancient musket thrusting out of the alluvial banks, still containing the echo of bangs and explosions, re-appearing like a banner pole, re-emerging out of the land. A ghost musket.

# 35.

I sat down at my desk in Sioux Lookout, trying to think of something riveting and astonishing to say about plans. The town was afloat in bright green leaves, shivering poplar leaves, and the ferny leaves of mountain ash. The new birch seeds dangled like fat britches hung out to dry. Things were very different in this part of northern Ontario. It was only a hundred and fifty miles from the American border, and pilots often flew their plans to Minneapolis for repairs. There were towns down here, and the railroad line. The Ojibway language sounded different even to my inexperienced ear. The history of settlement, the lines of trade were distinct from the remoter northern areas. There were roads and cars and big chain grocery stores and banks. The paper money was fresher, as it were, and actually crisp. There was beer and movies. There were *tourists*.

The newspaper was a going concern. It had been started by David Pezhiki, Oldman Woman's nephew. They were nearly the same age, and they even looked alike. David had a round face, a ready smile and a love of verbal jokes, puns, gossip, and stories. He was a natural journalist. He had begun the newspaper with no training, just guts. He had recently attended a six-week crash course in journalism at the University of Western Ontario and was now head of the Wawatay Ojibway radio network, and shared stories with the newspaper people.

Kathy Whiteshell was the editor of the newspaper. She was coming upstairs with the mail. There were all kinds of letters to the newspaper, some of them in English, and some in syllabics. Kathy was completely unflappable. She had a calm attentiveness to her, besides being pretty and possessed of a long silky fall of blue-black hair. She had been a powwow dancer all through high school. She sat down quietly and began ripping open the letters in delicate, calm rips.

The spiky syllabic texts were texts of listening. They were texts of occurrences, of beauty and fear, regret and loss, of ordinary community events and memories, of an especially bountiful potato harvest or fierce objections to the story in the last issue about a community's dock, its rotting condition and loose planks.

The newspaper came out once a month. The photographs were, at first, blurry and low-contrast but they quickly improved. I had always been impatient of mechanical devices, they seemed satanically impelled to screw me up, fling parts, short out, strip their threads. But these cameras were valuable and, once broken, they would take scarce dollars to repair. *Wawatay News* was operating on a shoestring. I learned, for once, to be patient. To sit down and figure it out. Focus had always been my problem. I loved doing things, moving forward at a brisk pace. The cameras took time.

The photographs were freeze-frames of life in northern villages and events in the native towns around Sioux Lookout. David put microphones in front of people's faces and drew laughter and had facts out of them, in Ojibway, for the radio network. We pasted up pictures and stories of hockey games and village celebrations, interviews with elders, bureaucratic tangles. The stories were typed up in syllabics by the translator, Victoria, who was also known as Piitonya.

The system of syllabic script grew out of trappers' marks, indigenous symbols carved onto trees that meant, "I'm trapping here. I, Missinaibi." Or whoever. Or the equivalent. A Methodist missionary, a Reverend Evans, in the latter part of the nineteenth century in Manitoba, used the symbols to construct a system far more amenable to Ojibway and Cree (which are as close as, say, Spanish and Portuguese) than is Roman orthography. Who ever said there was any logic to the way we use that alphabet in English anyway? And every white person who went north and transcribed Cree or Ojibway words had had a different way of spelling them. Into this maddening jumble, Reverend Evans carved his way with trappers' symbols.

It's easy. At first. Like playing guitar, it seems quite easy at first, but why not? Otherwise you'd get discouraged.

The symbol $\wedge$ is a *P* sound. In this position, $\vee$, it is pronounced "pay." In this one, ∧ "pee," in this one, ⟩ "po," and in this one, ⟨ "pah." Thus:

∨ ∧ ⟩ ⟨

pay     pee    po   pah

The *T* sound looks like a *U*. It took me a long time to stop thinking of it as having a *U* sound. It, like all of the symbols, changes its vowel with varying positions.

U ∩ ⊃ ⊂

tay   tee   toe   tah

There are pure vowels; △ is the sumbol for a vowel, and it too changes according to its position.

▽ △ ▷ ◁

ay   ee   oh   ah

There are a few diacritical marks. ◁ with a dot in front, •◁, is "wah." The symbol denotes a light, breathy *H*.

▽̇ △̇ ▷• •◁

way   wee   wo   wah

So read this; •◁ •◁ U

However, every time I tried to help set out the headlines in syllabic Letraset, I got myself in trouble. Piitonya was impatient.

"Leave them alone or you'll get us sued one of these days," she said. "You'll say something you don't mean and then it's going to be Katy Bar The Door."

But I kept trying and once reversed the ◁ symbol on the banner, leaving us with a newspaper called Wowotay.

All six thousand copies.

I said, "Okay, but what does Wowotay mean?"

"It means you'd better not touch those syllabic headlines unless I'm here," she said. "Listen to me and we'll all live through this."

The syllabics were used by the northern Cree and Ojibway people, but the more southerly nations hadn't learned them, I suppose because the Catholics, who, in the main, came to the Ojibway people along the

Minnesota border, regarded syllabics as the invention of a Protestant and therefore schismatic and probably boring.

The Inuit people use them too, so when we ordered Letraset in syllabics (Letraset makes its sticky letters in all sorts of scripts) we got all the additional symbols used by the Inuit people in their language. Nobody could figure out what they sounded like. There was a ⏶⟍ and other things. I sat around making up sounds for them, horrible sounds, livening up our late hours, as we ground out column after column in the summer dusks. Jackets and purses and boxes of Pampers crowded the layout room. Never could tell when somebody was going to bring their baby along.

Letters would come to the newspaper for Piitonya. She opened them in her office, and sometimes told everybody what was in them.

"Uh-oh." Oldman Woman was drawing a Turtle cartoon, Mikinak, the joker. "Piitonya's got another Ojibway-gram."

Piitonya leaned out of her tiny office.

"Somebody come and get the translation. I've got an obituary here." Piitonya knew everybody and their family trees.

I bent over my typewriter. I remembered the Lazarus Error and was determined to stay away from obituaries.

I said, "For sure?"

"Yep. It's an elder. Mrs. Mindemoya."

I jumped up and went to her office.

"Really? Really? From North Spirit?"

"Yes, really. Here, I'll translate."

I said, "Get Kathy to do it."

I went back to my typewriter and burst into tears. I cried and cried. The office was suddenly silent. She had been the mentor of one of the most intense times of my life. And at the very end of her life, a hardworking life, suddenly this strange white person had appeared next door and needed yet more help, and she had responded as if there were no end to her strength, her ability to be generous, understanding.

I went into the darkroom and ran films for the afternoon.

Piitonya was trilingual. She spoke English, Cree, and Ojibway. Her original language was Woods Cree, but she could speak Swampy Cree easily. Maybe she was quadrilingual. Piitonya had a neat, short perm, two strikingly beautiful daughters, and she lived in town since her husband was head mechanic at one of the bush airlines. She had her own office, she wrote up her own page all in Ojibway syllabics and wouldn't translate it for anybody.

"Everybody writes their story in English and then gives it to me to translate," she said "It should work the other way around, too. Fair is fair."

Piitonya's daughter, Anne, worked for the newspaper part-time. She was still in high school. She had saved her money for two years and had gone on a tour of Europe, and apparently everyone on the tour refused to believe she was native Canadian. She kept getting letters from France and Germany addressed to Tokyo Rice Mitsubishi and Heavenly Flower Sanyo Kowasaki. Since we often had another Anne working for the organization somewhere, she was called Tokyo Rose.

Tokyo first started as part-time help, dropping in after high school to clean the darkroom and paste up a few strips. Eventually she obtained a degree in journalism from Carleton University in Ottawa.

Elizabeth Peyton had discovered that the Olivetti Typewriter Company made typewriters in scripts other than Roman. She spent a great deal of time and effort, and in her very polite English-Canadian way ground down with relentless pressure on funding sources, smiling sweetly, for money to purchase special typewriters. She came up with two typewriters with Ojibway syllabic fonts. It was magical to see Piitonya strike a key and suddenly one of the angled syllabics would appear neat, edged, impersonal. Before the Olivettis, syllabics had always been in a recognizable hand — the rounded script of Oldman Woman, Nathan's hurried slant.

Nathan was busy with paper in his downstairs office. It seemed odd for him to be here in a town, in town shoes and a sports coat rather than in North Spirit, cutting wood or starting his snowmobile or carefully reading through a book on the Hudson's Bay Company. He would sit and stare at the list of stories. He was going through the complications and ramifications: Crees or Ojibways? Related to whom? It mattered who a person's father was, what family they were related to on their mother's side. When a village appeared on the list, he was perhaps thinking, we passed through there on our way to the trap line when I was twelve, or my father went there with the York boats. The complex interrelatedness of the north, which I would never quite grasp; instead, I had learned to be cautious.

I wrote everything on a sturdy IBM Selectric, frequently checking *The Compleat Reporter.*

Nathan stuck his head in my door right in the middle of "three young men wielding knives took two nurses hostage. . . ."

"What?"

"We've got a new consultant coming."

I said, "Releasing them seven hours later when the police . . . the police what?"

"No, a consultant. Brad MacInnis. He's going to help us get started with TV video cameras."

I looked up from the drudgery of typing out a story. Not only was the dreaded television arriving in the north, but someday soon *Wawatay* would be helping it along.

It seemed to me that even the newspaper, by itself, would bring about great changes.

Every month when the bundles of newspapers came back from the printers at Dryden, it seemed miraculous. The paper was actually type-set. The banner, *Wawatay News,* in English script and Ojibway/Cree syllabics, streaked across the top of the front page, asserting the language and the lives of the people of Anishinabe-Aski. Here was Mr. Whitesky at the tiller of his freight canoe on the Sand River, Oldman Woman's photo of a screaming child getting a diphtheria inoculation.

The speech of the northern people was jacketed in print now; occurrences which were worthy of a tale moved from the spoken word into the written.

The newspaper had become a sort of archive, and the lives of ordinary people in the villages, in the towns, were suddenly deserving of a well-written story; and they were ordinary people leading extraordinary lives.

There was a shift in focus, in emphasis, that began to occur; a sudden jump from the oral story to the written. Data was accumulating, like snow on a doorstep. The Cree and Ojibway people walked into the world of print.

Lives no longer subsided into the dim past without a mark of their passing; of their passing as individuals. In the times before Print, the stories of their lives, after two or three generations, were incorporated into Fable. People who live beyond the edge of reportage find themselves in the web of legend and myth; but with literacy and preserved documents, people remain individuals forever, long after their deaths.

Data was accumulating, there for the taking. It was separating itself from Experience. The scholar, the poet, the bureaucrat stays at home in a study, accumulating data about the world from books. The soldier and the explorer and the refugee go out into the world and are battered by Experience and Time, and so there come to be two separate ways of understanding. The change is profound. It is primary. It happened to us, a thousand years ago, in the dim dark ages of Europe, and when knowledge bifurcated, we said goodbye to magic.

But the requirement of turning all these tales into prose, within the strict rules of journalism, was good for me. Sometimes the angelic presence hidden in the mind, which has been called the Muse, broke out of its secret place and I found myself writing things on scraps of paper; poetry. Musings.

I sat down at my desk and wrote, quickly.

*"You don't remember me," she goes, "but I remember you."*

*But I do remember her, and every time I see her, she arrives with the news of starships.*

*They say she lives on the other side of the mountains. They say she lives in the ruins of fallen cities and all-night cafes. Once I saw her sitting in an abandoned car, and when she lit her cigarette, the match-light shone on all the rusty dials.*

*She says, "You don't remember me, but I remember you."*

# 36.

The summer thunderheads, the Kitche-Pinesewak, Great Birds, moved in on the north on flat bottoms, their peaks towering up to thirty-thousand feet, filled with lightning and interior convection currents of immense power. They were massive atmospheric disturbances, trailing long robes of rain. They paced across the sky in regal processions, infused with air, with energy, vitality, power. Pilots avoided them, and planes sat safely on the ground until they had passed over. There was no disputing their mastery of the air. Sometimes they held back their rain and sent down dry lightning. Then forest fires started up and began to run downwind.

I woke up in the early summer mornings and I leapt out of bed and straight into my parka to start the fire. In town, during the day, the air warmed up. I returned at night to the silence and peace of the lakeshore. Sometimes I felt full of objective thoughts and facts, like a brain-balloon peppered over with asterisks. I missed listening to the legends. I came home at night and worried about the next story. This was when I watched whiskey jacks. Soon the male bird would sit on my finger and snatch at pieces of bacon or cheese or attempt to fly off with my entire finger.

Despite the sailing thunderheads, there had been very little rain and the fire season was upon us. My cabin sat in the middle of crackling-dry spruce woods. Pretty soon there would be a fire story.

I remembered Nathan's admonition.

> *Now Puanets, you must understand why legends are never told in the summer. It is because the frogs and the snakes and the turtles have come out of hibernation, and they will tell the*

*Thunder People that we are talking about them, telling stories*
*about them. The Thunder Beings don't like to be talked about*
*by human beings.*

I had published one book of poetry and wondered if I would ever pub-
lish another one. Oldman Woman had also given up her painting to
work on our translations and cartoons. Hard news and excitement had
taken over our artistic lives.

I have a Polaroid photo of me and Oldman Woman standing outside
the toilet-sized newspaper office. I think David took it. Oldman Woman
and I are both skinny, have long hair and jeans and big sweaters. Poetry
is flying out of the top of my head in an invisible ray, and the stanzas are
still in unlatticed photons. Unpainted paintings in bewitched forms are
in wait in the spruce shadows and, in the high background, ravens sit
on top of the telephone poles and strike bell-like tones in single notes
as if they were clocks telling geological time.

# 37.

Summertime, when people lived by the seasons, used to be the dreaming time, the time one fell into relaxation, and did not work to keep warm, when the people traveled by canoe over reflective lakes. But we are in a different work time now, this century has a new, different rhythm, and the newspaper kept revealing its stories, and the stories must be changed over to print, as one would change money from one country to the next.

Kathy Whiteshell and her family were on their way to a summer powwow, down near the American border at Whitefish Bay.

"You come along too, and cover it for the paper," she said.

I said, "Why me? You're a dancer, you were raised on powwows, I don't know a thing about it. I'll get it all wrong. Tokyo Rose would probably like to go. She needs a little story to cover. Something to practice on." Tokyo was taking a summer journalism class offered by the high school, starting in on the reporting business.

Kathy laughed.

"Come on! There's nothing to get wrong. Just take a lot of pictures. Write down the names of the winners in each category."

"What are the categories?"

"Traditional, jingle dress, fancy dance, grand entry, sneak up. Sneak up is the men's dance. Jingle dress is for women. Men and women always dance in separate events, but then there's men's fancy, women's fancy, men's traditional, and women's traditional. It's easy."

I was writing notes as quickly as I could.

"What are the criteria for winners?"

She said, "Well, in traditional, women move very slowly, and one foot is always on the ground. You have an eagle-wing fan, and you fan yourself, and that's to keep the fringes on your shawl moving." She thought for a moment. "It's like, you're at peace, you're in contact with Mother Earth. In fancy dance, both feet can leave the ground at the same time. Same with jingle dress. Only Ojibways do jingle dress."

"Are there just going to be Ojibways?"

"Yes. I think. Usually just Ojibways come to Whitefish Bay."

"And what's a sneak up?"

"Okay, that's really focused. They move their eyes, watching all the time. Focusing on enemies. You dance half bent over and you *looook* . . ." Kathy demonstrated. "The enemies are inside you, too. You're real alert, focused. You'll see."

"What about etiquette?"

"You're not supposed to talk about negative things, and women aren't supposed to touch the drum. No drugs, no alcohol."

"Oh gee, I can't bring all my whiskey and cocaine."

"You need to go, Paulette. You need to unwind."

"I still don't know why you don't cover it." I was packing up gear: camera bag, jacket. I would have to borrow a tent.

"Because I'm dancing."

There were perhaps a thousand people.

I was the only non-native person there.

The drums went half the night; I lay in my tent and listened. The frail, high cries of Indian song drifted through the camp. Smoke lay low, tangled, unraveled itself, moved up and evaporated in the night.

Girls in jingle dresses walked past in the dark, clashing with musical notes, laughing and whispering. The midsummer stars appeared in the eastern sky and the smoke of campfires poured upwards, into the heavens. There were fires everywhere. I suddenly felt I didn't need anything more than the borrowed tent and some money and some blankets.

I thought, I don't even need a job, really.

Disastrous thought.

The drumbeats were without any accents; it was a steady, unmarked beat. The drum clubs scattered around the camping meadows, put up their tents and drummed together, sang together. Fires erupted in noiseless sparks, a thin moon came up, a fine gold.

The next day I tried to take pictures, but I was entranced by the drums.

The arena was packed with people from Minnesota reservations and Ontario reserves. The small matter of an invisible international boundary was forgotten. Some people were in traditional or fancy dress, others in ordinary whitemen's clothes. The drums kept on and kept on and kept on. In the arena, first one drum group and then another took up the production of these heartbeats, dancers moved out onto the flattened grass. Women in long dark dresses and brilliant shawls with silk fringe a foot long slowly moved eagle-feather fans in front of their faces. Men with dark bands of paint across their eyes, carrying rifles and tomahawks, rattling with eagle-bone chokers, danced with such light movements, it was like flight. Young people walked past in the heat, eating dripping snow cones. Grandmothers sat in lawn chairs, fanning themselves with paper fans, discussing vital tribal things, making decisions.

The drum group called Northwest Angle was playing when I started taking pictures. The husband of a friend of mine was playing with that group.

He was a tall man with long gray and white braids. He was holding a pink umbrella with one hand and drumming with the other. The men were in perfect unison, looking into one another's eyes, singing strenuously in a tight-throated, high-pitched chant.

I watched Kathy dance in the traditional category. She wore two eagle-down puffs in her hair. She moved to the voice of the drum with faultless rhythm, her foot-long silk fringes swayed in aligned waves, she fanned herself delicately with the eagle-wing fan and paid attention to her interior state with the silver coins, *shuniamin*, of serene dance steps. Each dancer was dancing for herself alone. Perhaps she would have won but her two-year-old son, spying his mother, ran yelling out onto the dance ground, breaking her concentration, and so she laughed and picked him up and walked out of the dance.

I took a picture of an elder woman leaning back in a camp chair, rolling snuff-tin lids into cones for a jingle dress.

The sun went down, the drums kept on until they were part of the fabric of the day, of its waning light, and then part of the arriving darkness, until they were the underlying rhythm of the appearance of stars in their sequences, a constant, vital heartbeat that was the low, comforting noise of the earth's interior. The songs were sung into the night air. I could never tell when they began or ended, where the melody was, or the timing. Maybe what Nathan meant when he said no legends were told in summer because Frog and Turtle would hear, and tell the Thunderbirds, was that the rising summer stars were now constellations called Turtle and Frog, a star-Mikinak, a stellar Frog. They would tell the Thunders a conversation about gossip between astral beings. A red star glittered, the system coalesced. The Stern Paddler, Oda-Ka-Daun, was rising at midnight or later. It was Odaëmini-Keesis, the Strawberry Moon.

I woke up the next morning to drums. Low, soft, introductory drums; one drum group or another, practicing. People ate breakfast in their trailers or RVs, their tents. Jingle-dress dancers crashed about, leaping little leaps, getting ready.

Somebody handed me a paper plate of eggs and bacon.

*Awenin kin?* Who are you?

*Wawatay News.*

Hey! Take my picture!

Grand Entry is when all dancers enter the arena, circling the brush arbor, circling with the sun, toward the right. Drum groups from Kenora, the James Bay Coast, Winnipeg, Red Lake Minnesota, began to tighten their drum heads.

One of the drums had a sticker; REPORT ALL INDIAN RAIDS HERE, it said.

I stood by Kathy and watched the men's traditional. In Reverend Wilson's dictionary, there is an entire page of entries under *Indian*. The *Dictionary of the Ojebway Tongue for Missionaries and Others Working Among the Ojebway Indians* was written in the 1870s. Rigorously fair, it contained words which might well have otherwise been forgotten. The Reverend would be scandalized by this pagan drumming. Or maybe not. At the end of his life, he surrendered to Anishinabe-Aski, he advised his superiors in the Methodist Church; *it doesn't work.* He said, *The Indians must be given their own nation.*

The process must have begun when he was listing the words: Indian dance; Anishinabe-wishemo. Indian religion; Anishinabe-ezhetawin.

Indian war club; *puhgumeygun*. Mythical bridge, over which the souls of the dead must pass; Kookokauzhegun.

The drummers would suddenly move into a crescendo, the men bent over and all the drumsticks with their long woolen heads flying in unison, louder and louder, and then there was an abrupt stop.

I looked around. People in the stands were shifting, watching the dance ground, and the drum was silent.

The arena master was shouting something. All the men dancers suddenly began inspecting their weapons, their headdresses. Then they were straying off the dance ground, undancing, a precipitous descent from the height of the focus and concentration of the scalp dance (*guhonaujewin*) to a vague, slack wandering off to the side.

Kathy looked around. "It's July, and there's been a lot of powwows."

"What's happening?"

Two men were standing and looking down at something on the flattened grass of the dance ground.

"Somebody dropped an eagle feather off their regalia."

"So everybody stops."

My editor fanned herself with her eagle-wing fan. "It's mid-season and the feathers work loose and then they drop off."

"So they clear the dance ground."

"An eagle feather should never touch the ground. When it does, it can only be picked up by a war veteran. Then it has to be given away as a gift to someone by the guy who dropped it. Listen."

The arena master was calling for a war veteran. A middle-aged man in Levis and a ball cap, with short hair and a RED LAKE BAIT AND TACKLE T-shirt moved up through the crowd, turning sideways to squeeze past the watching dancers who always formed the front rank of spectators, through the jingle dresses and the stiff-standing feather bustles, the shaking red-tipped deer-roach headdresses. His ball cap had a POW-MIA crest.

The arena master waited. The Vietnam Vet bent down and picked up the eagle feather, then he stood and held it over his head. It was aloft again, where it belonged.

The man who dropped it called out a name. The man in the POW-MIA cap walked over to an elderly man and handed him the eagle feather, and then eased back into the crowd. There was a round of applause.

The arena master said, in crackles and buzzes over the PA system; "I don't want to have to stop this dance anymore, everybody check their regalia, please."

It was a sort of pleasant hypnotism, a dream of plenitude, peace, the heartbeats of the north itself, pure water in the lake and clean air around one, the bright scent of spruce and pine, of wood smoke.

I lay down on a blanket, listening to the heightened drumming of the jingle-dress songs, to the frantic clashing of the dancers, high-energy young girls flying into the air in crazily enthusiastic leaps.

I felt someone sit down beside me.

I looked up. It was a man's face, painted in black and white, with a high deer-skin roach, and an eagle-bone choker. He was carrying a rifle and a tomahawk.

He said, pleasantly, "Do you have any identification?"

I sat bolt upright.

If somebody carrying a rifle and a tomahawk asks me for identification, I always produce it. Imagine my gratitude for the wonderful new press cards Nathan had printed up for us all, with our pictures and everything. The photograph made me look as if I had been struck by an electrical charge.

"Yes, I certainly do."

He lay down the tomahawk and looked carefully at my *Wawatay* press pass.

"Good. Alright. I'm from Red Lake Minnesota. You've heard about the trouble there."

"Yes, I have."

Two tribal factions had come to blows over resource allocation; the reservation was rich in phosphate. A big corporation was willing to pay millions to mine it. The two factions of tribal people had taken to shooting at one another. It was a mess.

"There's always a lot of FBI around, taking pictures. You white people do stand out."

He handed my ID back. He got up.

"Thanks," he said. He smiled; or, I think he smiled. Face paint, expertly done, is a marvelously effective mask. "I'm camped over there," he said. He nodded toward a group of RVs and tents. "That's my drum group." He paused. "I'll probably run into you again."

I said, "Yes, I'm sure." I looked at him again. He was quite good-looking.

Then he was back into the crowd of dancers, red-tipped roach shaking like a Legionnaire's plumes, and the drums picked up their thread and began weaving the world again.

The brush arbour and its greenery and its center post was the axle of the world. Time was a concept of repetition, the same summer moved past us, the same year of stars repeated itself, and inside this everlasting year, this eternal legend-year, we grow up, grow old, make mistakes, have children or not, learn things, unlearn them. Third created, after the drumming shaman-frog, we walk on the circling earth as it moves past us, driven by time. Some sort of vessel is moving with us in it, bearing us away.

At dawn I woke up; Kathy's husband, Tom, was calling me. A drum group somewhere was greeting the first light.

"Come have coffee!" Tom said.

I could have been there at the dancing place for a month and not realized days were passing. I could have gone to find the Red Lake man without his rifle and face-paint. I could have done a lot of things but mostly I was engaged with the sensation of descending like a diver into the deep liquids of sleep and dance and drumming.

I took the steaming cup of coffee. The morning was still chilly. The Silver-Throated sparrow sang *O Canada Canada Canada.* Pearly Everlasting spread dusty flowers in cream velour under the birch.

"New word for you," said Tom. "This is *piitabin,* first light. Look, people are at the lake. Most of the elders have a song to greet first light. I know you were up in North Spirit for a year; most people are very Anglican up there. They don't care for drumming. But down here, a lot of people practice the older ways."

I said, "What do you think about that?"

Tom said, "What I was told was that it is wrong to criticize anyone else's beliefs."

My camera released its images in the dark room. I kept copies of most of them: the drummers, the moon, the campfires. Kept the memory of sweetgrass and pine, lake water, high floating notes of

Ojibway songs, sparkling crashing noises of jingle dresses, a handsome man in a high roach, the drum moving, the drum moving the world, the drum moving the world on its circular way, the circular way of songs, hearts, missed opportunities.

# 38.

The interlude of peace and music of the powwow at Whitefish Bay was soon swallowed up by the emergencies of fire season. The low, steady insistence of drums with their unmarked beat gave way to ringing phones and the constant overhead noises of aircraft; the spotter planes, single-engined Otters and turbo Beavers, and heavy crew helicopters bearing men away to the fire fronts.

It was an extremely dry summer and the forests all around the town of Sioux Lookout seemed to burst into flames.

By early August, Red Lake, a mining town of two thousand people slightly north of Sioux, had to be evacuated. At first the townspeople were getting out by surface vehicles, but then the fire burnt across the graveled road and cut off the road connection. The people remaining were flown out by Canadian Forces Hercules and by any bush planes available.

Smoke rolled across the universe and the sunrises were volcanic. It was Meen-Keesis, the Bilberry Moon, and the round rising moon was the color of a Pikanjikum sunset.

Nathan and David walked around making lists of what we would save if we were forced to evacuate Sioux Lookout.

It could all go up in smoke.

"Jiles, go out to Savant Lake, to the fire base out there," said David. "The MNR fire fighters are taking reporters up in a helicopter. If we're going to get burnt out, we might as well get pictures of the fire that did it."

The town seemed suspended in smoke. Everybody was waiting for the evacuation siren to go off. There was a frenetic feel to life. I was sitting behind my typewriter writing a poem called "The Ship's Boy." It had seized me and said, Write me now. I couldn't stop myself.

I said, "I'm on my way."

*He dreams of cinnamon factories and people in the glassy*
*forest who lie down each night with friendly griffins.*

The entire town smelled like barbecue. It made your hair stand on
end.

David said, "You and Bradley MacInnis. Okay. Cameras; we can throw
those in the files."

I put the typed sheets of poem in my back pocket. "Don't bother with
loading anything, let's all just run out in a brainless panic."

He went back to his lists.

"I'm about halfway there now."

The Ministry of Natural Resources' fire base, near the railroad town
of Savant Lake, at Fire Number 46, was a tangled mess of hoses and
trucks and pumps out in the forests east of Sioux Lookout. This was the
fire that would eat us up in rushes of red silks and laser heat, it would
gallop down on Sioux like a tidal wave if the east wind kept up.

The PR man for the Ministry was yelling instructions at the reporters.
The fires of northern Ontario had brought reporters from everywhere,
from the Toronto *Globe and Mail,* the *Detroit Free Press* and the *Los Angeles*
*Times.*

They were heavy reporters. They looked like the kind of professionals
who could think up a gag lead in a minute, people to whom the inverted pyramid was meat and drink, people with enormous per diem and
expense accounts, you could bet their editors weren't sitting around
thinking how much equipment they could get in the back of a pickup.
These were people with *desks*; city desks, foreign desks, national desks.
We all stood around in the clearing, among the ground-up birch limbs
and deep ruts in the dirt, amid the noise of machines: pickup trucks,
pumps, helicopters dipping down to the lake surface to drag their buckets through the water, like bees racing off with a load of honey.

I thought, it's going to be a miracle if I get on that helicopter.

Bradley MacInnis was thin but he could bully people. I was about to
fall in love with him. I liked working with him. He was fierce and bony
and red-bearded, he plunged into work with Glaswegian energy. But

Bradley loved his work. That's why he was good to work with. That's why he lived by himself and had a motorcycle and would probably always live by himself.

Among all these reporters from Los Angeles and Detroit and Toronto, I was the only woman.

"We'll take you up two at a time!" The helicopter was a little bubble-front job. "You two, and then you two . . . "

There was an odd number of reporters, and I could see from the way he was counting us off that I was going to get left out. Women reporters should stay in the city and report on feminist issues. He was going to exclude the sole female in the crowd. Bradley grabbed me by the collar and pushed forward.

"She's my partner," he said. "We go together. We're with *Wawatay News.*"

This is how I got on.

"Okay, we'll take you two now," the PR man said, quickly. "But listen to me! When you approach this copter, *bend over*. The blades drop when it's sitting on the ground and it will take the top of your head off."

I noted a big sign at the side of the landing pad. It was a terrifically graphic hand-painted depiction of a man's head being sliced off by a rotor blade.

Brad and I ran up to the little helicopter bent over, blasted with the rotor wash and all the things rotor wash can pick up and fling at you at a fire base: chips and sticks and gravel. I got in all bent over and then Brad got in bent way over.

We were aloft in one of the Little Bony Flying Things, moving in any direction. It was shamanistic flight, flight without effort, without price.

The wind shook my clothing and smoke blew through the rotors in streams. Somewhere below there were flames. On the far horizon blue reaches of spruce flowed in every direction. Hot air rose up to us, smells of gasoline, and burning wood. It was the hot beauty of the north world in summer. They would never cut all this down, I thought, it can't be done. Bright lakes shone in blue bosses, scattered across the landscape like Wimshoosh stepping-stones. The spruce trees looked like expanding fat ladies from overhead, with pointy crowns.

"Helicopters are like divine beings!" Bradley had to shout over the noise of the engines and rotors. "When people come up to get on them, they bend over and bow and grovel!" He was laughing. "And they rise and descend *vertically*, you know, airplanes take off in a long glide but these things drop out of heaven! They just flat take off straight up!"

"Right!" We were flat taking off straight up.

"And when you come down, with that rotor wash, people avert their faces! From the Presence!"

The pilot turned around to us.

"Headphones!" he yelled. He pointed. There were headphones beside us. We put them on, and then we could hear one another over the intercom. The headphones had long, thick, curly wires.

They had taken the doors off the machine so reporters could bend out in their safety harnesses and take pictures and scare themselves. From an altitude of about eight hundred feet we could see all the rolling hills fading away to the horizon. The fire was leaping through the rich, dry forests near the highway in long smoky strings. There was no front.

It was running in streaks before an east wind. It flowed in an initial, light wash of quick flame over the duff and crisping needles, and then a deeper flame stayed behind to begin eating at the trunks.

When enough of these trunks are thoroughly on fire in a tight group, the fire begins to take on its own momentum. It starts sucking oxygen into itself, along with anything that's loose, and it begins to immolate whole trees in seconds, it becomes a fire storm. It becomes a furnace. Farther to the east, just beyond Sioux, a cloud the shape of an atomic explosion was booming steadily upwards, something in its dark-red heart feeding it. This was the center of the main fire.

Fire leapt onto a great, tall fir directly beneath us, and the tree burst into flame all over in one bright flash from root to crown, its resins turned into expanding gases in the intense ambient heat, flinging its spruce cones like hot grenades in all directions.

"That's what you call torching," said the pilot. "That tree just torched."

Ahead of us, in the air, two helicopters were flying bucket-bombs, big rubber containers strung beneath the machine, which dropped three hundred and fifty gallons at a dump. They were hitting hot spots, trying to douse the smoldering punks of duff before they burst into flame.

"This is a natural thing," said the pilot. "These trees have to be subjected to fire before the cones will open. Then the seeds get out. However, we're looking at too much of a good thing."

Maybe that's how we all are, I thought. Maybe we have to be burnt over somehow, forged in some kind of intense heat, torched, and then we break open. Then we become wise through experience, or not. Something takes us by the neck and roars flame at us. Then we fall in love or are fallen in love with, or not. Maybe we don't really carry a seed, perhaps we're a dud cone. Maybe sometimes we don't survive.

"Hello, Jiles, wake up, the pilot's yelling at us."

The pilot was saying,"Where do you want to go?"

Two helicopters paced us on each side, trailing their three-hundred-and-fifty-gallon buckets. The one on the port side suddenly shot ahead and dumped its water. I got the picture. The hot wind, laden with smoke and ash, was tearing at my face and clothing from the doorless doorway.

"Could we get one of the forward camps?" Bradley asked. "I want a shot of the guys and the hoses."

"Right-o," said the pilot. "These guys up here are getting out. The fire's headed toward them."

We pressed forward even closer to the main fire. There was a clearing below us. In this country, a clearing means bog. There were men down there in tan coveralls, dragging hoses and rolling them up on spools, squashing through the *terre tremblant* and semi-liquid earth.

"Looks like some kind of weird religious cult," said Bradley. His voice was electronic and thin, it was weird to see his lips move and hear his voice in a radio crackle. "Snake worshippers!"

I said, "The Rolly Hosers."

Brad laughed so hard he had to lean back and clutch his camera.

As I leaned out to look, my camera bag swung forward and out of the side pocket, my little book light pitched out, hung for a moment in the air and then went tumbling end over end down the chute of the smoky wind, flashing once or twice and then disappearing into the unburnt green of the spruce below us.

"Brad, Brad, I dropped my book light!"

"Your what?"

"I dropped my little book light that I read at night with!"

"What the hell are you carrying that for?"

"What if we had to stay overnight here or something? I brought *Idylls of the King* with me!"

"Just shut up about the damn thing, god, Jiles, we're on a *shoot*!"

Next I'd lose my little folding binoculars; I zipped my bag shut.

The helicopter settled down lightly on a firm stretch of ground where the men were extracting a pump from a bog pool. As we came down, they took off their hard-hats and bowed down, covering their faces with their hats, turning their heads to one side to avoid the rotor wash. It was the closest one can come to feeling like the Goddess, like Ashtar, An-Lil, the divinity of wind and fire descending vertically out of the blue heavens.

"What do you want?" shouted the crew boss. "We're pulling out of here!"

"Photographers!" yelled the pilot.

Brad jumped out and started at a run to get a picture. He was in such a hurry he forgot and left his headphones on. I realized that as soon as he hit the end of the curly cord, with the headphones still clamped to his ears, he would be startled and jerk upright, right into the rotors.

I dropped my camera and leaned out and grabbed the cord with both hands and gave it a terrific jerk, snatching the headphones half off his head before he got to the end of the cord. Brad's hands went to his earphones and he dropped straight to his knees. The fire crew were also yelling at him.

He looked back, white and startled. He took the headphones off, dropped them, and then bent over and ran out clear of the rotors.

"That was close," said the pilot, conversationally.

I reeled in the headphones by their difficult cord.

"He owes me his life now," I said, dramatically. "I'll make up stories about this and tell them in the bar and make myself look good."

"Right-o," said the pilot. "'There is a destiny that shapes our ends, rough-hew them how we will.'"

"That's very appropriate," I said.

"Yes. I was the one that did the sign at the landing pad; do you like it?"

"It's to die for," I said.

"Thanks."

Brad got back in in a rush of headphone and cords and camera straps. He stared out at the fire crew. They were heaving up long lengths of hose like sausages or flat tubes and then rolling the hose up. Somebody would have to come and lift them out. A big crew helicopter would come, a Bell-Sikorsky, long and heavy, with a tail rotor.

The fire was moving; not fast, but still waltzing forward at route step. The men's tan coveralls were streaked with black and their Day-Glo hard hats were rimmed with fingerprints of ash. They snatched their hard hats off and put them over their faces, bent over, turned slightly away as we rose into the air again, spewing cotton-grass heads and water spray and sticks into the clearing. We made the water in the bog pool twill itself into a glittering weave, we rose on a column of disturbed dust.

I said, "You're welcome."

"Thanks for jerking on my headphones," he said.

"If I ever find a man that really appreciates me," I said, "I'd do anything for him. Even save his life."

"I don't guilt."

"I hope to hell we don't get stuck overnight here," I said. "I'd end up reading Tennyson by candlelight."

We rotored back to the fire base in order to let some other reporters have a turn at flying up in the air. If I weren't flying on helicopters, I realized, I would be living entirely in my head. I would be like one of those medieval queens in a pack of cards, severe and dry, drawn thin with figuring. Like them, I had to be in a field of movement, I needed to be near the fire. Songs of Experience.

# 39.

Unlike poetry, theater is a present-moment sport; one lives in its immediate occurrence as if it were hockey or dancing or preaching or storytelling. It is not a reflective activity; you are joined with an entire crowd of people around you in emotions of joy, disgust, boredom, fear and are led perhaps by the spellbinding voice of the Shaman of North Spirit. You surrender your critical mind for awhile, and in return, you expect great things. You expect to be lifted out of your seat, seized by the moment. And recently videos, played on VCRs attached to a television, powered by Honda generators, had arrived in northern villages. Videos are magic stories impelled by light, and in the north country light is valuable and sacred. Theater, in any form, is image hypnosis, and to break out of that hypnosis into the present moment is the duty of the critic, but when the audience breaks out it is the misfortune of the actor, the playwright.

Now theater was coming to Sioux Lookout and I was being involved in it, willy-nilly. One thing happens and then another thing. I didn't know if this play was a good thing or not. I was always sure I was a storyteller, but then I could never manage to face the silent hours staring at a keyboard. I was lazy and undisciplined. It required more focus and ability to live in one's head than I was able to endure without rushing away from the typewriter screaming.

I was unpacking cameras and files out of their boxes. We would not have to evacuate after all. The fire had stopped fifteen miles short of town. The wind had changed, pushing it back over the area it had already burnt, and so it destroyed itself, like somebody repeating the same compulsive habit over and over.

Nathan was in the layout room inspecting Piitonya's all-Ojibway page for improprieties. He did not always have time to do this. When he did, he sometimes found things that caused long, exceedingly polite conversations in Ojibway between himself and the elder woman.

He called me over and said, "Sarah Winnepetonga is coming down for a few months to work on the newspaper. She needs some money to buy a snowmobile for this coming winter."

He paused, again, and smiled his reserved smile. The responsibility of managing the expanding organization, which included technicians as well as creative freaks like me, white people and natives, Treaty Indians and Métis, men and women, city folks and people raised on trap lines, was wearing him thin. He always seemed pinned to the edge of a scrupulous diplomacy. "You'll help her start out with writing, won't you?"

"Yes, yes!"

"And, um, something else. There are some people who are wanting to start up a native theater group. A Toronto theater company. Come on and help us out. They got me on the board of directors. As if I didn't have enough on my plate."

"Why are they coming up here?"

"I don't know. I guess that's what they do, they do community theater. Help community theaters get started."

Every summer, evangelical groups from northern Minnesota head into the Canadian wilderness to do the work of saving souls for Christ. Specifically, saving them for wildcat Pentecostal churches. They bring gospel choirs, musical instruments with enormous speakers, full sound systems in which the preachers pour out their stream of talk. They are not so deluded that they think the native people haven't been exposed to the Catholic teachings or the Anglican teachings for centuries. Nor do they believe they are saving the Indians from pagan practices; no. They want to steal the congregations away from the Catholics and the Anglicans.

But only temporarily.

They don't want the Indians to come *home* with them or anything.

What is truly appreciated is the contributions made to the collection plate.

One of these crowd inciters was preaching at a nearby reserve. He and a couple of other, unknown, generic-type Pentecostals had driven down the dusty, late-summer main street of Sioux Lookout in a ten-year-old Ford with a big sign painted on the side: WEIGHT LIFTER FOR CHRIST.

He had so excited the more gullible members of the nearby reserve community with his evangelical skills that a large band of newly converted, hard-shell primitive Pentecostals had gone about the village, rushing into people's homes, smashing televisions, and throwing the women's makeup out the windows. There went the Maybelline, there goes the Sanyo.

"I could *kill* people like that!" said Sarah. She was writhing in her seat she was so incensed. "They *prey* on people's good will, they're *white* guys who come up and impress ordinary people with all this talk, and gospel music! They take in thousands."

I said, "I can't wait to hear this sermon."

"Did I ever show you my pictures of the Holy Land?" said Sarah.

I said, "No! You went to Israel?"

Sarah nodded.

"Yes, I did. Egypt, too. You know . . . " she laid her notebook on the seat and turned to me. "There's been so many put-downs of religion, you know, that the Anglican church is just the white man's religion and all that, I mean even white people are saying it, and they're the ones who brought it *up* here! White culture is so *unstable.* I went to see for myself. To see where Christ had walked. To think about it."

This was wonderful; I could see Sarah, Indiana Winnepetonga, striding among the pyramids, fading off into the desert on a camel, in search of truths. I found this admirable. And also admirable because she had gone there on a philosophical or perhaps a spiritual quest. It's so easy, especially for women, to simply think what you're told to think.

But Sarah had saved her money and had flown to the Middle East to answer the great questions for herself. To come to a decision about her personal beliefs; not to debate these beliefs with other people, or to argue down an opponent, despite her summer clash with the Weight Lifter for Christ. That was a matter of defending people against a fraud.

Which fraud we were even now approaching. The road led out of Sioux Lookout, a logging road, dusty and late-summery. The road was tapestried with fireweed and Indian paintbrush, black-eyed Susans, and, in the shade of the spruce and pine, the buff pales of pearly ever-lasting. It was actually hot.

Sarah said, "My father, you know, he's been an Anglican minister for years, and he says, 'Your work for the Lord is pastoral work.' These guys whip people up, grab the money and go. They make people stop thinking, they just stop thinking. Oh, I am so mad."

In the little community log church, set back among birches at the edge of the reserve village, the white Pentecostal preacher was calling out with the voice of a grieving parent to erring children. He was an older man, bald-headed, but his voice was apocalyptically strong and he wore a muscle shirt in order to display his holy biceps. The erring children were all native people, sitting soberly and quietly in the pews, listening with a grave and willing attention. Outside, children ran around shrieking and yelling *bang bang*.

The preacher had a set of weights on the stage. Weight-lifting-for-Christ equipment; the guy was a fundamentalist on steroids.

"*Satan* is a *deceiver!* And the Deceiver has traps and snares and the glitter that is not gold, brothers and sisters! Satan was the Son of the Morning, he is Lucifer, beauteous to behold, but mind him not!"

Sarah and I crept in and slipped into a back pew, bringing out our notebooks. *Satan is a deceiver*, I wrote.

I said, "We'll have to interview him."

She whispered, "Why?"

"Because it's the rules. You can't just go to print and say he's an asshole. You have to give him a chance to speak for himself."

"I don't know why not. What is he doing with that dumbbell?"

The preacher reached down and grasped his dumbbells.

"Now see what strength God has given me, people! If God were not at my side, if he were not giving me strength and help in my ministry on this sinful earth, in the fleshpots of Minneapolis and among the lost souls of the Canadian reservations, would I be able to pick up this weight? No!"

He reached down and lifted the weights. I had no idea if they were made of rubber or lead. He held the weights over his head. I was praying he would drop them, or drive himself through the floor. God works in mysterious ways his wonders to perform. The people shifted, looked at one another, looked back. Outside the northern summer ran rampant with foxtail grasses and dragonflies cruising like miniature helicopters for mosquitoes. Two of the children outside fell into an audible argument over who the plastic Batman belonged to; it was an alarming mixture of Ojibway and English.

"*Ni*-Batman, *nin*! *Minshin*!"

"*Ahte* let go of it. Ev-ver! Hey stupid!"

"The Lord has sent me, he has sent me unto . . . " he paused. He had forgotten the name of the community. "Unto Caesaria! And there may be people who do not *believe*! The *non-believers*, like those two women back there in the back row! No, no, they sit and they sneer at God's work and God's powers and God's people whom he has chosen to be led into the Promised Land at the Day of Judgment when the Goats shall sit on the right hand of the Lord and the Sheep on the left!"

"Goats on the right . . . !" Sarah snorted.

We watched as the collection plate was passed and people put in five-dollar bills, dropped them in the plate with hands muscled by hard work with axes and ice chisels, scarred with gill-net cuts and powder burns. It was awful to watch. Fives, tens, ones. There went dinner, there went the kids' gum-boot money.

Afterwards, outside, Sarah stood with her pen poised over her notebook.

"Where did you get the idea to come up here and ask Indian people for money?" she said. "I'm interested."

When he saw we were from a newspaper, he became bluff and threatening.

"I don't know who you're writing for but you better tell the truth."

But Sarah doesn't scare easily. She started writing.

"I'm being objective," she said, primly. "Reporters have to be objective. Now, I'd like to hear about how much money you got out of these people and if you're an alcoholic or a pederast or anything. Have you ever been arrested for moral turpitude?"

"Young woman!" he said. "The revenge of the Lord upon the unbelievers can be terrible! You will be drowned in your sins like the Philistines in Jordan's billowing flood!"

"Bullshit," said Sarah. "The Jordan is about as big as a drainage ditch, and I'm Ojibway, not Philistine. Come on, how much did you get from these people?"

I said, "I thought you guys did stuff in the confessions line. You know,

'I was a slobbering drunk for twenty years and then God saved me.'"

He said, "Well, I do that too."

I said, "Are you a minister of the Pentecostal Church?"

"Which one? There's forty of them."

"I guess you make forty-one," said Sarah.

He shrugged and surrendered whatever pretensions he had to legitimacy.

"Ah, you know how it is," he said. "I preach good, why shouldn't people pay for some entertainment?"

We found that he had heard from "some guy" at the Salvation Army men's hostel in Minneapolis, where he normally lived, that there was the Lord's work to be done in Canada. He traveled around the country doing this all the time he said, easily, chewing gum. Like, from this bunch, he made about a hundred dollars. As for the weight lifting, it can be summed up in one quote; "If that don't fetch them, I don't know Arkansas."

Sarah sat down at her desk at the office and wrote a blazing report; she was not only not in the least objective, but she salted the article with Bible quotes of her own, concerning Saul's calling up the Witch of Endor and others about false prophets. The pages smoked.

Then we went out for a beer.

The next morning, Nathan called us both into his office.

"David referred this to me," he said, looking at Sarah's story. "You know we can't, under any circumstances, disagree with other people's personal beliefs."

"But you know how people are!" cried Sarah. "They'll sit and sit and listen and listen to be polite, that's how people [she meant native people] are, a white guy comes along and they *believe* him on those little . . . "

Nathan held up his hand.

"The elders, the board of directors, would have a *fit*, Sarah."

I stood and listened.

"Look what he's doing, he's causing trouble, taking their money . . . "

"You know better than this." He handed her back the story. "You know it is very wrong to ever disagree with somebody else's spiritual beliefs. Ever."

The story was cut, edited, watered down, and printed; it had about as much excitement as a soldering iron. I thought about it. No matter how much trouble the guy was causing, one didn't attack others' beliefs. Nathan had decided that principles were not to be sacrificed.

"It doesn't mean we have to sacrifice any standards of theatrical excellence," said Keith Turnbull. "But if you guys want to start a native theater here, we're going to have to make do. The vital thing is a script that . . . "

I said, "Standards of theatrical excellence? Does this mean you want us to write a skit or a passion play or maybe we could do vaudeville? A peep show? How do we get costumes?"

Nathan and I and Oldman Woman and Sarah and David and several other people were all sitting around my cabin. I liked it. I liked it to be full of people.

Keith Turnbull was the director of the NDWT Theatre Company of Toronto. He had a stand-up-straight haircut that looked like a badly mowed wheat field, an alert expression, and a great smile; he smoked incessantly and coughed. The fire roared and a tortoiseshell cat, who had adopted me, marched solidly along the countertop, looking for the can opener.

"Tuberculosis," he said.

"Well, stop smoking!" said Sarah. "You'll kill yourself."

I said, "What do we do about costumes and sets and a script?"

"I'd stop smoking if I were you," said Sarah.

"Don't mind if I do," he said. He lit up. "Well, costumes and sets are the least of the problem. You guys have to start a non-profit corporation, so we can get funding to you. You have to do your paperwork. We apply for funds for a season's play, and we forward it to you guys. As a non-profit corporation. You have to pay actors and travel and so forth and so on. A script . . . "

"Travel?" cried Oldman Woman. "Travel to where?"

"To as many northern communities as we can. By airplane. It's really quite doable, I think. What we have to have is a secure, workable script that . . . "

I said, "But where do you play the play? In the HBC stores?"

Keith said, "Aren't there community halls? If a script is written so that . . . "

I said, "Well, somebody better come up with one."

Nathan hesitated, and then said, "That's what we are actually talking about, here, Puanets. *You* are going to write the script."

"Oh sure. Sure. I'll just rip one right off here. Excuse me a minute while I dash back to the typewriter."

Keith said, "It's not as hard as you think."

"But this is native theater."

"Just think of it as an interim solution. As *northern theater.* Theater is illusion, it's magic. You address a special part of the mind with gesture, with speech."

"Sounds to me something like that Weight Lifter for Christ was doing," said Sarah. "That was a real performance."

"What Weight Lifter for Christ?" He seemed startled.

"Oh, one of those Pentecostals, they come up here every summer," said Sarah.

"I swear, we're not an apostolic movement, here," said Keith. "But that's exactly what I mean. You've just seen it. It was theater. Only community theater is about community stories. You have to think of yourself as a magician. You trigger something in people's minds, and the mind is as real as anything else."

Nathan listened intently.

He said, "I always thought of white people as so completely materialistic."

Keith smiled his beatific, amused smile. "We have our little ways," he said.

I said, "Well, when am I supposed to have this script?"

"Well, not next week or anything. Over the winter we'll put the non-profit papers together, so you'll have an incorporated theater group. Then next summer, we'll have the actors hired, and start rehearsing. Late summer, fall. Then by that winter, we'll be on tour. There's lots of time for a script. This is late August. Let's say a year from now we'll start rehearsing."

Great. Lots of time.

I had always wanted to be an entertainer, a ham, a Skit-Writer For Thespia. If that lunatic with his dumb-bells could do it, so could I.

# 40.

Fire season was nearly over; another month and the fall rains would come. I realized that the stories in the newspaper would change with the seasons; and seasons, in the north, run the world through extreme changes, enormous swings in temperature. One travels by canoe and then, suddenly, one is walking on water. Deep blankets of snow change the entire landscape. Leaves were whirling down in spirals now, yellow and red.

I had tried to write some sort of plot for this play, but grew bored with thinking up things and then throwing them away. I left my attic study and went outside to see which stars were rising.

I don't know why I agreed to do it. I would rather have used my nonwork hours to write down a few ideas for poems, or sit in the Sioux Hotel pub and gossip or go to a movie. The movie theater would fill up with any local group that felt it had a special interest in the current attraction. *Airplane II* drew a big crowd of pilots and bush-airline employees who laughed uproariously and applauded when the nose of the passenger jet smashed through the glass of the airport lounge. *Windwalker* drew so many young native people at an afternoon matinee that they made the showing unendurable with their flirting, yelling, and rushing back for more popcorn to throw at each other and the villain twin. I finally gave up and left them to their enjoyment and came back at an evening showing, along with the silent, grave native adults who took in every nuance, every motion and gesture of this light show.

This was of course far better than sitting alone, in isolation without any images except those engendered in your head, and no popcorn to throw at the villain. But the hours at the office, battering out stories, had somehow done me good. I could keep at it longer now. After a while, I listened to the dog barking, and I thought, hey, maybe it's a wolf, and dropped my pen and hurried outside to shine my flashlight into the thick spruce, or the wraith-like bodies of the birch, thin as spirits, pale as departed ones. Then my dog and I would sit on the stone of the lakefront, watching Fisher circle around the Bow Paddler, high above Sioux Lookout, over North Spirit Rapids and all those entrancing lands farther north; even farther than Hudson Bay. Axel Heiberg, Coronation Gulf, Greenland.

For a month or so things were quite calm at the newspaper. This was a welcome respite from the fire season and bogus "apostolic" weight lifters.

One pleasant day in mid-September, I sat behind my desk scribbling a few lines for a poem that I had decided to call "Northern Radio." I had my typewriter and some Ministry of Natural Resources reports in front of the paper so nobody could tell what I was doing.

I heard somebody coming up the stairs, yelling, "WHERE'S PAULETTE JILES??"

Oh dear. It sounded like a pilot. A big angry pilot.

The pilot was big indeed. He stalked into the hall, in canoe-sized unlaced Greb Kodiak boots and greasy hands and a quilted green vest with rips all over the ripstop nylon and little feathers falling out.

"Where is she? I'll tear her limb from limb."

"She's not here!" I called, cheerfully. I slid down behind the desk and kept the typewriter safely in front of me.

"No, you won't," said Kathy. "I'm the editor and you'll deal with me first." I continued to scribble, desperate for one more line. Good for you, Kath! "And if you don't like dealing with me, there's Nathan Nanokeesic down stairs. He's the overall manager."

The pilot stopped, momentarily confused, and then turned to me again.

"You!" he said.

"Yes? You're interrupting an important report I'm writing here," I said. I had just got a nice line about *brain music*. "I suppose you're objecting to the fact that I wrote something about your sinking that miserable little machine at the dock in Kingfisher?"

"By god, you damn near got me fired! I don't want to get fired! That's my *job* !"

"Tsk," I said. "Minor. Think of the Coral Rapids crash. Twelve people dead. It was before I came, but think of it anyway."

"It was just the pontoons!" he said. "I just had a hole in the pontoons!"

Kathy paused and said, "If there are any problems, you'll speak with me."

"Right," said the pilot. He looked rather dejected. Kathy squared her shoulders, smiled her radiant, happy smile, and went back to her office.

"What about the pontoons," I said.

"Well, you know. It's a dry year."

He sighed and sat down on a broken chair. "It's dry and so there's low water. There's rocks sticking up now where there weren't any last year. So I bang into them. Everybody bangs into them. And the pontoons get holes and cracks and I was sitting in the Kingfisher Lake band office, waiting for the chief to get on, I was three pages into a murder mystery and somebody yells, 'Your plane is down!' And by god, she was."

I said, "Right."

He said, "No harm done, really. Why did you have to report it in the paper?"

"Because . . . "

"I know, I know. Well, just get off my ass, okay? You know something, if you keep this up, Jiles, none of the pilots up here are going to fly you anywhere again."

"Promise?"

"It's serious."

"If you think I'm not fair, talk to the editor."

He hesitated. He had no desire to face Kathy's intimidating, gracious calm again. He was trying to back out of the confrontation but somehow I had to back out too. A mutual retreat.

"Well, I will, by god," he said.

"Okay, maybe I gave it too much play. It's not like there was a passenger aboard. I mean, it just *sank* in shallow water."

"Right!" he said. "Well, we understand each other."

"I can see how you'd be mad," I said. "It's the mechanic's job to check those pontoons."

"'Well, kind of," he said. "Can I buy you a beer sometime?"

Thus we had well'd each other and kind-of'ed each other into a state of declining hostility until there was a thin friendliness. He stomped out. I looked down at the poem.

Why did I continue with these things? Why was poetry important? It described small reflections, tiny feelings. It didn't comfort anybody. The pilot walked into the dusty streets of Sioux Lookout, down to the docks of the airline water base, or to one of the bars. The half-lines of the stanza looked frail and sparse beside the fat, heavy columns of news reports. The Coral Rapids crash, the mercury-plated river, the Inuit freighter that had gone ashore at Fort Severn, the native political organizations' struggle to obtain more reserve land, to writhe free of the bureaucratic arms of the Ministry of Natural Resources. These were stories of true-life confessions, tragedies, heroic rescues. The life of the villages, the tales of the Spontaneously Created People contained so much more vitality than what I was writing down in half-lines on a single sheet of paper.

Alright, start the play.

Outside the second-story window of the office, taxis dusted past, voices of small-town northern life. We are surrounded by forests here, and the trees are alive.

"Are you alive in there?" Kathy called down the hall.

"No. Hack hack hack. Arrgh."

"I thought he wasn't going to leave without your scalp."

"Nevertheless," I said. I was doing a Katherine Hepburn; the scene in *African Queen* where the German commander says, YOU CAN'T POSSIBLY HAVE KUMM TROO DOSE SCHVAMPS!! and she says, *Nevertheless.*

# 41.

The wild rice harvest was coming in by late September.

Kathy said, "Paulette, why don't you go out and do the traditional-style harvesting thing. I'll send somebody else to the professional outfits, and we'll do a big thing about comparing the two. Or would you rather stay in town and take this story on the Native Women's Organization?"

"I'm gone. Adios." I sat there, scribbling poetry.

"Well, take the old Ford. You can reach Eagle Lake by road. They have a woman chief. Down on the Trans-Canada, behind the Dryden airport."

Dryden, the paper-mill town, had the only jet-capable airport between Thunder Bay and Winnipeg.

"Okay, I'll pack right up."

> *Nothing can jar me from this attentive position, this pen hesitating over the paper is a cardiogram needle, the page will be full of spikes and hesitations.*

"Well, gas up at Jim's Taxi. He'll bill us."

"Right. I'm gone."

An old friend from Toronto had called; a publisher wanted to see my poetry manuscript, if I had one, and wasn't it true that I had one? Yes, but the manuscript looked as if it had been slept in by an untidy brain. It had coffee stains, and many of the poems were handwritten on the back of press releases. I would send it to her as soon as it was all retyped. Or rethought.

How did one write about the north in a poem? What about the Thunder Beings, the fearsome Missepijou, Grandmother Underwater Panther, the one living beneath the rapids?

*Elder Wapiquae will tell me about stars, this is for the young people who are forgetting the traditions of their ancestors, she says they run around and drink and throw knives at each other. I will make you appear just as you are in our pages, no distortion, the hostages, the elder, those at the wild rice camps and loons and stars. And all this time (I am sitting here) my heart is talking to itself, all its valves and dull arterial thuds, it is a high-ranking defector, under all this nodding and quotes it says Listen to me. Only to me. Listen.*

Nathan said, "New word for you, Puanets. *Monomin-kauning.*"

The place of wild rice.

Native cooperatives harvested wide paddies of wild rice with large machines that thumped and thudded their way through the watery fields. They had enormous blades, like a steamboat paddlewheel, bolted to an airboat from the Florida Everglades, with a big pushing propeller high in the back. Rice flew into the flat-bottomed boat and then it was cleaned and dried and sacked in warehouses owned by the reserve.

By contrast, the traditional way was difficult, not very productive, and a great deal of fun.

I crashed along the potholed road, back around behind the Dryden airport, to a lake far back in the spruce and granite. Jets roared off overhead, Air Canada creatures with red tails, heading on short flights for Thunder Bay, Winnipeg. Connections to Toronto, Montreal, Vancouver, Hong Kong, London.

I could smell the wood smoke before I got there; a camp of people, tents and pickups, a radio playing, laughter and talk among the spruce and poplar.

The woman chief was young, enthusiastic, welcoming.

"We do it strictly according to tradition," she said. "Here, get a picture of this man."

She led me over to where an elder man was standing in a two-foot hole in the ground. "There, take that picture. Good. He's treading on the parched rice to get the hulls off. His moccasins are specially made new just for this. They won't be used again. The women don't do it because women must never step on food, put food beneath our feet. Now get a picture of this woman."

I watched the man treading on the grain. It was marvelous, this burial of the seed king or spirit, its death and rebirth. I went around snapping photos, all of elders.

"People really like photos of their elders in the newspaper," she said. "They cut them out and keep them."

I was fed boiled wild rice, cooked with salt pork, and Spam and Coke and then a pan full of strange white seeds or puffs. They were using an old copy of *Wawatay News*, the one with my prize-winning shot of the helicopter dumping its bucket on the fire, to clean the skillets.

"That's popped wild rice," a man told me. He laughed at me, as I picked it up and tasted it. "Watch me do it."

He dropped parched, dried wild rice into a skillet of hot grease and it foamed up into tiny pops the size of bugle beads.

I said, "Who is your feast-master?"

The young woman chief said, "Over here."

I walked with her to a Winnebago motor home. An elder woman sat at the step in a plastic lawn chair, busy with work; she was stripping out *watap*, spruce root, into long threads.

"This is Mrs. Makwa," she said.

We shook hands and greeted one another.

I said, "Well, would somebody take an amateur out in a canoe?"

We glided over the still surface of the water in a sixteen-foot canoe, drifting into stands of wild rice with their feathery, grassy heads. My boatman was a woman, a boatperson, young and picturesque. I took photo after photo of her, the sun piercing her straw hat, light falling through a rent, painting her cheek. She bent a stand of stalks over the canoe with one carved stick, and struck it with an identical stick in the other hand.

The blackflies were gone now, and the lake was a lifting, mesmerizing plate of precious metal. These ceremonies of harvest had gone on for thousands of years. Like this; the pile of grains growing and growing in the middle of the canoe, the sticks swishing and the shatter of the grains falling in a heap. The canoe getting more and more unstable as the center of gravity shifts with the height of the pile, the watery voice of the stern paddler, moving the canoe here and there.

Overhead, another jet took off for Toronto or Winnipeg, full of carefully dressed travelers, who were eating little lunches of tiny food made up somewhere; liquid pipe dope and Spork with cheese product.

Back at the camp, women were tossing the hulled grains in a large flat basket, letting the breeze carry the hulls away. It made a whushing noise at it flew up and then settled, flew up and then settled. Flaky gold hulls coated the nearby bushes.

When I started home, the chief handed me a sack full of homemade wild rice. Hand-gathered, hand-toasted, hand-hulled and sacked.

"Hope you got good photos!" she said.

I couldn't wait to develop my film.

In the hot, stifling darkroom I could already see what I had taken. It was all in my mind's eye. And that's where it would stay.

Tokyo, in a burst of energy and generosity, had decided to clean up the darkroom for everybody, and had poured out the old, crystallising D-76, and put water in the bottle to soak it clean.

I was running my negatives with water.

I walked into Kathy's office, stretching out a roll of negatives that was completely clear.

"That means you have to go back," she sighed. "More gas money. Get another mileage sheet. And don't tell me whose fault it was."

"Never. But her initials are T-O-K-Y-O."

"Last name Rose."

"Right."

I made the thousand-year journey once again, from the jet-noisy airport, around it on a potholed road, to the aboriginal camp, to Turtle Island.

There was no radio. No talking. It was silent. I got out of my car, already apologizing for having to ask somebody to take me out again.

The air was glacial.

I went up to the young chief.

"I lost my film," I said, nervously. "I hope it's alright if I come back."

"Well, yes."

*Bonk,* said a raven. It looked at the camp with one eye, and then the other eye. Turtle Island moved slightly and the raven was waiting at the entrance to the lower world.

"We had a drowning here last night," said the chief. She hesitated. I looked quickly around; there, to my relief, was the woman whose picture I had taken, and then lost.

A young man had come out to the camp drunk. He insisted on going out in an unstable, sixteen-foot canoe. Nobody stopped him, nobody disagreed. Nobody has the right to tell other people what to do with their lives, drunk or sober. One's mind is one's own. The Great Spirit gave each one of us our own path, and so he flipped overboard and tangled in the reeds and he drowned.

"I think Mr. Kiidawso better take you." She led me over to an elder, who was white-haired, handsome. "He's very experienced in canoes."

Mr. Kiidawso shot the canoe out into the lake with a few hard strokes. A stern paddler of great skill: one of the best portraits I ever got in the north.

With a 50-millimeter lens, I had to lean far back in the canoe to get a full frame; he kept reaching out toward me. He was nervous.

"We just lost a young man to drowning," he said.

We stabilized, and he bent some reeds over the boat and pretended to beat at them with the traditional carved sticks, smiling for the camera.

It had been like a fairy tale, this little camp, and now a young man was dead. Dead of drink, really.

I jumped out in a few feet of water and helped walk the loaded canoe in.

Mr. Kiidawso said, "This is a special lake, you know."

I said, "Yes. There's a lot of rice here."

He said, "They say you can't whistle on this lake."

I said, "I see." By this time I knew one mustn't whistle near sacred things. Or whistling was a sacred signal, a magical summons, and, of course, you might not want what you summoned up.

"It's a sacred lake."

I said, "Yes."

He sloshed through the last few inches of lake to the rocky shore. "And people should be respectful, because there are powers here."

Between us we pulled the laden canoe all the way up on shore. I was sloshing and banging with camera equipment and my khakis were wet to the knees.

I said, "Yes?"

"There are rock paintings here. Look." He pointed with his lower lip, toward the far side of the lake. I looked, and on the far side of the small lake, where the water exited in a fast rapid, was a bluff of granite with an overhang, and a dark area in the shadows.

I carried a small pair of binoculars; I looked. It was Missepijou.

I shook hands with Mr. Kiidawso, the chief and the councillors, and drove off feeling low.

We printed the picture of Mr. Kiidawso large and ran a sidebar on the drowning small.

Kathy laid out the wild rice issue. The shots of the commercial operations were very good; mountains of wild rice in warehouses, heading south to America, to the big Canadian cities. Stories on the big machines, figures, poundages, tonnages, salaries and profits going to native-owned businesses. Somewhere there were native accountants sitting over the books, sometimes cooking the books, mostly balancing profit and loss with probity and rectitude, paying salaries out, taking payments in. Somewhere the red-ocher figure of Missepijou, the Underwater Panther, a perilous creature of rectitude and sobriety, of exaction and Karma, of terrible power, painted on a granite wall, looked out over the ripe harvest of seeds and souls.

# 42.

It was getting crisp outside; a light, winey smell was in the air from fermenting leaves that had fallen in yellow heaps; poplar and the violent reds and burgundies of the mountain ash.

It was past wild-rice harvest time. The three stars of Orion's belt, called the Stern Paddler, were rising in the early hours of the morning, and so he was invisible, never seen.

There were three marvelous films — all shot by Tokyo. She was becoming a splendid photographer. We had just been on a trip to a very small village called Winter Fisher, and I was in the darkroom developing her negatives.

I was supposed to be training young Tokyo, so I made her hang out of an airplane. This was to build character and teach her the joys of a reporter's life.

When we started off on our trip to Winter Fisher, Piitonya came out into the layout room. Tokyo and I were packed up: camera bags, knapsacks with nightgowns and candles and paperback novels, extra film and rubber boots (fall time, like spring, was rain time) and ponchos and notebooks and pens. Winter Fisher had a sawmill; the chief had obtained a great deal of funding from the Indian Affairs program for native-owned businesses and then had allowed the sawmill to collapse. Nobody knew where the money went. We were going to take aerial photos, if we could get there. First job was to get to North Spirit.

"Get my daughter in a plane crash and your life isn't worth a plugged nickle," said Piitonya.

I said, "No ma'am. Won't let any guys near her either."

"I'm serious."

"Really, Piitonya, I'll look out for her."

*****

"Splinter" villages continually form, take shape, establish themselves. People fed up with a certain chief in a certain village will leave by families, in snowmobiles, and go live somewhere else. They completely ignore the surveyed lines, they trundle off into the bright snow, pulling *djabanak* (animate plural sleds) behind their snowmobiles, little kids packed into blankets among the tools and traps, and somewhere a sort of secret, unadministered village springs up. Usually this happens in the far northern areas, so far north that the MNR can do little about it. Like a paper pop-up village on a greeting card, small one-room cabins spring up in a few days as if they were a sort of natural growth, the women set their gill nets at a likely stream-mouth, and then there is a tiny community full of activity: gossip, skinning, the drying of meat and fish into *pemaigun* and *nokahiikan.* An approaching visitor can hear the steady whacking noise of someone cutting wood, a tape cassette playing the latest Inuit rock group, arguments and shouts.

Muskrat Dam started as one of these splinter villages. Others were MacDowell Lake, Summer Beaver, Winter Fisher, the East End of Sandy Lake and then there were small settlements out in the forests surrounding Sioux Lookout. I had always wanted to visit one of them, to discover how people made their own towns, their own little world in unofficial mini-towns. Why they went there, how they lived.

But not this time. We were merely going to fly over Winter Fisher and return. Another time.

We had a good, smooth flight into North Spirit. We would change planes there, if there was another one to rent.

From North Spirit we got a small Cessna 185 or 175, I forget which, to fly us over Winter Fisher. It was good weather, clear skies. I wore a bright Pendleton wool shirt, the sleeves rolled up past the elbows. This was so they could spot me in the bush if I fell out of the plane.

I put Tokyo in the front seat, the copilot's seat.

The little Skywagon tore off downwind, crushing the wave-tops, and rose, and we were airborne.

The pilot yelled, "Want me to take the door off?"

"No!!" screamed Tokyo. "My mother will kill you!"

"It's safe!" said the young pilot. "You'll be strapped in!"

"No!" yelled Tokyo. "Another time! When I'm old and don't care if I die!"

We flew over the sawmill and the pilot tipped the plane sideways to give Tokyo a good shot. I leaned forward and forced the window open. With astonishment, I noticed that my skin was rippling up my arm like a silk shirtsleeve.

Below us, there was a large opening in the forests, and an abandoned sawmill. Its funding and its machines were all gone to hell. Maybe everybody had moved somewhere else. The *matagwans*, tipis made of logs, looked deserted.

"Shoot!" I yelled. "Tokyo, shoot!"

Tokyo paused and looked down and gave a little shriek, and then leaned her small self out the window and grit her teeth and looked through the lens. She was, after all, Piitonya's daughter. She put her mind and her eye behind the camera and started shooting, the wind tearing at the camera, trying to snatch it out of her hands, the camera-strap smacking her in the forehead. She was brave. It's cool to be a trainer.

When we returned to North Spirit, I pulled on my mountaineer jacket and wrapped a wool shawl around my neck. I went past my old cabin, now jammed full with a family of three kids. Mrs. Mindemoya's cabin was empty, the windows blank and sad. The weather balloon rose up from the bluff and trailed off into the atmosphere, a silvery disappearing tadpole gone skyward like Frog about to be reborn in the zodiac.

I walked all over, from house to house, surprising people: Mrs. Half-A-Day, Chief Makepeace, Eno and Bruce and all the radio guys. I looked around at the radio station, where I had spent nearly a year. The Canadian flag draped over the window as a curtain, the photo of the prime minister, the old oil stove.

"You guys are doing some theater down there, I hear," said Eno.

"Yes, we need a script! Think you could write one?"

"Not this time."

Shit.

I went for a long walk through the light grasses of the shore. How beautiful it was! It had just last night frozen over the bay behind the Blackhawk Store, a slick glass surface over which children were skating, and the ice was so thin, so transparent, it seemed they were walking on water. Older people walked out on it in timorous baby steps, full of qualms, as if they were about to be shot. An elder man bent over and said,

"*Mii o-ooh!*" Here it is! My hatchet! The hatchet he lost this summer, overboard, as they were taking off for Angling Lake or the Deep Hole where the trout lie. And then there were other adults, grandmothers who didn't trust themselves on the slick, thin surface, urging grandchildren out onto the ice: Look for the tea strainer I dropped overboard! Go see if you can find your brother's sunglasses!

I slid out on the ice myself, peering down. It was as if I were in a glass-bottomed boat. I saw the waving bottom-weeds, fields of granite pebbles, occasional tin cans, a Pilot Biscuits box.

An elder woman was yelling at me. It was with great pleasure I realized it was Nathan's mother, Mrs. Nanokeesic, and I understood her. I looked up from my prone position, decorated with shawl fringes.

"Do you see my long knife?"

For a minute I thought she said, "my American," which in Ojibway translates as "Long Knives." *Kitche Mokoman.*

I said, "I *am* a Long Knife."

She paused a moment; rotund, strong, healthy, astonished. Then she said, "Really?" And slapped both hands on her thighs and fell into hilarity.

At the Ministry of Natural Resources guest-house, where Tokyo and I were spending the night before returning to Sioux the next day, I spread out a few sheets of play plot. In the next room, a radio was on; North Spirit radio, rapid Ojibway I couldn't understand. Let us say, then, that the protagonist is a young man who has returned to the north from the city. Long years in city pent, longing for that bee-loud glade. He's got a college education and he's coming home to tell the elders how the cow ate the cabbage. He's going to run the trapping program of the completely planned village in an urban, modern way, yes, it's Global Village time.

Tokyo said, "Um, Paulette?"

"Here."

"I got an interview, just sort of wandered around and picked one up."

"Who with?"

"A lady called Sarah Pijou. It's really interesting. I just said to myself, well, go ask somebody for an interview. I really like it. It's about stars."

"Really?" I had met Sarah Pijou once; a small, neat lady of about fifty, very shy, who had arrived at the radio station with beadwork to sell. She had come over from Winter Fisher by snowmobile. It was beautiful beadwork and I had bought a pair of high-top moccasins from her as a gift for someone.

I looked at Tokyo's notes.

Sarah Pijou, small and shy, spoke out of the quick notations. The Big Dipper is what we call *Ojig*. The Fisher. He has a broken tail. He circles around and around the Nail Star, who is also called . . .

"Called what?" I said.

"I didn't get it." Little Tokyo bent eagerly over her notes, her finger on the paper. She was wrapped up in a parka liner, the duffle part. "I didn't get it from the translator and she was talking so fast . . . kind of like 'nematode' or something. Nah. That's an algae, isn't it? Or a pseudopod or something. Anyway, the North Star is the Bow Paddler, and she says he stays steady, he's the steady point in life. He doesn't change. He's kind of, you know, secure. It's neat, isn't it?"

I said, "Wait. I know what it is. *Nemetahamun*, the Bow Paddler. Mrs. Mindemoya told me, once."

Ojig circles around and around the Bow Paddler, the pivot of the heavens, who can only be Polaris, and Ojig's tail was broken because he rescued the Girls Who Married Stars from the tallest tree in the world. They fell into the tree when they fell out of heaven. Out of the hole in the sky.

I said, "The hole in the sky."

"Can we use it?"

"I bet Akewence will draw something beautiful, a sky-map, for this," I said.

In the darkroom back at the Wawatay office, I looked at Tokyo's photos of Sarah Pijou; the small woman's face was electric with storytelling, relating the great oral works of the Spontaneously Created People, her hands were both raised and open. She swam up out of the developer like a visitation, as if she had arrived, like the Girls Who Married Stars, out of the celestial realms, full of startling information.

I took a clothespin and pinned the photo to the overhead line, and prepared to go home to feed my cat and my dog and my whiskey jack.

# 43.

Ace Lawson was wrenching the pontoons off a Beechcraft with any number of tools. I was at the airport to interview one of the airline owners about something. It was a crackling fall day, near the freezing mark. Ace had left off flying cargo in DC-3s for the temporarily more lucrative job of flying out wild rice harvests from remote lakes.

The north froze in a series of steps like ladders. First Fort Severn, then a week later down to North Spirit Rapids, and so on.

I said, "Are you flying out the rice from Lac Seul?"

"Hi, Skinny. How's my white Indian?"

"Good. Looking for stories. Ace, if you weren't married, I'd take you out for a drink of whiskey. Maybe a bucket of it."

His long face was marked with age and freeze scars and grease.

"I don't know why a man gets married, what with good-looking women like you running loose. Yes, yes, I did indeed fly out the rice from Lac Seul, and got stuck on Little Eagle Lake north of there yesterday. I came in on pontoons to get their rice out and it froze on me."

"But everybody knows Little Eagle was freezing up!"

"Don't tell an old pilot his business, Skinny. If they don't get it out, they don't get their money."

"How'd you get out?"

"I revved them goddamned engines like you never seen. They were smoking. I jumped her up on the ice on those pontoons and took off skating, sliding . . . it was a real carnival ride. But I got up. And then came in to Lac Seul, and since that's a hundred miles south, I could land on pontoons, because they weren't froze up yet."

Oldman Woman and I sat on a point of pines at Lac Seul, and watched the water describe the fall wind that moved across it, and drank

Drambuie, and saw the geese go south in shattered lines, and we waved at Ace, flying overhead in his silver Beechcraft with its battered pontoons.

We were still up at ten o'clock, it was the first of November, we were squashing headlines into columns, thinking of short words, long words, any words.

Another story from Fort MacPherson; a shooting at a Halloween dance. A man became incensed because his girlfriend was dancing with another man, went out and got his .22, and shot his rival in the leg.

ALTERCATION AT HALLOWEEN DANCE? SHOOTING AT HALLOWEEN SHINDIG? It was one column wide by about two attention-spans long. The trouble was the word, "Halloween." It was almost longer than the story. It was the last snag holding us up.

"Oh think of something!" said Kathy. "Think of anything, let's just get it *done.* Tom's at home with the baby and here I am, fussing with this."

Tokyo said, "I've got it!"

"What? What?"

She smiled. "Trigger Treat!"

# 44.

When the lakes freeze, they make big booming sounds, roars. I don't know what causes it. You can hear them at night, in the late fall, when the temperatures drop, and a thin glass pane of fresh-water ice suddenly spreads, and crystallizes, and then something goes off like a cannon shot.

It will startle you out of bed.

One day, just when the freezing lakes were booming with night noises, Celeste, from North Spirit, called from the airport. Could she come and stay for a while? Her baby was named Tina Marie, just a month old, and she and her husband had been fighting. It was mid-November; the Freezing Moon.

The baby was a girl with a head the size of a teacup and fingers with pearls on the ends. She was tucked into a *tikinagan*, a cradle board, laced in tight with moose-hide thongs. There were yards of embroidered baby-sheet flowing out around her face, edged with lace. She looked like the center of an exotic bloom.

Celeste got out of a taxi in front of my cabin with a plastic suitcase and the baby. I remembered her then; she had gone to the school meeting with Jeannie and Sarah and me. She was very quiet. I gave her the guest room and she wordlessly settled in.

Celeste spent most of her time tracing over the illustrations in a book of flowers, thinking of another baby-sheet. She talked to the baby in low tones.

She was married, had a baby, and was separated. She was only eighteen.

In the evenings, I would climb a steep stair — a ladder, really — to a little space under the eaves where I had my desk and a typewriter. No matter how many people came to stay I now had a little private space to bore myself silly trying to think up a play.

It was late at night. The sun had fainted out of the sky in a low haze of ground-blow, sifting the season's first heavy fall. I was in the middle of a long, dull dialogue. Why did I just not throw this shit out the window?

Downstairs, Celeste started screaming.

I shoved away from my desk and papers as if they were on fire. I turned to the steep ladder and I was three steps down when the door to the attic stairs came open and Celeste was on the bottom step, and the baby was in her arms, and it was dead.

"Paulette, Paulette, the baby, the baby!"

Her hair was in a wild tangle of permanent curls, she was dressed in an old nightgown with a blanket thrown over her shoulders, the dim light from the kitchen coming in behind her and outlining the limp, dead little girl in her arms. I hope never to see a sight like that again in my life.

She was screaming with such intensity that she was shaking all over. I saw very quickly that the baby was dead and Celeste was out of control.

She was walking up the stairs, screaming.

I said, "Give me the baby."

She gave me the baby very gently, still screaming with all her strength. The noise of her voice was filling the cabin, the night sky. I ran down the stairs with it for years. It seemed to take years and years to get to the bottom of the stairs. I was trapped in the dim light on a narrow, precipitate ladder with a dead child in my arms and I ran on and on and on.

I seemed to have made it to Celeste's bedroom, laying the little girl on the bed.

I said, "Stay there, Celeste, I'll try . . . "

What would I try? The child was dead and lost, blue, gone, absent, her half-open eyes jelled and dull. Something had evaporated from her. I pinched the tiny nose shut, opened her mouth and blew. There was no response. I couldn't make myself do that twice.

Crib death is something that comes in sleep, in dreams, and no one ever catches it as it approaches. It is invisible. It is strange, isn't it, how it waits until one is sound asleep, preoccupied, unguarded.

I folded her hands together as best I could.

I called the police and the doctor, a doctor who was a friend of nearly everyone in the community.

Celeste was walking around the room, saying, "I just walked in to look at her and she was dead. I just fell asleep, I should have been watching her . . . "

I left the little girl in Celeste's bedroom and shut the door. The dead are not only the color of limestone, but they are dangerous. I stood with my back to the door. It was as if I felt that the dead child would try to get out and speak to us without her spirit, and I had to guard against this happening.

It was dark night, and we were far from town, and the winter cold had settled in, grinding.

The doctor came in a spray of snow powder and crunched to a halt in the driveway. Celeste and I turned to him as flowers turn to the sun.

A good doctor is supposed to put a hand on your shoulder and say, "I'll take over now." They are supposed to say, "She was a healthy baby, there was nothing you could do. She was well-cared for." They should say, "This is absolutely terrible."

He did all those things.

The ambulance drove away, and all the big systems took over. The hospital, the police report, the funeral director. The ambulance drove away down the snowy road and darkness fell and fell and fell.


While Celeste was at the funeral home, I rearranged every stick of furniture in the house. I moved everything. I thought, nothing should remind her of where she saw the baby first, or where she sat, or even the blanket she was wearing.

I changed all the bed linens and pulled down the curtains and put up some of my printed sheets instead. I started an enormous stockpot full of soup, and began laying out all the dishes I had.

Her husband's relatives all came from the reserve down near the American border, and her mother from North Spirit.

She said, "This was right. This is what Indian people do — change everything. You did just right."

Her relatives came to stay at the cabin: elderly people and young people, quiet, hushed. There were some ceremonies to go through, I didn't have any idea what they were, all I knew was that a year from now there would be a give-away feast for the soul of the dead person. Celeste's father had been to see a shaman, or perhaps he was a shaman, I never knew and didn't ask for fear of being rude. In the meantime, I made beds and cooked.

The morning of the funeral, Celeste walked out to the shores of the lake behind my cabin into the banks of diamond willow. She wandered and stopped, broke off a branch, wandered on.

She came in and kicked snow from her moccasins.

"I'm cutting red willow for a bow and arrow. She has to have it to cross into the Villages of the Dead. They are always dancing there. There's a fierce dog that guards the bridge." She spoke in her strange, low whisper. "She has gone to be with my grandmother, I know. I am sure of it."

That evening, when the snow was still and thick and marked with starlight, a gathering of stored light in the starshine and the deep, new cold, someone showed me a hand-drawn map to the Villages of the Dead. It was reassuring. The map said, *the child is on a journey.* The map said, *the way is perilous and it is also a matter of peril to look into these things.* It said, *leave this to the people who know.* A medicine man named James Redsky has drawn a map to the Villages of the Dead. It is known as a ghost scroll.

The funeral home was full. Oldman Woman was there, and David, and Nathan, and all of Celeste's people, and the young, distraught husband. Celeste walked up to the small white coffin and laid the bow and two arrows securely in the little girl's hands, she leaned down and spoke to her. They shut the lid. The little girl drifted away and turned her face resolutely to the great river and the bridge. She held her red willow bow in her left hand and the two arrows in her right. There was a path toward a meadow of sweet fruits, but nothing tempted her. There was a startling rattle of gourd rattles, but nothing distracted her. She passed beneath the stone gaze of the Four Winds Manitous. A long bridge made of one narrow log crossed the rapids. At the other end was a fierce dog with yellow eyes. She lifted her bow, she fired, and the way lay open to the Villages of the Dead.

True maps are made of experiences, and to move into this unknown geography the explorer must have the courage of a new soul or spirit, even that of an infant girl. I have always wanted that inestimable gift of doing the right thing, and sometimes I think I manage. I hesitated to tell this sad story but it is like picking up a heavy pack. You must understand how useless a map is. You must also study them with great care.

# 45.

"You need nine poles," said Piitonya. "Nine. Well, hurry up, chop it down." She was Sacajawea, the woman of many languages, persuasive, bullying, wise, an elder.

I chopped down one more birch tree and watched it fall. We were building a tipi. She was showing me how. The smoke poured down out of my chimney and, inside, the lamps glowed in the dim, cloudy day.

Piitonya had come out to my cabin to borrow something, I don't remember what, and then saw I was clearing some slim white, peeling birches from my view of the lake, and then she started talking about the way her mother had built a tipi when she was young, and I said, Let's build one, and she said, You build it and I'll supervise.

We worked most of the afternoon, wading through new snow, Piitonya talking happily about how it went this way, and then that way, and then the three poles were tied, and then one leg was walked up, an ungainly giant water-spider, and then the other leg, and it was a tripod. Then three times three is nine, and the smoke rises up from the fire, the same fire since the world began, this world (there are others, she says), and the poles have to be laid into the notch of the tripod, and then the rope slung and lassoed around them.

This is the doorway where human beings enter, bowed over, to the realms of fire and meat and warm furs. These are the two door-poles, that hold a skin between them.

These are the places where people sit; each person has a place. The old men sit at the very back, the old women beside them. The younger people sit closer to the door and to the cold, and the youngest woman with a baby sits right beside the door. Each person has an exact place, according to their station. This is the etiquette of the circle of people sitting inside a tipi.

And every day you shake out your bedding, your night thoughts, and freshen yourself to a new day, hanging the bedding on tree limbs, and the work of life begins, or no work, maybe just lying around.

"If I were looking for arrowheads in the summer," she said, "I would look for a point out onto a lake, where a cool breeze comes up. That's where somebody would have sat to work, under a tree, chipping flint." Our breath steamed up into the spruce. Piitonya had on an electric-blue parka with white fox trim around the hood, and leather gloves.

She said, "Now we used to make fruit leather by mashing blueberries, and spreading it on a sun-hot rock beside the lake, and we would come back and roll it up, and put it in birchbark containers, and store it somewhere. That wasn't so very long ago."

We sat inside our tipi, which was covered with plastic, and looked at the lake. The inside was soon crispy with breath-frost.

"You're interested in legends," she said. "You must know about the *pawakan.*"

"No. What's that?"

Piitonya was in a talkative mood. I was delighted with my tipi. It was a correct tipi. And all the people of my imagination had a place inside.

"It's a skeleton-child, that flies from tree to tree. It has these awful cries." She paused. "People who have lost a child, or seen a child die, are carried away by the *pawakan.* They run after it. And a medicine man has to tell them, leave it alone. Let it go back."

I said, "I see."

"When I was three or four, I had a little sister that died. She died when we were out on the trap line. And my dad, he was really a good Anglican, he said we had to take her back to the Hudson's Bay post for the minister to bury her. So he made a coffin, and a little canoe, and we paddled back all the way to the village, pulling that little canoe and coffin behind us. She was like following us. It scared me to death. It was like the *pawakan.* You must let it go, let it go back."

I said, "What happens to people in the Villages of the Dead?"

She thought a minute and said, "I've heard they're reborn here on this earth, but I could never figure that out, because the whole population is growing so much, so where are all the new people coming from?"

I said, "You got me."

# 46.

It was a relief to have a good hard freeze. Now the lakes were solid and could be crossed if you knew the places to avoid, the thin place where a current kept sanding away at the underside. Oldman Woman walked with me from my cabin to town one morning, after coming out to visit and then staying up half the night to talk about spirit things by the wood stove. She had spent the night and now it was time to go to work.

Instead of taking the car, we walked across the lake. My dog followed after. The lake was a brilliant field of white, our breath streamed away from our mouths to the south. The snowshoes dipped into the light powder like beaters. I slogged forward hardily.

We were in the midst of stories, at the newspaper, about government. The MNR was being asked to concede hunting rights to native people and not apply southern rules; Indian Affairs was being pressed to present better teaching plans with native content, the federal government was stalling on admitting native treaty rights into the new constitution. I was sick of government. I had never had to deal with government so much in my life. It was everywhere, it made up rules for every aspect of one's life. All these government agents and ministers and assistant secretaries had to be paid high salaries with travel and per diems. Why did we put up with them? Why were they so necessary? Where did they *come* from? Were they from outer space? Have they all just taken over our brains?

I said, "I've got to get started on some damn story about Community and Social Services plans to institute workshops on co-dependency, can you believe that?"

Oldman Woman said, "It's better out here on the lake."

"And my dog will want to come in and sleep on my feet and fart."

She said, "You know, all these organizations and dogs. It makes me think of a story."

"Tell it."

We plunged on through the powdery snow, cheeks bright red, a clean wind whipping down from the north. Snow powder crusted the wrinkles in my jeans, my fat moccasin-feet disappeared repeatedly.

"It's about why dogs always sniff each other's assholes."

I started laughing.

"You know there was the big conference of animals? When Frog stole summer?"

"I don't really remember." I did remember; I just wanted to hear it again. The far shore was drawing closer, and then we would pass into the trees, and we would be at the rail lines, thank god. I was not adept at snowshoes.

"I'm sure I told you this. Anyway, Frog stole summer, and there was a sort of war between the winter animals and summer animals, and then they thought they would have a big treaty meeting. They had it in a huge skin lodge, and they hung summer up in a bag, suspended from the lodge poles, so nobody could grab it until it was decided who would get it. Well, they decided to share it. The winter animals would get summer for a few months, and the summer animals would get it for a few months. Anyway, this went on and on, it's a long story about the meeting.

"But somebody forgot to invite the dogs. Nobody told them there was a big meeting to decide about the possession of summer. So the dogs got mad. They were all very insulted." Oldman Woman stopped to wipe her nose. Cold makes your nose run. The wind was biting. "So they said, well, we'll have our *own* conference! They set up a lodge, which they thought was very grand, and to make sure they were all *very* proper, and mannerly, they made a rule that everybody who came in had to hang up their asshole at the door." Oldman Woman put her hand over her mouth and laughed in a snorting giggle. "Stupid dogs! They were trying to be very high-toned." We snowshoed on again, I walked with my head to one side to hear her over the wind. The dog ran beside us, prancing and important. "So right in the middle of their conference, the lodge caught fire! And they all started running to get out, and as they rushed out, they just grabbed any old asshole . . . " I was laughing in shouts, in the high wind, hurrying toward the tree line and laughing. "So they all got their assholes mixed up! Now when one dog meets a strange dog, he runs up and sniffs the other guy's asshole, like 'Have you got my asshole?'"

We passed through the belt of trees, and crossed the rail line, took off our snowshoes and walked down the main street of town toward the Wawatay offices. My dog dashed ahead down the street, looking forward to meeting all the town dogs, forever looking for his asshole that he lost in the lodge fire when the Conference of Governmental Representatives on Alternate Summer Possession broke up and scattered them forever into the world of men with the wrong fundament, a story about a conference gone utterly wrong, and the origin of the expression, usually shouted out when a citizen is ensnared by some mindless government rule, "Those *assholes!*"

We walked into the busyness of the newspaper office, its telephones and emergencies.

# 47.

A plane from Winter Fisher was down.

"What??"

We rushed into Piitonya's office. People always called her with news first, it seemed.

"A woman . . . Sarah Pijou and the nurse's aide, Serena Southwind. They took off late, got toward Thunder Bay and then went off the radar."

Sarah Pijou, the tiny woman whom Tokyo had interviewed about Ojig, the Fisher who was the Big Dipper with his broken tail who had saved the Girls Who Fell Out of the Sky. Sarah Pijou had had an accident on a snowmobile. She was coming home from the trap line with her husband and had somehow injured her hip.

They took her to the nursing station in Winter Fisher, and the nurses felt she should be flown out to the hospital in Thunder Bay for an X ray.

The head nurse called around for the first available plane, and got one in Red Lake. The pilot was George Sutherland, the flying bank robber.

But everybody liked him because it had been many years since he had robbed a bank, and anyway, he'd spent his time in jail, and also, it's another story.

He was an excellent pilot.

They put Sarah aboard and then also Serena Southwind, the nurse's aide. Sarah didn't speak English and would need a translator when she got to the hospital in Thunder Bay.

"Why Thunder Bay?" I asked. "Why didn't they send her here? They have X-ray machines here."

"I don't know," said David. "I have no idea. Listen to the rest of it. Last night about ten o'clock Thunder Bay radio picked them up.

Sutherland said he was switching from Red Lake radio to the Thunder Bay beam. He went off the Red Lake frequency and then there was just silence. He was about twenty-five miles north of Thunder Bay."

Almost as bad as a crashed plane is a missing plane. No matter how many anxious questions you ask, it is still missing. The questions are not really questions. They are demands.

Didn't he carry an Emergency Locater Transmitter in the tail? Those things are required by law. Aren't they picking it up? The ELTs are supposed to start broadcasting automatically on impact. Are they searching? Of course they're searching. Well, what color was the plane? White, of course. White as the snow, white as stars. Why aren't those damned planes required to have International Orange strips painted on the top? How does anybody think searchers can see a white plane in the white snow?

While the Canadian Forces Hercules search planes flew their patterns over the forests just north of Thunder Bay, reporters turned back to their telephones. We ran Tokyo's striking portrait of Sarah Pijou on the front page.

Days stretched into weeks, and they were still missing.

Temperatures fell to forty below and farther.

# 48.

The town steamed, people came to work in volumes of clothes. I seemed to live in my muskox parka. I hoped that the play would take shape like the crystals of fragile ice at the first freeze. Lowered to a certain temperature, structures formed in isolation, and then began to lock together, and then formed a whole thing. Maybe it would sort of happen, organically, and I wouldn't have to really work at it.

I sat in my attic room typing and freezing and freezing and typing. Why did I hide out up here? Well, it seemed sort of private. Away from wood stoves and the telephone and the hateful oil stove. It was like entering my brain. This was my brain. I sorted through various lobes trying to find the play script. I had an electric typewriter and, as the temperatures dropped, I suddenly found that if I typed an *H*, the metal letter would fly off the striker arm and go whizzing across the attic. I would grope for it on my hands and knees and try to do wit out an  . Then the *P* went, and the *G*.

"Do you have a wood stove, by any chance?" the repairman asked.

"Yes, I do."

"That's the trouble. The heat goes up and down. From freezing to warm. And so the solder on the striker arms expands and contracts, and whoosh! It's loose, and it goes flying."

So I put it on an electric heating pad every night, covered tightly with a piece of plastic. The protagonists had decided to make their sojourn trapped in the Hudson's Bay Store more endurable by snatching up a fiddle and playing "Ste. Anne's Reel" with one light bulb. They all danced, including the Hollywood actress, who broke into a fast jig during the fiddle break on "Hen and Chickens." It turned out that the pilot, who had sunk his plane at the dock while on the third page of a murder mystery, had been a reporter at a northern newspaper, and was secretly reporting on everybody.

Not.

I threw the script back into its paper bag and went for water.

My oil stove was refusing to work. Every time I made a trip, I came home to a frozen-up cabin. It was so cold even things in the refrigerator had frozen through. The beer was a brewy smelling alcoholic mush. It was enough to work at the strict and formal requirements of journalism all day — I was, after all, a poet — but then to come back to solid beer was more than I felt I should have to bear. The days were short and dim. It was nearly Christmas.

It had to be something wrong with the feed line in the oil stove. In the twenty below zero cold, I rolled up my parka sleeves and took a wrench and began to unscrew the bolts that held the feed line. I put a three-pound empty coffee can under the intake to catch the fuel oil as it spilled out of the reservoir.

The oil ran all over my hands. Oil at the temperature of twenty below. I had to stop repeatedly and wipe my hands and then hold them in front of the little electric heater.

Then I was suddenly seized by an attack of culture fatigue. It came without warning. It is a well-known psychological phenomenon that attacks people who are living in another culture and another climate for extended lengths of time, always confused as to the functioning of various machines, tools, instruments, social rules. It happens to people who find themselves the perpetual outsider, never allowing themselves a spontaneous reaction to anything, totally and infernally one step behind the curve that everybody else seems to be skating on without effort.

I swabbed oil off the floor with an old copy of the newspaper, smearing photos of the Whitefish Bay powwow, the handsome Red Lake man with his deer-tail roach.

I felt myself hating the north. I felt myself suddenly hating Sioux Lookout with its Darth Vader blue town lights glowing in the distance, I found myself overtaken by impatience and fury at the thought of the dangerous bush planes, with their pilots who weren't even old enough to shave, flying me to bush strips with dogs and stumps all over them, and the noisy isometric exercises of the switch engines on the Sioux Lookout tracks, and my typewriter flinging its frozen letters all over the cabin.

I wrenched at the fuel line. I was sick of the staggering trip back from the hole in the ice with full buckets slopping all over my moccasins, the northern lights were just an irritating mistake on the part of the Light God who couldn't keep a straight line if he had to, Spork was a revolting concoction of pink rubber invented by food sadists.

Culture fatigue is a rejection of reality by someone who is intellectually pooped by constant contention with difference: difference in language, manners, clothing, food, and habits. Who needs a rest.

I sat in front of the electric fire for a moment and warmed up. The culture fatigue attack passed. Never mind. I love this place. I wrenched my wrench and the fuel oil poured out its cold iridescent coagulation and I pulled out the copper pipe. Then I threw the thing out into a snowbank and built a fire.

Normality returned at the office.

The coffeepot was full in the downstairs coffee room. It was hot and strong. There was light and heat, light and heat without effort. Good, good, I poured a great deal of sugar and cream into my cup.

David came down the stairs.

I said, "I just had an awful night. My oil stove gave out. I hated everything and everybody. It was like I was some other person."

"Yup," said David. "That happened to me when I went out to high school in Thunder Bay. One day I walked out of a movie and I hated the entire white world. Cities, oil stoves, movies, streets, cars, straight lines, flat surfaces, everything."

"Oh. Good to hear it."

"I have an assignment for you."

"Cool. To Bermuda, maybe?"

"You said you were interested in those little splinter villages. There's some people near here who are trying to get reserve land. Come on up to my office, I'll show you where it is."

David sat down at his desk and picked up a telephone message from somebody named Michikan.

# 49.

"Go and visit the Michikan family," said David. "They've just built a new community hall for the native people in Vermillion Bluff. They're going to have a grand opening."

I said, "I thought Vermillion Bluff was a white town. You know, there's a motel and a gas station, a lot of the people who work in the logging industry live there."

David said, "You know, there are little Indian communities all around down here. None of them on reserve land. They're sort of 'unofficial,' I guess. You know Sioux Mountain?"

That was a high hill that stood between Sioux Lookout and the reserve of Lac Suel, David and Oldman Woman's reserve. It overlooked the town.

"Yes, certainly."

"There's an Ojibway community up there on Sioux Mountain."

"Really?"

He paused.

"It's complicated. These small villages around here, they've always been there. Always. But they never got any reserve land." He looked up at the map over his desk. "When we signed the Treaty at Lac Seul in the 1870s, the Ojibway people from all around the area came over to where the signing was being held. The heads of families, at any rate. Lots of those families had never lived at Lac Seul and never would, I mean, did the Treaty commissioners think we lived all bunched up in a mob at one place? They just came over for the Treaty signing. So the commissioners got their signatures and wrote them down on the rolls and said, 'Okay, this is your reserve.' They just ignored them and went home. I mean, they never understood that the government thought they should *live* at Lac Seul, and that their own home area was now

Crown land. So they went back to their own little villages and suddenly they found themselves pressured by government agents to conform to the laws of Crown land. So now, they're applying for official reserve land. And they want the goodwill of the white people over there. They've built this community hall to get the native community together. It'll be a big celebration."

"Good! I'll be there for a feast, right? Great."

He cleared his throat and grinned.

"The Michikan family wants you to go trapping with them, too. The feast is at night."

"Right. How do I get there?"

"On the train. Try to talk the conductor into letting you off at Vermillion Bluff."

# 50.

Vermillion Bluff was thirty miles to the east of Sioux Lookout along the rail line. I was traveling with my snowshoes this time, and a backpack and the camera bag and my tote with the lock on it. The heavy old train with its 1950s cars trundled down the rail bed, swaying from side to side. The conductor came by.

I said, "Say, could you stop at Vermillion Bluff and let me off?"

He was very natty in his conductor's navy-blue uniform, a metal band around his cap, iron-gray hair.

"Young woman, what are you doing getting off at Vermillion Bluff? There's nothing there."

I said, "I'm a fungologist. I collect samples of fungus for the University of Newfoundland's Furred Plant Department. They're trying to discover how fungi survive the winter."

"Why am I not believing you?" He punched holes in tickets as if he were forcing them to confess.

"Actually, I'm a reporter for the Toronto *Globe and Mail*. I'm investigating some white-collar crime. I can't tell you about it."

"Go on," he said. He took tickets away from a young mother with three perfectly savage young children, blond and tired and sticky, who were pulling on each other's ears. "I'll let you off anyway. How do you expect to get back to Toronto?" He drove holes in their tickets.

"People said you used to stop at Vermillion Bluff," I said, "if they put up a red flag. Couldn't I just put up a red flag and catch this train going back to Sioux?"

"Give it a try," he said. He unhooked his walkie-talkie from his belt and began to say things in trainman's language to the engineer.

The Canadian transcontinental began to slow down a mile ahead of the old Vermillion Bluff stop, howling, and the spruce slid past more and more slowly until finally we came to a halt.

I jumped off the step into the knee-deep snow.

"Good luck," said the conductor. "Have fun with your fungus or whatever it was."

Chuck and Bernice Michikan were waiting for me in a big crew-cab pickup. Chuck was a round-faced man with a lock of hair that continually fell over one eye. Bernice was stout, short, and strong-looking. She was fair-skinned, with hazel eyes and light-brown hair.

"They hardly ever use that stop any more," said Chuck. "Because there's a road now between here and Sioux Lookout."

I said, "I talked him into it."

Bernice said, "Everybody calls me Neesa, so you might as well too. Ready to go trapping in the morning?"

"I brought my snowshoes."

"Good! We'll run the trap line, it's about twelve miles or so. You'll see what a trap line is like." Chuck put the truck in gear. "And why it's part of our traditions."

Native life went on inside and around the edges of the small town of Vermillion Bluff. White people owned the store, the motel and the gas station. They owned several fishing lodges nearby. White people were the agents of the Ministry of Natural Resources, the government bureaucracy in control of Crown, or publicly owned land.

We drove to an area at the edge of the little town of five hundred people, where the Michikans had their home. It was a new frame house with electricity and running water. Nearby were the houses of Chuck's parents, a brother and sister-in-law, some cousins.

I slept on the couch, and the next morning managed to get dressed in semi-privacy by writhing into my clothes under my sleeping bag. The entire household was up and busy by six-thirty.

It was time to get on the trail. We drove up a logging road to the trailhead. Everybody put on their snowshoes and backpacks. The day was diamond-brilliant in the new sun, and by full sunrise we were snowshoeing determinedly across an unmarked lake. I had no idea how everybody knew where they were going. The northern taiga is a world of great beauty, but there is a sameness to it. Dark green hills, thick with spruce, and then a clean white slash of lake, then more hills, more spruce, another white lake, then hill forest lake *hillforestlake*. It was like a mantra or chant sung in a clean, sweet voice, hypnotic.

"Watch it," said Neesa. We came to a steep slope down into another lake. I thought I should sit down and slide down on my snowshoes, and tried it, and pitched forward and fell over my snowshoes and somehow ended up on my face with my butt in the air and my snowshoes crossed in an *X*.

Neesa pulled me up.

I said, "Don't laugh, don't laugh."

"Okay, I'm not laughing."

Chuck and his father and the teenage son were far ahead of us. At least they didn't see me. I got up by rolling over on my back in the deep powder and then uncrossing my snowshoes and wallowing to my feet.

"Okay, let's go."

We started off in a hurry. Ahead, Chuck and his son and his father were swinging forward in a rolling, sailor-like gait that ate up the miles, the pace of men who have spent a lifetime on snowshoes. I pushed into the blazing day to catch up.

I said, "Oh wait, I lost my sunglasses!" I stopped and patted myself. Without sunglasses I could well go snowblind in this brilliant light.

"Let's go back," said Neesa. She clomped in a wide circle and pushed back to the lake-slope where I had fallen. I hurried after her. I hardly knew who to follow, although I supposed they all knew where they were. Neesa had a long free stride, and she never looked back.

"Look at this!" she said. I came up beside her in a burst of energy. I looked down where I had fallen. There was the imprint of my face, and my sunglasses sat over the nose-imprint. It was kind of ghost-face jammed into the snow, an anti-person. "I can't believe it." She was laughing and slapping her hands together. "Incredible."

Okay, okay, I said to myself. We've got ten miles or so to go. I can do it.

"Here, I've got some snares in that little grove of poplars," said Neesa. "Rabbits. We need them for the feast tonight. We're serving traditional Indian food — rabbit soup and moose meat and things." She turned into a whippy grove of poplar trees, they were like olive-green lines against the snow. "Can you skin a rabbit?"

I was breathing hard and wobbly on my snowshoes.

"Sure," I said. "I think I remember how."

"Good, good, we need all the hands we can get." She jammed herself through the wire-thin, tough branches. "We want to make the white guys feel welcome, so they won't holler when we go for reserve land."

A rabbit hung by its neck from the snare like a voodoo doll, dusted with snow. She wrestled it out of the noose and stuffed it in the backpack. Her mitts were commercially-made leather ones, and instead of parkas, as in North Spirit, she and Chuck both wore big padded mackinaws. She turned back to the main trail, happy with her catch, and I hurried after her, anxious to catch up to the guys. What if I fell through the ice somewhere? Snowshoes and all? It would take at least four people to get me out.

By the time we caught up to the men, Neesa had seven snowshoe hares, all of them banging together in her backpack like wooden sculptures, frozen stiff.

I fell to the business of snowshoeing, lifting my knees high, dragging the snowshoe tails.

"Lean forward more," said Neesa. "You can lean forward farther than you think you can."

There; it was just mental. One could lean forward like a cartoon character in a high wind, loaded with a pack and a camera, borne up by one's amazingly long feet. It was like having yard-long feet that were not really well attached but were always falling off your heels. They sank into the powder snow and then reappeared. It was like having *disappearing* yard-long feet, that were never there when you really needed them.

Neesa and I plunged forward into the short and brilliant day. We caught up to the men by main force on my part and a natural easy pace on Neesa's part.

We were strung out in a sort of pattern, I realized: Chuck, the strongest adult male, was breaking trail, and behind him came the elder, Mr. Michikan, a man of about sixty who was traveling on snowshoes twice the size of mine. Neesa and I, the women, came behind. To one side, setting his own trail in a burst of youthful strength and independence, came the teenage son. The snowshoe tracks were like petals. They were petal-shaped as if they were flowering snow-blossoms that bloomed out of the aboriginal trail.

I fell down again. Nobody paid any attention to me. I pushed my glasses back onto my face with a snow mitt, uncrossed my Xd snowshoes and hurried to catch up.

Neesa turned back to call to me. She was biting back an attack of laughter.

"Hurry, we're coming to the first beaver set."

Far ahead, at the end of the narrow, long lake, was a mountainous pile of sticks that indicated a beaver lodge. It looked like a messy wooden wig and it was capped with a little beanie of snow. Pointed ends stuck out, poplar branches chewed to spear-sharp ends. Maybe it was a new beaver technique of defense.

"Maybe there aren't any beaver," I said.

"No, it's a live beaver lodge," said Neesa. "Look at the top. See the heat waves? It's their body heat rising up?"

I stood and squinted against the light. The spruce trees behind the lodge, on shore, were wavering. It was the heat waves from the lodge hole.

"Do you get beaver out of here every year?" I asked. I got out the camera. I kept it under my parka, which made me look like a pouter pigeon, but it kept the film warm and the camera out of the snow.

"No, about every other year. There's about two or three young males or females in there now, I expect. Two years ago, we trapped a female beaver here, and when I skinned it, there were six babies inside." Neesa paused and shoved her light-brown hair back up inside her woolen toque. "I felt really bad. There went six beavers we could have had over the next year or two." She made a wry face and shrugged.

"So you skipped a year."

"Yep. We always skip a year anyway. I thought we should skip two years on this one but Chuck didn't."

Chuck and his father and his teenage son were cutting spruce limbs with a hatchet and throwing them down on the snow around the lodge. They had taken off their snowshoes and were stomping on the spruce limbs.

I said, "What are they doing that for?"

Neesa looked at me as if I were simpleminded, or maybe I was kidding her.

"So they can walk around," she said. "You can't get on your knees and dig out the trap with snowshoes on."

Well, I was relieved to hear it. I had begun to think the Michikan family could fly with snowshoes on.

The men were talking and working. They spoke in Ojibway, in low tones, and the ice chisel made thunking, chipping sounds as Chuck drove it again and again into the ice. The teenage boy shovelled away the snow and ice-chips, and then he was on his knees on the spruce limbs dipping out ice-chunks with a tea strainer. It was as if they were mining water; driving through several feet of ice, and then the lakewater came boiling up. They had jammed their snowshoes into the snow tail-first, and their rifles butt-first. It made a palisade around them.

"*Asha!*" said the elder Michikan.

They pulled up a chain, and at the end of the chain was a goggle-eyed beaver, dead in the bars of a Conibear trap.

Chuck was blowing deep breaths of cloud and mist, it wafted out into the crisp day on a light breeze and disappeared.

"This breaks their necks," he said. I started taking pictures. The film in my camera had turned a bright blue. "It kills them in a second." He took the long bars of the trap and pried them apart in his large, strong hands. "Put your arm in there."

I said, "I don't think I can lift my arm."

"It's a young male," said Neesa. "One of the young males." She sounded relieved. I didn't know how she could tell. Young males are always sticking their necks out, though. Maybe that's how. The elder Michikan wallowed the beaver around in the snow to mop up the water from the fur. He said something in the light, musical Ojibway of this area. So different from the flat intonations and rapid-fire delivery of North Spirit.

We sat down on the spruce limbs and ate hardtack and Spork, drank hot tea from a thermos. A feast of the dead, a feast of gratitude and success. I experienced a strange feeling; a rush of energy, as if I had taken some drug. I realized it was the fat in the Spork, pouring its calories into my bloodstream. I was experiencing a food rush. It was as if I had stood beside a warm fire.

We moved on through the afternoon like figures on an old map, the maps with fat-faced winds blowing in the corners, dragons appearing in loops out of stiff waves, and the edge of the known world indicated by a ship falling off the edge. These Ojibway people were surrounded by white culture, they lived a hidden life in the forests, they held onto these trails and this knowledge that was sacred to them, because it was who they were.

"Every stretch of lake or river has a different name," said Neesa. She was swinging along comfortably on a forest trail. She held back the low spruce branches for me. We appeared at the edge of yet another long narrow lake. "We knew these lakes by the things that happened here. This one is called in Ojibway, 'the place where the old man spilled loon grease on his pants.'"

I laughed. "Really? What happened?"

She shrugged. "Nobody knows. It would be fun to know. But I guess it's an old story that people forgot."

I fell down again, sideways. It was embarrassing. Someday I would have to learn the trick of going downhill on snowshoes. Flat surfaces were more or less okay. It was the slopes that did me in.

At their home outside Vermillion Bluff, in the "native town," the Anishinabe village-inside-a-village, we finally took off our yard-long footgear and stood flatfooted on the snow. Neesa took the beaver and threw it on top of the woodshed where the dogs couldn't get it, and the rabbits went beside the automatic washing machines.

She said, "Come on in. I'm fleshing a beaver skin. I'll show you how to do it. I'll get that one tomorrow."

Their house had a television, a dishwasher, and a washer and dryer. There was a big oil stove, the living-room floor was covered with burgundy carpeting. There was a shelf of reference books, and the kitchen had a tiled floor. It was comfortable, bright, and efficient. On the walls were religious pictures. Jesus, semi-transparent, bent over the shoulder of a young sailor at the tiller of a ship in a howling storm; male guidance for young men who would go about sticking their adventurous necks into traps.

Neesa and I sat on the kitchen floor with a beaver skin stretched on a hoop.

"See here, you get this inner tissue off without cutting the skin. If your knife slips, you lose about a hundred dollars."

She was using a skinning knife with a rounded tip. The beaver skin was turning into something to wear, instead of an animal. The way cows turned into shoes and belts and bookbindings and luggage and glue and chemicals for photographic processes and fertilizer and purses, only this wasn't an automated process far from the eyes of the general public. This was done by hand, at home, and with strenuous efforts.

I said, "Where do people here come from?"

"From *here*," said Chuck. "Are we supposed to wear feathers and moccasins to convince people we're from here? The MNR and Indian Affairs and everybody else said we moved here from Lac Seul. That's why they won't give us reserve land. How can we prove we're from here and we've always been from here?"

I wiped my hands and got up, sat at the table to take notes.

I said, "What if you could prove your aboriginal residency here by means of language? You said that lake was called 'the place where the old man spilled loon grease on his pants.' It's funny, right? It's some very old story. You can tell by the loon grease thing; nobody boils down a loon for the fat any more." The more I thought about it, the better it seemed. "And what about place names here in Vermillion Bluff? What are the street names?"

"Hmmm," said Chuck. "Main Street, Dryden Street, Railroad Street."

"So, what do you call this place?"

"In Ojibway, we call Vermillion Bluff, 'the long portage.' That's because this is the height-of-land between the Great Lakes watershed and the Albany watershed. And the town, I don't remember." He turned to his father and mother, and the three of them had a long discussion.

Names, place names, long phrases that told a story about something that happened in aboriginal times. The gray light outside faded into an aluminum color, and I could see lights coming on in small cabins all around. It was about four o'clock. Smoke poured out of the chimneys of small cabins like banners; *this is the free world.*

"Here, listen," said Chuck. He poured himself more tea. "There was *kwapshka-dongawa* near here, on Vermillion Lake. That means 'long sandy beach.' Everybody knows it. Another place is called, 'the place where the girl didn't want to get married.' Maybe she had an arranged marriage and ran away.'

"Right!" Neesa brightened up. "There's that other place called 'the place where the old woman had her fish trap.' I remember my grandmother joking about it."

I said, "How do you say fish trap?"

Chuck laughed. "*Michikan.* That's our name."

I wrote as quickly as I could. Name after name appeared out of memory, a cartography of events, ancient stories fossilized by place names, the story of the native people's tenure of the land for thousands of years.

Maybe it would help, maybe not.

In the living room, I heard the teenage daughter on the phone.

"She fell down three times," said the girl to, I supposed, a girlfriend. "Three times down."

Neesa said, "How about 'the trail where the white woman fell down three times?'"

I said, "Come on. Come on."

But it was no good. Once the teenagers start making up names for you it's all over.

# 51.

We went by pickup to the new community hall beside Vermillion Lake. It sat in a grove of poplars, and had been put together by the volunteer labor of the entire community. It was of log, and heated with a fifty-five gallon steel drum stove. There were tables and benches, a group of women hurrying in and out on various chores, and behind the hall, in the snow, was a stack of dead rabbits. It was as high as my head.

The frozen rabbits, or more properly snowshoe hares, were patchy brown and white and their legs stuck up in every direction. Young women and elder women dashed in and out of the door carrying in dead rabbits.

I went in, rolled up my sleeves and sat down on a bench, ready to work.

"Like this," said an elder woman beside me. "Watch me."

She first ripped out their guts by shoving her forefinger up behind the sternum and then taking out the rabbit's entire digestive and reproductive system in one clean jerk.

Neesa passed by, cheerful and happy, carrying a pail of hot water. Sunset light streamed through the new glass panes in the windows, the hall was steamy with women's work.

She said, "Watch it and don't break the gall bladder. The meat will be ruined if you do." She smiled an amused and tolerant smile. "There, see? Be sure and save the hearts and livers."

This was different from any rabbit-skinning I had ever done. But then these were snowshoe hares, not cottontails. I had attempted this entrail-removing as the elder woman had done, and a dreadful smell began wafting around my rabbit.

"No good," the elder woman said, and took it from me and flung it out the door. Dogs peered from behind trees, watchful and hungry.

They didn't mind a little gall bladder. Gall bladders were salt and butter to them.

I tried again and was far more careful.

"No good. Look. Still guts," said the elder woman.

She flung that one out the door too.

I tried again, blood and fur up to my elbows.

"Okay." She grasped the rabbit corpse away from me before I had time to damage it further and flung it into the bucket of hot water. It was bright red with silky-cream stripes of tendons and connective tissue. There were more than sixty of these things to process. I snatched up another one and this time I got the whole works out intact, apparently, and then began to undress it. A strip joint.

"Around, around, make a long strip," said the elder woman. There was a way to start cutting the skin in a long spiral around and around the body, to make one long strip, but I was not managing to do this. "I will make a blanket." She made knitting motions. "A blanket."

I nodded. I didn't have the vocabulary for this at all. But I knew that somehow, in the very old days, the women made blankets and coats out of rabbit fur by twining strips of fur into long strings, and then knitting it together.

I nodded, "*Ni kendan, ni kendan.*" I was being rude and using the word "I," *nin* to an elder but it couldn't be helped. I carefully began to peel back the fur. The community hall was full of laughter and high hopes, work and blood and fur and entrails. In a washtub at our feet, a heap of entrails was growing bigger and bigger.

I refused to throw up. I was a country girl. I remembered helping slaughter two hundred chickens when I was twelve years old. But that was then, y'all. This is now. The thin skin tore to pieces in my sticky hands. All I had left was a handful of rabbit rags.

I said, in an Elmer Fudd voice, "Wascawwy wabbit."

"No good," said the elder woman. She took the wad of torn skin and tossed it in the washtub with all the guts. "*Mina, minawah.*" Again, try again.

I grasped another frozen, goggle-eyed hare between my legs and snatched its half-frozen inner works out, turned it upside down and started again. When I got the fur down to the front legs, it all came apart.

"*Asha gistuun, nokom,*" I said. All screwed up.

"*Mina,*" she said, determinedly. She needed strips for a rabbit-skin blanket; where else would there be a pile of sixty or more snowshoe hares to mine for fur-strips? Ten or eleven skins, reasonably whole, lay draped across the bench beside her like the abandoned fur coats of little elves.

She watched as I peeled my present rabbit of its worldly fur down to the front legs.

"Now pu-u-u-ll easy easy."

I pulled carefully and came away with an intact skin. I thought, I should quit now before I tear the rest of them to pieces. But I did reasonably well, and the little fur coats began to pile up, more and more rabbit carcasses were plunged into the boiling soup-water along with salt and oatmeal, with the livers and the hearts, and finally the feast was ready.

Neesa, her teenage daughter and I ran home to wash up and comb our hair.

The hall that night was full of cheerful happy people; they had made their own community meeting-place, they were coming out of isolation as a community, they were wealthy enough and strong enough to have a big celebration, to invite all the important white people. Soon they would start down the tangled road of bureaucracy, papers, lawyers, treaty rights; they would ask for reserve land.

I took my bowl of rabbit-and-oatmeal soup and sat down with it. There were electric lights, powdered by a little gasoline generator outside that thumped and thundered along in a steady rhythm. The liver and heart swam among the flakes of oatmeal and pieces of rabbit meat, hard and dark like vitamin pills. The speeches by the white mayor in English and the elder Mr. Michikan in Ojibway were all well-received. They had been lengthy and heartfelt. Full of good wishes. Hooray for the new community hall. Across from me, a white woman was staring uneasily at her rabbit-and-oatmeal soup. She leaned across the table and whispered, in all the noise and steam and screaming children, "Hi. I'm Mrs. Baxter. My husband and I run the motel."

I said, "Hi there! I'm from *Wawatay News.*"

"Oh. I see. That's that Indian newspaper." She looked to one side and then the other, and then said, "Um, are you eating your soup?"

"Sure am!" I spooned down a big mouthful. "The heads are really good."

"Well." She paused again. "What are these little hard dark things?" She looked down at a rabbit heart.

I said, mercilessly, "That's a rabbit beetle. They live inside the rabbits and legend has it that they give the rabbits advice as to directions, marital difficulties and so on. But that's just legend. Actually, scientifically, they're quite nutritious."

She said, "You're pulling my leg."

"That's right, I am. Actually, they're hairballs."

She folded her hands and waited until the Jell-O and cake came around. At least you could see through the Jell-O and observe what might be in it.

The native people of Vermillion Bluff, or, perhaps, the Ojibway community which called itself "The Height-of-Land People," had stayed in one place while the white world moved in on the railroad, a world of straight edges and flat surfaces, internal combustion engines and then image-generators. The native children were becoming absorbed by the life systems of white children through the school, becoming addicted to television and movies and videos which offer thrills and violence without price. Priceless stimulation to bodiless brains. Would they become like urban children, whose minds were overstimulated, who were then lost and frightened in a real world where their bodies must withstand heat and cold, small and large dangers?

Only two percent of the population still lives on and with the land. "The land" becomes more and more a distant place, a strange tale, a weird idea. The Ojibway people of this small community were determined to get the land back, to use it, to be in it.

I shook hands with Neesa at the railroad tracks.

"I'm sure you'll get your land," I said.

She waved. "I hope so! Goodbye, come back."

I hung a red woolen scarf up on a bush beside the railroad tracks. I had a notebook full of place names and stories. Neesa had sent me off with a fresh loaf of bannock and a paper sack of pemmican. Far down the tracks I heard the transcontinental approaching. In the early, snowy morning I could see its one headlight, and I heard the changed note of the engine as it slowed down and prepared to stop. I waved.

Amazingly enough, the great machine ground down to a halt in front of me on the tracks, pouring out billows of steam into the cold air. It was stopping for me, a small, ordinary person standing and waving beside the rail line with a notebook full of pre-Columbian place names and frail snowshoes. I knew they were going to get their reserve land; even the most powerful machines can be made to stop somehow, with enough determination and thought.

"Well, here you are, young woman," said the conductor. "Where's all the fungus?"

"I got hungry," I said. "I ate it."

The next morning I drove into work with all my film, ready to face the typewriter. I took a cup of coffee up to my desk, and listened as Nathan came running up the stairs.

"Helicopter down on the coast," he said.

"Is there a photo?" I asked as I reached for the telephone.

# 52.

Keith Turnbull came up to Sioux Lookout and went over the script with me. What there was of it. We sat in the noisy pub of the Sioux Hotel. It was like something out of Central Casting: loggers and pilots and guys from the native organizations in intense conversations, writing things down on napkins.

"Okay, this is called a 'book' in theater parlance." He smoked furiously. So did I. "We've nearly got the paperwork done. We're hiring the actors now."

"Who are they?"

"Well, any suggestions?"

"Yes. There's this neat, funny woman in North Spirit named Doris Linklater."

"I'll ask her to fly out this spring, and see if she can do rehearsals. Ah, this script isn't going to work. Try . . . um . . . let's see. There has to be an expectation of something happening in the minds of the audience."

"What's wrong with them recovering this lost gold and going to Hollywood to protest the anti-fur lobby?"

"It just seems a little, well, far-fetched."

"Okay. I'll figure something out."

The helicopter crash was positively heartwarming.

This time nobody was dead; it was one of those amazing rescues. Near-disaster averted by quick thinking.

The quick thinker was a man named Crow, a trapper, who was diddybopping along on his trap line, alongside the shores of Hudson Bay, sifting snow through the meshes of his animate, hardworking snowshoes, when he saw a glinting flash from out on the ice of the Bay.

The helicopter had been cruising too close to the ice, had caught a sudden down-draft, and smacked down on the broken jumbles of land-fast ice.

A pilot, copilot, and geologist found themselves sitting miraculously alive in the middle of the wreckage, the scattered instruments, splintered Plexiglass. Broken limbs, yes, but alive.

Mr. Crow put up their emergency tent, made hot tea for them, laid them out as comfortably as possible, and then raced back to his trap-line cabin.

He called for help on his Wawatay HF radio, then grabbed his Polaroid and ran back and took a picture for *Wawatay News*.

It was a black Rorshach surrounded by glaring white. We ran it on the front page.

"Where's some film?" David was rummaging around in the camera bags stored in the file room. "Nathan is going to North Spirit. He's going to get pictures and interviews."

"Of what?"

"The crash. Didn't you hear? A plane hit the radio tower. Killed three people."

"Who? Who?"

In my selfishness, I instantly hoped it was nobody I knew. Not Emasiah or Sarah Winnepetonga or Mrs. Nanokeesic or, god forbid, children or anybody at all, ideally.

I handed him four rolls of film and felt as if I were hanging in midair as I waited for names.

David said, "Killed the pilot and the copilot and the passenger, there was just one passenger. A guy going up to repair furnaces at the school."

I sat down, rested my face in my hands.

"I know," said David. "Remember when my two brothers were in that plane that sank and they had to swim for it?"

That had been one of the *minor* incidents that winter.

I said, "Let's run a history of every damn crash in the north. Just a big list."

"Good. I want two full pages. List them all. There must have been ones going back — ones the old people remember — that never made the papers anywhere." He thought for a moment. "Yeah, yeah, there was a plane in 1967 that sank at the dock at . . . where was it? Drowned an entire family. Six people. I'll call my dad."

David walked off to the phone, stiff with his own subdued brand of complete rage.

The plane that went down in North Spirit was a Twin Otter; it had been pushing weather, flying on a margin of safety, reluctant to lose a flight. They were in a hurry, pressing forward to get into the North Spirit airstrip before heavy snow shut the strip down.

They had come in too low in a fog, struck the radio tower, and cartwheeled into the bay just beyond my old cabin.

Nathan flew back to Sioux Lookout the next day.

"There were pieces of airplane all over the place," he said. "Shit scattered all over the place. Windshields, wires, tires . . . "

The village men had taken their lives in their hands to shove boats into the water, paddle out into broken ice to retrieve the bodies. Ordinary people rising to the need, to the demands of decency, committing themselves to extraordinary risks. Because it was the right thing to do.

# 53.

One night, in mid-December, there was a forty-mile-an-hour wind, and the temperature stood at forty below Fahrenheit. I had given up on the oil stove. The wind tore through the cabin as if it were cheesecloth. It came straight off the lake like a rapids, and blew across the top of my chimney pipe, making howling noises and sucking the heat out of the wood stove and straight up into the sky. I couldn't keep the wood cut fast enough to feed the stove. I was up all night, hammering again and again at frozen green birch, and even though I had become skilled at sinking my light ax into just the right spot, somehow the stove and the wind ate wood faster than I could cut it. December was Manido-Keezisoons, the Moon of Little Spirits.

I drew hard breaths, sucking in the forty-below air. My windpipe was frostbitten.

When I woke up the next day I was still cold. I felt very lightheaded and dizzy. I got up, with effort, and called Kathy at the newspaper, coughing, and said I wouldn't be in.

Then, all of a sudden, I was hot. I felt restless and airborne and pleasantly unconcerned. I felt light as a gram of talcum. My legs stuck up out of my duffle socks and moccasins like thin sticks. The cat came up on the covers and made herself into an apostrophe. The beautiful creamy snow built up on the window ledges as if constructing a house of diamonds. The dog sat on the porch and barked at the door. I walked out onto the porch and took up a handful of snow to press against my face. I felt very hot. My dog pranced into the house in a happy parade gait, shook himself free of snow like a big mop-spinner in a car wash, and clicked straight to the kitchen area, where he put his paws up on the counter and ate a box of cookies. I could have cared less. I wasn't in the least hungry.

I felt I was sailing somewhere interesting without effort. That night I didn't bother with the fire again, but turned on the inadequate electric heater, and went back and forth between chills and fever as if in a binary number system, where there was only zero or one.

The next day the nice doctor who had come when Celeste's baby had died was sitting on the edge of my bed handing me a cup of hot tea and some pills the size of rubber erasers. The cabin seemed full of people. What did I care? Somebody might call me from British Columbia and then I would go out there where it was warm, and here was a cup of hot tea, and a load of wood, already split, being ejected from a truck outside, and I was sleepy again.

There were big, leaping waterfalls of northern lights during the windstorm. It seemed as if they were full of beings, beautiful and shoeless, wandering down the corridors of the aurora, and there was a kind of singing sound, like a chorus of delighted, entranced voices whose notes were made of the evaporating colors.

> *Starshine strikes like the appearance of aliens. The aurora is a piano, playing blues in green neon. Shut up, wait for the angel or the airplane disguised as an angel to descend with silent twin propellers out of the madonna-blue evening, wait for your cue, your moment to appear in the zodiacal footlights of this special and dreadful one-man show.*

And so a week passed, and with the week my pneumonia, and I was never able to endure the cold so well again.

# 54.

"Hey, you should come to Muskrat Dam for Christmas," said Stan Winnepetonga. Stan was one of the younger chiefs, aged thirty or so, and, like his cousin Sarah, he had several years of college. "Come up and do a story on the festivities. You can stay with Sarah and her mom."

Stan was hanging around the newspaper office. He was short and energetic. I was drifting from desk to telephone to layout table.

I said, "Is Sarah still in Muskrat Dam?"

Stan laughed.

"That's where she's from! All the Winnepetongas are from Muskrat Dam. It's a really traditional Indian Christmas, and you can do a spread for the newspaper."

I wanted to be home in Missouri, but I couldn't afford it. Brad the Scotsman was flying home to Glasgow and Oldman Woman and Garnet were deep in conversation about vast, extended-family holiday plans at Lac Seul.

I was pasting up my own story about the Ojibway people at Vermillion Bluff; the height-of-land people. It hadn't been that hard to do, surprisingly. I had spent hours at the typewriter without bolting. Probably because I was floaty and weak from the pneumonia.

I drew blue lines on things; slowly, carefully, out of energy.

Stan was very enterprising, always looking for ways to promote native culture, establish native businesses, strengthen native political organizations. He was electric with energy, dressed in a bomber jacket and fur cap. His wife, Nelly, was a teacher.

He strode around the layout room, his fur earflaps turned up, his beaded moose-hide mitts stuffed into his pockets.

"So this is how you do it," he said. "You write in your titles in blue . . ."

"Headlines."

"Hmmm. And then they print it."

"Right."

"And under the photos, you write in little headlines too."

"Cutlines."

"This newspaper is very influential," he said. "And the all-Ojibway page, the elders really enjoy reading it. Especially when Piitonya and her sister start in on somebody."

"Start in on somebody??"

"Yeah." He grinned. "You can't read it, can you? You guys never know what they really say. You better have Nathan or somebody check that page carefully."

"Right."

The X-rated moose sausage had been the last photo to go on that page, but what had they *said?*

"Come to Muskrat Dam, and have Nathan pay your way. It'll be a newspaper trip."

It was a kind invitation, and I accepted it gratefully.

# 55.

I took the script and the poetry manuscript with me. Now that all this might see the light of day I started taking it seriously. I kept looking at them. I couldn't stop. Exposed to air.

When I was packed up and ready to go, waiting for a taxi to take me to the airport (Sioux Lookout now had an "airport" rather than an "airstrip;" it also had a waiting room and Coke machines and bathrooms), Nathan came in.

"You know what?"

I said, "Another plane is down."

"No. Do you remember Nimrod Kanakakeesic? The old chief, the man who spoke on the radio in North Spirit and you broadcast him by accident? With Beethoven's Ninth?"

"How could I forget?"

"Well, he's missing."

"Well, where'd he go?" Stupid question.

"Evidently people saw him dragging his canoe out into the snow, and his drum, and other things, his most treasured possessions. And setting fire to them. About a week ago. That's the last time anybody saw him."

I said, "Why?"

Nathan sat down with his coffee cup in his hand.

"You know where he lived? Across the other side of the bay, across from your old cabin. Isolated houses." Nathan hesitated.

"I never knew him. Don't think I ever even saw him at the, *ahi*, store."

I had been talking with Oldman Woman on the phone and I was starting to talk *like* her. Like.

"No. He was a loner." *Tap tap tap*, Nathan's fingers did a little number on the plastic tablecloth. "And his daughter, he never let her go anywhere."

I said, "He was a shaman."

Nathan nodded. "That's what people say. They say it comes back on you after a while."

"What does?"

"The bad stuff. Well, I thought I'd tell you. Have a good trip."

"Nathan, have you got twenty dollars?"

He reached in his pocket.

"Starving poets," he said.

# 56.

I stood in front of the microphone and sang, "Oh Little Town Of Bethlehem" while Sarah and her sisters boiled over with choked snorts in the background.

Muskrat Dam was bent on having a good Christmas. The tiny radio station was a room in her brother's house; the transmitters for a one-watt FM were now no bigger than a suitcase. All the guests in the village had to come and sing a song.

I watched the children blow soap bubbles; the bubbles froze in the air, drifted and, when they struck something, shattered in fragile, glassy shards and tinkled down onto the hardpacked trails.

The candy throw and dance and give-away was in the community hall. There was an immense pile of gifts, and it was with surprise and pleasure I heard my name called. One of the Morrises, Roy, I think, had drawn my name and he and his wife gave me a set of glasses and a set of towels. I still have the set of towels.

Candy flew into the air, bright little packages, and instead of children, it was the elder women who scrambled for them. The log hall resounded with shouts, yells, cries of encouragement and flying bodies. Juliette Winnepetonga, Sarah's aunt, seemed to have won, snatching up the largest number of hard candies by hurling other, older, ladies aside. She stood up out of the scramble in her bright flowered headscarf and many layers of cotton stockings.

"I won!" She was saying this in Ojibway. "Now I get to marry Santa Claus!"

Santa Claus, whoever it was, fled out the door.

It turned out it was her husband.

*****

Sarah's mother was elderly, mild, soft-spoken. She pieced me together a pair of emergency moccasins, as the pair I had were wearing out. She made them with canvas tops, quickly. They were the everyday, working footwear of the north.

In trying to tell her what I wanted, I said "tin-can moccasins" instead of "stove-pipe moccasins." She was grateful for a good laugh. I have never heard the end of my tin-can moccasins.

I sat and watched as she stitched. The pattern was complex. The strong moose hide was smoky-smelling, soft and pale brown. Again I was struck by the image of creation, of making people.

"Tin-can moccasins," laughed Mrs. Winnepetonga. "I swear."

I was nervous about flying home.

There was an accident waiting for me somewhere.

Sarah and I went out to her nets. We went on two snowmobiles. Her parka hood with its wolf-fur trim was snugged tightly around her face like an Elizabethan ruff, and we tore through veils of ground-blow. I could hardly stay on my machine. Sarah was travelling fast, and I am light, and tend to fly off the seat when charging over the humps and bluffs in the trails, through the little, snow-plated spruce with their drooping arms, out onto the lake.

Her nets were out in the middle of the river-lake, the broad Severn, the poles jammed down through safe ice.

We cut through several feet of ice and began to draw up the net.

"It's been good for me, Puanets," she said. "To come home here. You know, I had been out to school all those years when I was a kid, and I didn't *know* anything. I didn't know how to live. And after that awful thing in North Spirit, when the elder women rejected that day care . . . that just crushed me. I thought, why did I go to school for two years? And my brothers said, 'come home.'"

"So you've been here learning from the elder women."

"Yes, and look, I can keep a net and make high tops and everything." We pulled the long spruce pole out of the hole, and the net came with it. It was hair-fine, a gill net, light as spider-silk. "I used to think everybody here was so ignorant. It was like when I went to the Holy Land."

"Like how?"

"I came back with all these slides. I wanted to show the people here, what the Holy Land was like, where Jesus really walked and everything. Land, the land, means something. So I set up a slide show. And they didn't *believe* me! Puanets, I'm not kid-ding! The elder men and the women said, 'Oh, that can't be Gesthemeni! It's too shabby looking! That's not the Mount of Olives! It's just a little hill!' And they all walked out of my slide show!"

I could hardly pull the net for laughing.

"So you thought, 'Wow, unsophisticated folks!'"

"I guess I got pretty arrogant about how I knew everything and the elders didn't. Then I came home. My brothers are big people, and they're *convincing*. They were looking out for me."

We dragged up the net between us. It crackled with instant frost, and far down in the depths, I saw the light shapes of fish, like thoughts. Arriving out of the realm of deep water, elements of the mind.

The big jacks fought and twisted, sometimes they froze solid in the midst of a flop, in a hard semicircle. I could have used them to hammer nails.

"Did your mother arrange a marriage for you?"

She started to laugh.

"I have respect for my elders, but you got to draw the line some-where! You should have *seen* this guy!"

"Tell me, tell me, who was it?"

"Oh, nobody you'd know, it was just awful. He was about a hundred pounds overweight, he was from God's Lake, he owned a little store and my mother thought he was my kind of guy. It was so embarrassing!"

I threw ice cobbles out of the hole we had created in the ice with a tea strainer. Sarah jammed the jackfish and the beautiful silver white-fish, *attikameg*, caribou fish, into a burlap bag.

"Look, there's more."

"More fish, more guys, what the hell," she said.

The lustrous, shining fish, arriving out of the black water, threw themselves about, and lost their color, and became like wood.

We threw the burlap bag on Sarah's sled.

"I heard you're writing some poetry."

I said, "Oh, I always write a little poetry. It's a stupid, useless occupa-tion. But maybe it'll get published. I don't know. If I live. These goddamned planes are falling out of the air like meteors."

Sarah tore at the starter cord. The ground-blow surged past us like a surf. I couldn't see the shore. Flying, wind-torn crêpes of snow, glittering white, obscuring, blinding.

"Stay close behind me!"

She was tall, square-shouldered, slim, sitting erect as a soldier on her machine, gliding off into the forests with her mitt-fringes flying, fearless and skilled.

We had fish for supper.

Sarah's enormous brothers came over, leaving their wives, and ate their way through four large jackfish. Furs were piled in the corner; her next-oldest brother was a fur dealer.

"We've done good in Muskrat Dam this year," he said. "We're the Independent Kingdom of Muskrat Dam, and when we trap, we trap."

"How's the play?" asked Sarah. We were playing 'Ninety-Nine' with her brothers.

"I got it figured out. You know, if you just settle down and say, 'I'm going to tell a good story,' then it's easy."

"What's it about?"

"Well — I've just thought about this now — a guy goes out onto his fishnets, and he comes on this plane that's gone down years and years before. He looks in it, and there's a satchel in there; it's gold bullion. He takes it back to the Hudson's Bay Store in the village, and then he and some other people get trapped in the fur storage room. Then this Hollywood actress flies up looking for her lost lover, who was this pilot, see? The thing is, it's got to have some music and dancing, some performance stuff in it, to entertain people. I haven't figured out how to do that yet."

"I see." Sarah cleared her throat.

At the tiny Anglican church, at midnight on Christmas Eve, I sat in a pew, packed in with the rest of the village, and listened to the women's choir sing "Silent Night" in Ojibway. Everyone wore their parkas and high-top moccasins, and took off their big caribou-hide mitts only to turn the pages of the hymnals. Our breath rose up in clouds. I couldn't read either the hymnals or the prayer-books quickly enough to keep up.

They were printed in Ojibway-Cree syllabics. Ice formed on the insides of the small pointed windows.

The choir sat behind a railing on a raised dias. This was very much an Anglican village.

Only the older women were allowed to be in the choir, as it was a position of great prestige. Whether one could sing or not was beside the point. Sarah's mother was there, small and gentle. Juliette Winnepetonga sat with her hymn book, large and imposing. It was a full squadron of elder women in brilliant headscarves and full flowered skirts. Their faces were lined and dark with sun and wind and snow-burn, their black eyes gazed over the coughing, restless crowd.

They sang the carol in the Indian way; high, strong falsettos. *The night is silent*, they sang. *The night is sacred, it is very calm, and the star-beings are shining. Over there, the virgin young woman is holding her child, who is sleeping in a calm manner.*

These were women who made people from the feet up.

# 57.

There were two small stores in Muskrat Dam, one owned by the Winnepetongas and another by a white guy called Carson. Perry Carson. He was a fuzzy-headed guy from Manitoba, with a Cessna 175 Skywagon. He agreed to fly me out to Weagamow, where I could catch the scheduled flight back to Sioux Lookout, with my camera bag full of films, like black eggs, ready to hatch out into images.

Sarah walked with me down to the snowpacked ice of the bay in front of the village.

"Now, we want to see this book of poetry," she said. "Tell me where I can get one."

I said, "It's really not even done yet."

"Never mind. It will be someday."

"I can't tell you how grateful I am for your hospitality, Sarah. It was a wonderful Christmas and New Year's."

"We're all happy you came. My mother loves to hear you try to speak Ojibway. She laughs about it for weeks afterwards."

Carson said, "Climb in." I stepped up on the little metal step on the copilot's side and saw that there was no copilot's seat.

Carson said, "I tore it out to make room for more cargo. It's okay. Don't worry about it. Just sit on the floor."

The bay was full of snowmobiles and people walking; people going home, the Spontaneously Created People heading back to trapping camps and to other villages, wandering around, saying their goodbyes.

Carson was a big ropy guy with hair he had obviously cut himself. Like most of the small traders in the north, he had hands with frostbite scars, blackened nails, a battered canvas coat over a down vest and wool shirt; a trader, a hustler, a survivor. A country boy, no doubt. If it could be held together with baling wire, it would fly.

He got in and pressed his thumb on the ignition and got a long, rhythmical grinding noise. He pulled out the choke and tried again.

Once again the starter whined hopelessly and refused to catch.

"I'm going to have to hand-start this son of a bitch," he said. He jumped out of the pilot's door. "Just a minute."

I said, "You're not hand-starting this machine with me in it." And I jumped out on the other side.

We were like a circus act.

On second thought, I reached up and pulled out my sleeping bag and my knapsack with the manuscripts in it.

I dragged my traps and gear around the tail of the 175 to the other side where I could watch what Carson was doing. He suddenly seemed like a Christmas demon, bent on destroying my poetry manuscript.

I dragged all my gear well away. I stood and watched as Carson laid hold of one of the propeller blades and gave it a flip. Happy voices sounded all around us — goodbye, *miiweh*, I had a good time, say hello to Aunt Dorcas — and it flipped over once and quit. He laid hold, reaching over his head, and flipped it again.

The twin blades spun into life, the engine roared. I stared at them. The engine was really in high gear. The plane trembled, and then started to move.

"Oh no!" Carson yelled at the plane as if it could hear him. "I left the choke out!" He turned away from the spinning props and ran back to the metal step, the door. But the plane was moving faster and faster, and the door passed him by. The 175 gathered speed, he ran beside it, his legs seemed to be spinning in circles like one of those cartoon characters, Wile E. Coyote perhaps, and then the plane was trundling down-bay at lift speed and he fell back.

The 175 carried on down the ice, heading toward the birch grove at the deep end of the bay, innocent of human control.

Everybody around me, and me too, watched openmouthed as the high-winged little plane, animate and free (Free I tell you! Free at last!) gathered speed, plunged past two people on a snowmobile, barely missed a fifty-five-gallon metal drum, frightened a teenager out of his wits, and then lifted off the snowpack.

"No," said Carson. "No no no."

It flew a hundred yards and then smashed head-on into the birch trees. The force of the impact made it bang backwards, the windshields popped out and baggage flew out after the windshields.

Carson put his face in his hands. His living gone up in busted metal. His cargo-carrier, his margin. By this time everybody was running toward the plane. I came to my senses and got my camera out of the bag.

Both sides of the windshield had popped out, the propellers were bent into big curls, one wing gestured upwards at a right angle, and a wheel was torn off.

I got some good pictures.

In a few moments, some children had gotten the windshields and were using them to slide down the snowbanks.

Another plane came in; it was a young Ojibway pilot from Weagamow, who had just gotten his license last year and was flying the village co-op plane. His name was Gary Kakekeyash, or, Forever Seagull.

I ran up to him. Like the children of Muskrat Dam, one must learn to seize opportunities when they present themselves.

"Can you take me to Weagamow? I'm trying to catch that sked flight to Sioux."

"Sure. What the hell happened to Carson's plane?"

"It wanted some birch for breakfast."

"Son-of-a-bitching bad luck," said Forever Seagull. He wore a natty navy-blue flight suit, with zippers all over like brass grins. He discharged his two passengers, and some cargo, and I heard tinking noises as his engine cooled down. It was New Year's Day, and minus forty degrees Fahrenheit, clear and bright. Last night all the guns of the village had gone off, all the rifles and shotguns, right at midnight, and the snow-packed ice was littered with brass shell casings, red plastic shotgun cartridges. "Anybody hurt?"

"Nobody was in it."

"Well, get on. Get in the copilot's seat."

Forever Seagull pressed the ignition button and once again I heard an engine respond with a grinding whine, cold, a non-starter.

He said, "Hell, I'm going to have to hand-start the props." He started to get out.

I grabbed Forever Seagull by the back of his navy-blue flight suit in a desperate grip.

"You're not going *anywhere* till you show me how to shut off this engine!"

I saw myself in sole possession of an airplane as it roared off down the snowpacked ice. I saw myself clutching the knapsack with the poetry and the play manuscripts in it as the plane rose fifteen feet and smashed into the birch. I saw myself flying through the empty windshield frames after the windshields themselves.

"Push in the white button and pull out the red button. Or just jump. What's the matter with you, afraid to jump?"

When I walked into the office in Sioux Lookout, David said, "Write up that story about Carson's plane, quick, and we can get it into this edition. Where's your film? Hurry, Kathy will run it for you."

I sat down behind my desk, still in my parka and tin-can moccasins, and started typing.

# 58.

Keith and the director had come up, and what was in preparation was a genuine, full-length play. There was a good part for Doris. Doris was slim and had rich dark hair and good features, she walked onstage like she belonged there. It's just that the part was for an old lady, a wise woman. She turned into a wise woman before my eyes. Now all I had to do was to complete the part where she and the bureaucrat from the Department of Misplaced Bullion and Fur Disposal start yelling at each other. Doris had an extremely long speech about knowledge that comes from experience that I thought could be cut a little.

Doris and Oldman Woman and Keith and I had gone to the Goodwill to find things to make costumes. We browsed around the piles of clothing sent up to the north by people of good will; we found fake green fur, and bright skirts, and old coats.

"Something can be made of all this," said Keith Turnbull, cheerfully. "You'd be amazed." He asked Oldman Woman, "Is there a color code in Ojibway culture? I mean, if we put Doris in green, would this be *symbolic* of something, like, you know . . . in the Middle Ages, green meant virginity."

"No," she said. "There's no color code. But . . . " She looked as if she thought it might be a great idea.

The clothing piled up in our arms, they would no longer be rags, they would become illusion and magic. They would become the leather jacket of Ace Lawson, the bright skirts of Jemimah Nanokeesic, the chief's ball cap, a bureaucrat's three-piece suit. They would arise and walk onstage and begin to speak.

The play was supposed to be the task of a native playwright, and I was neither one.

"It's alright," said Keith. "We have to have a play, and you can do it, and stop biting your nails."

I dreamed I was on a trail from one place to another; a dream-trail to dream-places, in the thick spruce, the low, scooping limbs bearing freights of snow that fell in light drifts even without a wind. Coming up the trail were the Nuns of Fort Albany, in full-length fur coats, their tall moccasins, walking in a line, cheerful, on their way to some destination that gave them heart and courage. They followed behind a *djaban*, the alive sled-being, with the dogs hitched in pairs. Their lively snowshoes threw up an airborne puff of powder snow before each footstep, their skirts were swinging as they walked.

*Te Deum*! they called out to me in dream-voices. *Salve Regina*!

# 59.

It was late winter, February, the Red Sucker Moon. We were over the most uninhabited stretch of the north, and we were losing altitude with sickening rapidity.

I sat beside Kathy and watched the propeller on the dead engine spin raggedly, and the night lay outside the windows of the Navajo in deep solid darks.

We were still a hundred miles from our destination, the Cree village of Attiwapiskat on the James Bay coast. Below, I saw the glowing lamplight of a trapping camp; any light at all stood out in this darkness.

We were going to Attiwapiskat on a story. A new telephone system was going in. It was a free ride, and we needed news from the coast, and now the twin-engined Navajo had lost one engine.

The pilot said we'd do fine with just one engine. The pilot was Ace Lawson.

The windows were vibrating with the strain, as the port engine held us in the air and provided forward momentum.

"We're just going slower with one engine," said Kathy, reasonably.

"If we lose the other one, we'll be up here the whole damn night," I said. Kathy laughed. It was an uneasy laugh. She was making a brave place in her heart.

The Navajo kept wanting to turn toward the dead engine, she kept having to be corrected. The pilot increased power on the remaining, port, engine, and it was consuming fuel wildly, gulping it. We were losing altitude slowly, inevitably.

My poetry manuscript was at home, in the cabin, along with assorted kittens and the mother cat, old copies of the *Atlantic Monthly*, and everything I owned and cared about, other than friends and family. Would they be able to sort it out?

The cowl flaps were trailing on the good engine. I don't know why. Some sort of procedure for when you lose an engine in mid-flight, on your way to a remote village, where there is an airstrip. I unbuckled and got out of my seat, went to the cockpit.

"Ace, I swear."

"Honey, we just *checked* this thing, I don't know how this happened. We just blew a *jug*."

"I'll blow my jug in a minute. Does Attiwapiskat know we're coming?"

"Ah, no. We got off late from Moosonee and I didn't have time to call them and now the guy has gone to bed, I bet. But he'll hear us coming."

"Great. What if he doesn't?"

"Then I'll land this sucker in the dark."

*Now Puanets, this is the story of the Girls Who Married Stars. It was doomed to failure. We leap up into the sky with great expectations and find ourselves in the remote dark, we want to come home, wherever home is on this planet. Do you know, yourself, where home is? Is there a certain smell in the air, of certain plants, or stone, or the shadows in the lake bottom, of springing caribou moss in the early Month of Breaking Snowshoes, or the feel of cool air rising from the last snowbanks when the sun is hot in May?*

*They wanted to marry stars, they thought, and two Star Men came down in a glittering rush of star-detritus and falling bits of light, and they were carried up to the sky country.*

*But the Star Men were gone all night, hunting in the corridors and the trails of the zodiac, stopping by lakes of fire and the thick tangles of nebulae to kill the mythical animals, and then they came home and slept all day in a blue-white lodge.*

*The girls slip away and wander across the flat, glittering plains of the sky world. They encounter Spider Woman, who sits over the hole in the sky. And the girls drift down to earth again on a thin, lustrous thread of spider-silk.*

*It is far more complex than this. They go up in the fall, and come down in the spring. Many more things happened than I can tell you.*

*They land in a tree and are rescued by Fisher, they are taken across a river by Grebe, there is trouble and soap operas and conflict. They arrive in a village in the spring. There were no permanent villages then. A village was an idea that was re-invented every spring at certain places where on the home planet people gathered out of their winter trapping camps at certain places and made a village. They made matagwans, tipis, and suddenly there was an actual village, besides the vil-lage that people carried in their imaginations. And young men and women looked at one another, marriages were arranged, everyone drove hard bargains with the Bay men, we drummed all night. The girls were descending on a spider-silk thread, their hair blowing out in the wind of those great altitudes that lie between heaven and earth.*

"Think positively," said Kathy.

The terrible hard planet was getting much, much closer.

One of the Bell Telephone men, PR guys from Toronto who were going up to inaugurate the new system, looked over at us. "Hey! We're losing altitude!"

"We lost an engine," said Kathy.

"Which engine?"

"This one I'm looking at," I said.

"By god, this should be reported!" The man was scared, and when people get scared they sound angry, like me.

*We are in the hands of the pilot and one engine. Icarus, our pilot and our downfall. Orion and his blue gems freeze in the southwest.*

We burned through the air, the remaining engine consuming fuel at an enormous rate, sliding sideways into Attiwapiskat, the village on the salt coast below Henley House, dark, glittering with roofs, pack-ice on the bay raftered and jumbled, shining, lustrous.

When we were skimming the tops off the spruce, sinking, the lights flashed on the runway. Everyone cheered.

They had heard us coming.

We slammed down onto the brilliantly lit snowpacked runway, and slid sideways, jewels of ice and snow flew everywhere, there were rains of snow, a deluge of flying powder. Ace was at his controls working and working, the tail straightened itself with a sudden roar from the port engine with the last remaining drops of fuel, we plunged on, the brakes snatched, held us, we stopped.

The airstrip manager walked out to the plane, a tall Cree in a long parka.

I trembled down the steps.

He held out his hand.

He said, "Welcome to Attiwapiskat."

Spider Woman had let us down easy, we were alive again.

# 60.

When a traveler is in a distant village, and the weather has closed down over the village like a lid of fog and wandering rain, and traveling is impossible, there is often a feeling of freedom, a kind of lightness. The traveler is a prisoner of the season. Then stories are told in their long versions, the version that has all the significant detail. Brevity and abstraction are the results of good weather. It was in a small Ojibway village on the Albany watershed that I finally learned about the paths of the Stern Paddler, and his long, stellar journey, and what it is he carries in his canoe.

I was in a place called Ogoki Post, on the banks of the Ogoki River. I had come up in search of a story about an assault. The postmistress, Hannah Achineepiniskum, unlocked the small cabin that had been meant for the Hudson's Bay clerk. I could stay there.

Hannah was a medium-tall woman with very good English, a quick sense of humor, and short, curling hair that writhed out of her woolen toque in loops.

"Do you have cigarettes?" she said.

"Sure." I gave her one. "Don't you?"

"No! That Bay Store has been closed down for a month, there's nothing in the village."

I found this astonishing.

"What about food?"

"The young guys are out hunting caribou," she said. She was throwing the bright blue Canada mail sacks into the storage room at the band office. A grainy rain stuttered at the window. "But we don't have dog teams anymore, you know. There's no *gas*. The Bay tanks are down to fifteen gallons. And when the snow goes, the guys won't even be able to get out on the snowmobiles."

Trapped in a village gone back in time; it was delightful. A band of people easing across the dangerous bridge of the seasons, between winter and not-winter.

It was early April, there was the smell of free water in the air, melting snow, the diamond-willow bushes by the river had blushed into a palisade of garnet-red sticks. The snow was made up of fat, water-soaked grains, and I had heard somebody say the river was breaking up now, downstream where the Ogoki and the Albany River joined.

The river was breaking already, out of the walls of winter, and the village was on its own. Twenty days ago the Hudson's Bay Store was closed down, and there had been no shipments of food into Ogoki Post in all that time. The village had returned to another, earlier way of existence. Without regular plane loads of canned goods, bread, oatmeal and sugar and Toastie Pops, wieners, footballs of frozen hamburger, all the noodles and rice and crates of Spork that it took to feed a village of three hundred people, they had once again become dependent on the land itself.

They had become dependent on the strength and skill of the young men. It was a deeper change than merely a change in the food supply. The young men were needed; they were keeping the village fed. The sense of severance they had been burdened with, of distance between themselves and their elders that the day school had brought about, was gone. This is how food was meant to be obtained in the north. The men roared into the village on snowmobiles, erect, heads high, mitt-fringes flying, with expressions of modest reticence, behind which was a joyous, barely concealed pride. Behind each snowmobile was a sled, and on it a dark woods caribou. Later the young men could get back to their studies of the world wars and health sciences. Later.

The Hudson's Bay manager's cabin looked as if it had been hastily abandoned. A deck of cards was scattered on a small table, there was a box of soup packages, a rubber boot.

I looked out the window. The village was thick with fog, the cabins were weathered to the color of brushed steel. Heavy figures moved about, lumpish and vague. I went out to find out what had happened to the Gentlemen Adventurers.

I walked down a path with my camera and backpack. An elder woman was stripping a caribou hide of its inner membranes, and the hair on the opposite side was flying. Caribou hair is loose, it sheds easily.

I said in Ojibway, "Would it bother you if I took your picture?"

Not at all, and as a matter of fact she had a few things to say to me, since I spoke Ojibway. The elder woman laid down the ax head and tore into a long, aggrieved speech about the foolishness of the young chief.

I said, "Yes, yes, um, what is your name?"

"I am his mother!"

The reason the Hudson's Bay Store had closed down was that the chief had fallen into a dispute with the manager, reputedly over a young woman they were both sparking. The young chief went home, loaded his .30-30, and fired at the Bay manager as he was coming out of the store. The manager saw a plane landing on the river, sacked up eleven thousand dollars in cash out of the antiquated safe, locked the store, and got on the plane, never to return. The Hudson's Bay Store, after two hundred years in Ogoki Post, was closing down.

Somewhere in the village a young girl was the cause of this sudden revision of village life, this reversal of the time-stream. Or perhaps, the cessation of progress. Of progressive consumerism. The rainy snow pelted down out of a low sky, and there were scents in the air that come only with the freeing of water. The smell of wet snow, and spruce, and earth, and stones beneath the snow, and roots within the earth. There was nothing to do now but wait the weather out.

I woke up in the middle of the night to strange, washing sounds. I stood on my bed in my nightgown, holding a candle, and the light of the candle slid in clusive, refractive waves off the surface of the water; there was two feet of water in the cabin. The snow was melting in one wild rush, flooding everything.

I sloshed around in gumboots and nightgown, stuffing things in my backpack. I hiked up the trail in the rain, carrying everything I could, falling down in the mud, getting back up, falling down, getting up. Hannah's house was up on the rise. I was lost, briefly, in a strange village, and developed a freaky, irrational fear of suddenly tumbling down onto the river ice and breaking through, and never coming up again.

A neat little cabin shone with lights and voices. I heard Hannah talking inside; this was it. By the time I got in, I was plastered with mud.

There were more people coming in; others whose houses were awash with snow-melt. They burst into the house where Hannah lived with her parents, sparkling with drops of rain on bright black hair, flinging water off themselves.

"Lots of rain! Who's that white woman? Where did she come from?"

"*Wawatay News.*"

"Ah."

Soon there were ten people in the small Achineepiniskum house, in various states of *deshabillé*, and the wood stove was cracking with hot knots of dry pine, and a kettle of tea was boiling. The coal-oil lamps gave a smooth buttery glow to hands, wet hair, black eyes, and there was the familiar and comforting smell of wet fur.

Hannah shoved a stack of newspapers and magazines from the couch, to make room. I saw an issue of *Wawatay*: there was Stan Winnepetonga at the dance, Carson's crashed plane in the birch.

I sat on the bed, listening to the running water, wadded up in a pile of blankets and sleeping bags. A very small lady sat on the bed next to me, a big shawl around her shoulders, laughing at the silliness of it all, everyone jammed into the Achineepiniskum house, wet and half-dressed. Two children were also on the bed, they had shucked themselves of parkas and moccasins, and one of them had hold of my hand and was tugging at a silver bracelet.

"*Minshin,*" she said. Give it to me.

I took it off and gave it to her. I said to the elder woman, "*Nokom* [grandmother], what is your name?"

"Antoinette. I am called Antoinette."

"Tell us a story."

"I'll translate for you," said Hannah. "She has wonderful stories."

"There was a family that starved to death during a bad breakup like this. Yes, it was the Henley House chief's family. They got up on an island in the river, waiting for the ice to break up and clear, but it didn't clear. They were trapped. It was all bog, you know. And she says, they ate their dogs . . . they found them . . . she says she changed her mind, she doesn't want to tell you that story.

"She says, but now that can't happen any more because they have helicopters."

I said, "Listen. It's really raining now." I curled up in the sleeping bag, the kids writhed up close to me like kittens, one little girl floundered and crawled up onto Antoinette's lap. A man got up, went outside, and came in with an armload of wet wood, chucked it into the wood stove.

Hannah said, "She says, there are geese on the open rapids down river. She's heard them."

The geese scouts, the ahead-geese, the ones that come before the main flocks, scouting out the open areas.

We sat, listening to the pleasant sound of rain, rain that might well trap me in Ogoki for another week. Or more.

I listened for the sound of geese.

I said, "Does she know any legends about stars? Or the names of stars? I'd like to put this in the paper for the young people."

Antoinette waved her hand, suddenly she was quite enthusiastic. The bed bounced. Firelight skittered along the wall.

"Yes, she says it is good that you ask. That's the very thing young people should know. We tell the seasons by the stars. And there is a long, long, story in them.

"She says, you see, now the world is changing. The rapids are breaking up and winter is going. At this time, the first stars you see rising in the evening are those three stars there, called Oda-Ka-Daun Anakwak. That means, um, a Stern Paddler." Hannah paused, thought, and then said, "Yes, it's a guy in the back of the canoe, the Stern Paddler."

"She says when those stars are the first ones rising at evening dark, then the geese are coming, and many important things are happening. At the time also, we see Makwa-Estiquan, just above the Stern Paddler. A group of seven stars."

"Ah, I know," I said. "The Pleiades."

"The what?"

"We call them the Seven Sisters."

"Okay. The Bear's Head rises just above the Stern Paddler. She means . . . what she means is, I mean, the Bear's Head, is that it's time for the people to gather in villages. You see, the Bear's Head is just peeking out of her den. She is looking for a mate. Spring is here. And then the people gather together in villages, you see, and then it was when the young people started, you know, seeing one another and dancing together. And the old people would arrange marriages."

*And we re-invent the idea of "village," at the places on the earth where it already exists in time, hidden in the complex pathways of time, the idea, "village."*

The Bear's Head, Makwa-Estiquan. Grumpy, huge, maternal.

"And the Bear's Head l-o-o-o-ks out of her denning place. We were all isolated in our winter camps, and now we come together. This all happens at the same time."

I said, "Hannah, would you ask her, who is the Bow Paddler?"

I already knew; the last thing Sarah Pijou had left with us before her death was the secret of the Bow Paddler, his faint, stellar steadiness. His holdfast point in the heavens.

"Yes, yes, you see, this is important. The Bow Paddler is what you white people call Keewatin-anak, the North Star. But we call it [she/he, the alive star-being] Nemetahamun, the Bow Paddler. And the Bow Paddler and the Stern Paddler are in a giant canoe, an immense canoe, and in this heavenly vessel are all the stars of the heavens, and every star is a legend."

I was astonished. I sat for a moment, suddenly struck with the immensity, the complexity of this notion. I had been puzzling over the star-concepts for two years, reading through Ruth Benedict, and Levi-Strauss, and nowhere could I find the names of the stars, the ideas or beliefs behind the names. Except in one place. A nineteenth century work which hinted that somewhere the northern plains peoples saw each rising star as the continuation of a story.

She was telling a meta-story. A story about stories, and the Stern Paddler was *il capo de tutti capi*. He and his great vessel full of figures, characters, plots, denouements and resolutions were flying down the time-stream, bearing us all away. Carrying us through season after season, through the dangerous time. Like now, the bridge between seasons. The most dangerous time in the north. And here we are in a village that had gone backwards, or perhaps had jumped sideways, however temporarily, out of the western civilization supply grid, into another state. A state of new rain and clean saffron lamplight, wood smoke and people sitting quietly, listening, lifting their mugs of tea.

I said, "Is Wimshoosh there?"

"Ah yes! Wimshoosh is there, and the Girls Who Married Stars, and their Star Husbands, the dim one and the white large one, and Spider Woman, and the Son of Ayash, and his mother, who became a chickadee and is a red star, and Loon and his ugly brother Grebe, and Wisekejac, and the otter who brought up the mud from the drowned earth, and the two children who ran away from the rolling head, and the twins of east and west; all of them."

"And which stars are they? I mean, for instance, which stars are Loon and Grebe?"

"She doesn't know. The old people used to know when she was young. But now people have forgotten which stars belong to which legends."

I found this startling and intriguing. It was such a rigorous system, demanding of memory, a commanding view of the heavens.

"Yes."

"And as new ones are seen first rising in the evenings, it's another story."

"Yes. And all the stories are interconnected. Do you know the story of First Man and First Woman?"

"Yes."

"She became a mad, greedy rolling head and chased her children through the world."

"Yes."

"They escape her, and do you know what happens?"

"No."

"They are adopted by Wimshoosh!" She laughed at my astonishment. "Yes, Wimshoosh's son-in-law, the one he abandons on a rocky island, is that boy grown up. The Girls Who Married Stars, they are let down by Spider Woman, and fall into the tallest tree in the world. They are rescued by Fisher, who has a broken tail."

I said, "Yes, I know. We call him the Big Dipper. He broke his tail getting them out of the tree."

"And so the Girls come to a river but they cannot get across. They are carried over by Grebe, who takes them to his village, and there they meet his brother Mang, and then begins the story of Mang and Grebe."

I said, "Do you know how they all connect?"

She laughed; her face was a map of experiences, of narrow escapes, of a young girl in love, a mother, a hunter, of years and stories.

"No one could tell them all. Nobody knows them all. In the old days, it would take four full days to tell the story of the Girls Who Married Stars and Loon and Grebe. And people sat! And listened!"

In the millennia before this time, this must have been the thought-system, the story roads, of our early history. The Greeks, who left us with their star stories, must have also told the tales of the rising stars in season. Hercules, Virgo, Aries, Orion. These stories were also interconnected. They must have told the stories of the rising stars all through the winters, in sequence. It must be a system as old as humanity.

I felt as if I had discovered some ancient legend-artifact, a paleolithic mental construct of great elegance, as if I had stumbled onto an imposing edifice in a clearing in the forests. A temple of strange dreams, nearly abandoned, but still standing, wrapped in snow and the night. But, like the ice palisades of winter itself in mid-April, it was beginning to shatter and crumble. It was being abandoned, forgotten. The Four Winds Manitous were waiting at the entrance. The traveler in a distant village approaches with caution.

I had never quite become fluent in Ojibway, but knowledge of the language helped me to speak through translators. I understood how best to put a thing in English in order to have it flow through the grammar and concepts of Ojibway more easily.

I said to Hanna, "Tell her I said, this is a thing of wonder."

*Mando*, the prefix used to indicate wondrous, magical, spiritual.

I heard Hannah use the prefix I wished.

"She says, yes, it is. But few people now can tell even one entire legend."

I said, "They are being recorded as much as possible."

Antoinette shook her head.

"She says that's not the important thing. People have to learn to tell these legends. Just like the young men going out for caribou to feed the village. They used to listen to us old people tell how we rarely got food from the store. Now they know!"

The great structure was cracked. Like winter, its buttresses and walls could no longer withstand the stresses, and it too would disintegrate, like ice. The new story roads were *Terminator 2*, "The Young and the Restless." "The Bold and the Beautiful," in images and light. Light was sacred, and there it was, on the television screen.

"What would help?"

"Get rid of television. She says, she's seen it in Henley House and Big Trout Lake. It makes everything stop. She says, the Stern Paddler moves and the Bow Paddler stays steady. She says, the Stern Paddler moves this way and that, and changes with time, and comes up now in the spring at dusk and in the middle of the night in summer, and another time in winter. But the Bow Paddler stays steady. We must have a place inside us that stays steady like that. And another part of our mind moves with the seasons and the things that happen to us. And so she says she looks up often at night, and thinks about this."

A temple of transparent thought. An edifice of crystal and stars.

And so we talked on, late into the spring night.

I woke up in a tangle of people. Somebody was frying fish on the wood stove. Yum! Fish for breakfast! I sat in my nightgown and took the cup of tea that was handed me.

Antoinette said, "Listen! A plane."

I wanted to stay here forever. But it might be the last plane in weeks. Hannah came in, beating watery snow from her ski pants.

"Get your bags, hurry."

The Otter landed on what was nearly glare ice. I waved to Hannah, clutching my camera bag. We made it off. It was close. Languages, like ice, can disintegrate and with them their enormous thought-structures. There's no retrieving them. I began to wonder what I was doing in the communications business.

# 61.

We cannot see into the Villages of the Dead, and to look for them, searching with the dark lens of the mind, is not the task of ordinary people.

In late March a shaman of Winter Fisher looked into the dark places, maybe it was the paths to the Villages of the Dead. He was searching for the missing plane. He was asking for the presences of Sarah Pijou and Serena Eastwind and George Sutherland. He found something, some trace, some indication, on those perilous trails.

The chief and band councillors of Winter Fisher said they were sending down their own search party, now that the Canadian Forces had given up, and could a *Wawatay* reporter go along to cover it?

"I get to go! I get to go!" Kathy Chisel was jumping up and down in the hall. "Nathan and David said I get to go with the searchers!"

The rest of us looked on with some envy as Kathy got into the *Wawatay* junker with her snowshoes, backpack, camera and emergency gear to drive down the Trans-Canada to a spot just north of Thunder Bay. From there, she and the Winter Fisher men would go into the bush and begin criss-crossing the terrain on snowshoes.

The seer of Winter Fisher had described a hillside, a beaver pond, a clearing. Kathy called back to the office several times over the three days of searching. She sounded frustrated, tired, and finally depressed. It was late in the season and the snow was so grainy and wet they could make very little distance without great effort. It was Onabuni-Keesis, the Moon of the Crust on the Snow, the month when snowshoes rattle and slip on the hard crust when the frames snap as you break through. When snow machines grind down to the snow under the crust and then down into the moss and earth; the snow is like wet salt, and machines burn out their engines and throw tracks.

David spoke to Kathy over the phone.

"She says he could describe it so well, but there's so many places with a clearing and a beaver pond and a hillside."

She came back with good photographs, but nothing about the missing plane. She had very much hoped that *Wawatay* and the northern men would be the ones to find the plane.

"You got to be raised in the bush to keep up with those guys," she said. "I damn near died. I'm just a city girl powwow dancer. Jesus."

We went out for beer after work.

In the loud bar, we shouted theories at one another.

Nathan said, "Maybe he just pretended to go off the radio band. Maybe he switched frequency and then turned off his radio, and flew on to the States."

I said, "Why would he do that?"

David said, "They never recovered that gold, you know. The gold bullion he pulled out of the Red Lake mines."

I said, "What did he do with it?"

We shouted around the noise of another rock band. This one had guys all dressed as bikers. They had helmets with horns on them and big black leather kidney belts with rivets all around and beards. They were probably all college students from a Toronto suburb, spending a year being Heavy Guys. The pub was full of the usual suspects; of both races, of all cultures, meeting here at the pub, the living room of the north.

Garnet said, "That's just it. What *did* he do with it? Maybe he hid it somewhere in Indiana. That's where the police found him after the heist. Maybe he's always just been looking for his chance to go back and get it."

"Ah, come on," said Kathy.

I said, "Then where are the women?"

"Maybe he took them along."

"Huh-uh," said Kathy, stoutly. "No way. The medicine man in Winter Fisher saw the crash site. They're down there somewhere, somewhere near Thunder Bay. If a medicine man says so, I believe him."

I said, "And speaking of medicine men, what about Nimrod Kanakakeesic?"

"No word of him, either."

It is a special interlude in the seasons when four feet of snow clears off the surface of the earth. It melts and reveals things that were lost. In the northern villages one can see people walking around bent over, peering closely at the newly bare ground. Pacing carefully around wood yards, in front of cabin doors, beside the community stores, down the paths to the school, the church, the outhouse, and the docks. People are squatted down in their gumboots drawing fingers through newly exposed dried grass, sifting through woodchips.

"I am looking for my wedding ring," they say. "I threw it out when I got mad at Mark last November." They say, "I lost my eyeglasses right here at Christmas. I know they've got to be here." And, "My knife fell out of my pocket when I was cutting wood in January." They say, "The baby was playing with my watch out here in February, I know she dropped it right about here."

The snow evaporates and the curtain comes down, it is the end of the search.

They found Sutherland's plane in several pieces at the end of March, in the forests just north of Thunder Bay. It was at the edge of a clearing, on a hillside, and at the foot of the hill was a beaver pond. At the bottom of the pond the Ontario Provincial Police searchers found George Sutherland's wallet.

Near the wreck, they discovered a jawbone. They weren't sure whose it was. Anyway, it was somebody's.

In late April, when the snows pulled back in North Spirit, three hundred miles further north, Nimrod Kanakakeesic's body was discovered.

It had been nearby all along, in a deep snowdrift behind the Blackhawk Store, the Free Trader's. A few hundred yards from Sarah Winnepetonga's little house. Within fifty yards of people coming and going with their purchases. He had hung himself from one of the small spruce trees behind the store. His body was on its knees. He had hung himself kneeling.

"But Nathan, that can't be done!"

"Yes, it can," said Nathan. "And he had extraordinary powers. But that's not all. He hung himself with one of the aileron wires from the Twin Otter crash. The one that hit the radio tower and scattered wires and stuff all over the village. He used the wire."

# 62.

The tipi stood for a long time outside my cabin, its opaque plastic rattling.

Time flew by more easily now, maybe I'd get pneumonia and a high temperature again, who knew? We were moving forward to the time when the actors would arrive, a theater group would begin.

The Stern Paddler was rising early in the evening with his three stars of high magnitude, the dusty galaxy in his paddle glowing across the light-years, on his changeable journey. Just ahead of him in the celestial vessel, the Bear's Head shone down. She was all crystal and light. Summer arrives quickly; the Stern Paddler shoves his celestial vessel into the current of warmth and lime-colored poplar leaves, loon's nests hidden in the reeds, the silk of cotton grass. Into Wabigoon-Keesis, the Moon of White Flowers.

And now the fire season was beginning again. It had been a dry spring, with less snow than usual, and the fires were starting early. As I drove into town, I saw the fire danger indicator at the MNR fire base was already into the red even though it was only late May.

Fires made the northern summer a time of heat and light and danger. In the farthest reaches, near the Hudson's Bay coast, in the interior, they simply burned themselves out. When they came near a village, then the MNR would send a Twin Otter with a crew, pumps, and fire hoses to attempt to protect the community but otherwise nothing could be done. Fire was part of the natural order. Fire was part of the human psyche, interior fires of sweeping, hot emotions that burnt through one's social training, burst out in irrational actions.

> *Puanets, remember that legends are not told in the summer-*
> *time, and remember that when the Son of Ayash returned from*

*his journey, his vision quest across the land, he came back to find his secretive, malicious father, or stepfather, abusing his mother. On his vision quest he had left his mother alone and unprotected. Remember the great fire that swept up out of the deep parts of the forest toward their lodge. And recall that the old man and his second wife said, "What shall we do? What shall we do to escape?" And the Son of Ayash told them, "Hide in these big birch-bark containers of oil that you've saved for the winter." The father of Ayash and his lazy second wife, who had so mistreated his mother, were burnt to white bones. And recall that they were changed into white wild ducks who swam off across the black, acidic surface of the lake, calling and calling. You can hear them yet, singing their songs of passion and jealousy.*

David called me up at seven in the morning on a bright, hot day.

"It's not time for work yet," I said.

I thought, "This is my second season of fire."

"I know, I know, but there's a fire at Cat Lake that's about to take the whole village. Meet me at the Granite Falls water base."

Granite Falls was the name of a small bush-airline operation. It was named for the small community where it had started out. It had moved its operations to Sioux Lookout but kept the name. I wasn't too keen on flying with them.

At the little airline's base on Abraham Lake, David met me. He stood by his parked car, waving at me.

"It's not a long ride, don't worry, I'll get you in there and back again tonight. That's a promise."

David shoved me toward the shabby, one-engined rusting 185 Cessna Skywagon. The pilot was a little skinny grinning bonehead who had pitched a 185 end-over-end the year before on a windy lake, and the gossip was that he'd only survived the sinking by grabbing at an empty gas can as it floated upwards out of the cargo door.

I dug in my heels.

"I'm not flying with that asshole!"

"We need the story!" said David. He propelled me toward the dock.

"You need me! Alive!"

"Have faith! This is a great story! One that you, Jiles, especially don't want to miss." He was hurling my camera bag and knapsack into the copilot's seat. "A story of passion and jealousy. The fire wasn't started by natural causes — an eighteen-year-old girl started it. She was seeing this married guy on the sly, you see, up there in Cat Lake, and he tried to cut off the affair, and so she tried to set fire to him and his wife's cabin. She ended up setting the whole village on fire."

He was right. I was hooked. I would never have refused an assignment anyway, not from my editor and certainly not from David, but I liked to think I was being hurled into danger by forces beyond my control. It always seemed more ladylike.

The goofy pilot revved up everything with wild enthusiasm; he was a nervous skinny fellow who did everything by jerks, like a squirrel. He snatched out the choke, banged the flaps, charged up the engine and the last I heard from David, as we ripped off across the lake, was a shout,

"I'll have you back by sunset! That's a promise!"

In the heat of summer, when the sun bears down for long, long, northern hours on the endless lakes, the light-absorbing spruce forests and the granite bosses, heat columns rise from the earth and toss airplanes around. There is so much light. There is as much light as there is in deserts. Hot winds and heat columns beat at us all the way to Cat Lake, a little village only one hundred miles north of Sioux Lookout. The small plane was a construction of struts and ripped fabric, a kind of kite blazing through sheets of water reflections. I could smell the hot sweat of the pilot. He wore a T-shirt and Levi's, a little crazy hard-working guy with grease ground into his knuckles. He said nothing and I said less. I was mentally trying to keep us on an even keel.

There was, in addition to the heat, a terrific wind. Big windstorms can come any time in the north; summer or winter. There are legends about them. They can blow for three days at a time at gale intensity, and this wind was building to gale force. Whatever fire there was in Cat Lake would fatten on this wind. I suddenly thought, what if it really does eat the village and I'm trapped there? What if we're smoked in?

The next problem was to get the airplane down. A light plane in a high wind has trouble returning to earth. Sometimes the pilots just can't get them down. My squirrel-pilot was now beginning to fight the plane for all he was worth, and the village of Cat Lake appeared on the horizon, a little collection of houses perched on the edge of the lake with the forest behind it. There was one lone column of smoke being whipped to rags by the wind. Apparently they had got it out.

All along the lakefront, on pontoons, and tied firmly to the docks, were the big International Orange Day-Glo planes of the Ministry of Natural Resources, the firefighters' planes. At one end was a white-and-navy blue airplane of the Ontario Provincial Police.

"They came to arrest that girl that started the fire!" said the pilot. We were jamming down on the hot, rising air. He was starting a long approach upwind, onto the jumping lake, and I could smell the smoke. "They got the fire out, but they're arresting her!"

The lake-surface was standing up in whitecaps. The plane struck the top of one big wave and I gave myself up for dead. But the tips of the pontoons did not, indeed, catch, but slid over, struck the next wave-top, and sank into the next wave-top, and then there was the sensation of the pontoons diving deep into the water, heaving and bouyant. We made it to the dock. I jumped out, the pilot threw me a line, and I tied on.

The story then became a simple matter of finding facts. So-and-so had been arrested and charged with various things; mischief, jealousy, dangerous use of matches, intent to cause excitement in a little village of one hundred and fifty people. It was a hot, sandy place. Cat Lake sat in the midst of a forest of small, surprisingly stunted pines. I suppose it was on an esker, for the little twisted pines grew straight up out of white sand and the red, dusty dirt that comes from aeons of pine-needle duff. Here and there granite extruded from the earth. The girl was gone, taken away on another airplane.

The wind howled red dust and ashes. I talked to the firefighters and was told again that the fire had been deliberately started, burnt fifteen acres, but with the whole village pitching in, they got it out.

I sat on a boulder — there were many boulders in this village — and wondered what more there was to a story here. I hadn't risked my neck on that plane for nothing, surely. And then there is always the simple human greed for scandal, the curiosity which possesses us all to understand tales of human passion. To understand people out of control, people who are willing to set fire to their married paramour's cabin because he wouldn't leave his wife, the details, the entertainment of imagining the eighteen-year-old girl in her long, dark hair, cheated and abandoned, pouring gasoline against the cabin wall and striking matches, running into the dark woods with her heart afire with revenge and satisfaction, *then let them die!*

However, none of this was going to get into the pages of *Wawatay News*. I stood in the roaring wind talking to the officer of the law, a Cree fellow from Thunder Bay, who had adopted the reasonable, quieting tones of a lawman. No, there was nothing to get excited about. No, no one was hurt. The girl was only being charged with mischief, not arson. She was terrified at what she'd done and repentant. No, I couldn't use her name, she was still a minor.

The firefighters were laughing as they rolled up their hoses and loaded them into the cargo bays of the two Twin Otters. No problem. A little bushfire. Yes, it could have gotten out of control, but then, on the other hand, it didn't get out of control. We got it out. Fires of passion, eh? Ha ha ha ha.


There is always one thing to do when one is in a northern village, having taken the time and the trouble to go there, the expense of going there, and come up with little or nothing. And that is to go interview an elder.

Our readers loved interviews with elders.

"Yes, go see Sam Mikinak. He's got lots of stories. People like to hear his stories. He lives over there."

A teenage boy in a jean jacket and baseball cap directed me to a house. I walked through the hot wind and glittering sun to a log cabin in among pines.

"Eh, *bojo*," I said. The man looked up at me. "*Wawatay Tepajemo Massaigan nint-anoki.*"

He laughed, hearing a white woman speaking Anishinabe.

"I speak English," he said.

I said, "Good." I sat down on a wooden chair. It was quiet in here. The wind-noise stopped. I wondered if I got stuck here in the village, if I could stay in this place. A woman of about forty came out of a bedroom and looked at me. She was dressed in a flowered print skirt and sneakers and a T-shirt and she was wrenchingly thin. She did not seem friendly. She had long hair.

I had always found these small cabins, in the summertime, had wonderful scents. The smell of pine, and scrubbed wooden floors, and freshly-washed clothes brought in from the sunshine, tea on the stove, the cool smell of long pike drifting in a bucket of water, ready for cleaning. However, I couldn't lean back and enjoy myself because of the unhappy, sulky glares of the woman of the house.

He said, "You're from the newspaper."

I said, "I came up for the story about the girl that set the fire. A story about jealousy."

He laughed. He nodded. He liked this forthrightness. Sometimes people do and sometimes they don't.

I said, "But it's pretty simple, and I wrote down all the facts. I thought maybe, before I left, I could talk with you. I could ask you about the old days. People like stories about the old days."

He nodded again.

He cleared his throat.

There was a mass of gill net on the floor in front of him. The gill nets always need repairing, and he had the hand-carved wooden shuttle in his hand.

The hot wind moved the daylight from place to place outside the open door, the village of Cat Lake had fallen back into its surface placidity. Outside a few people wandered around, looking at the patches of burned brush and pine, remarking what a close thing it had been; there was still a heavy odor in the air of wood smoke and charcoal. A young girl, perhaps ten, walked in to see what was going on. She wore jeans and a T-shirt with Spiderman on it.

"This is my daughter," the elder said, with a smile.

He seemed old to have a daughter that young. The girl stared at me for a minute and then walked back to the room where the woman was. I didn't know what she was doing there. There was no laughter in this house; and maybe where there is no laugher, there can't be any wisdom either.

We'd had many men elders in the pages of the newspaper. They were men with men's hands, hard and scarred with life and effort, men who had handled weapons since an early age — men who were quiet, or boisterous, who had been teetotalers or alcoholics, patient or impulsive; but always men who had taken on a man's burden and lived to tell what happened to them.

He said, "Sometimes when you talk to a stranger, you are more comfortable telling things about your life."

I should have known something was coming. I said, "I would be glad to hear about your life. The young people want wisdom from elders, you know."

He said, "I know that." He was a handsome man. He was of medium height, with a dark complexion burned teak by a life in the outdoors. I was always in search of the great cycle of star-legends that nobody seemed to know anymore. Maybe he would have one of the missing links. His nose was sharp, aquiline, as if he had Plains blood, he wore a dark shirt and ordinary, dark pants. He picked up the mass of gill netting and began to repair the torn places.

# 63.

The wind sailed into the open window in a square blast and blew a paper bag across the floor. The woman came out of the back room and went out the door without a word, the girl following behind. Neither one of them looked at the elder.

He said, "That is my wife and my daughter," as if perhaps I hadn't heard him the first time.

I liked him. I felt comfortable here with him. I had all day before David sent up the Granite Falls Cherokee 206, flown by Matt Mitchell, if indeed Matt could make it in with this wind. I might be here for the night, in the village of Cat, which is a poor translation of *pijou*, the Lynx.

These elder men have a quiet, unpretentious wisdom sometimes, that comes from humility. Their advice comes from experience. They have lived through time, made their journeys through the segments called *years*, have been on vision quests or have gone to war, many different kinds of wars.

I wrote down the facts of his life; hoping for some adventure, something unusual. A young man came to the door from the band office with a message from David. He had his baseball cap down tight around his forehead, and was formal with the importance of delivering a message from Sioux Lookout.

"David called on the HF," he said. "He said to tell you that he will get you out today."

I said, "Thanks."

But the day had worn on past noon and then toward three o'clock. The wind was as bad as ever. I didn't know how anybody would get in; the lake was boiling with whitecaps.

I said, "What was your most important lesson in life as a young man?"

He said, "I killed a man when I was younger."

I said, "Ah!", startled and shocked and suddenly cautious.

He threaded the hair-fine strands.

I said, wondering if he were up to killing people again, "What happened?"

We believe in this concept, "Native Elder"; and I think our greatest delusion is that they have always lived exemplary lives and therefore have something to teach us about how to live a blameless life. But that's not it, at all.

I was stiff with caution. I sat and waited.

The man looked up and then down again. He looked out the window.

He said, "I was a wanderer when I was young, you know. I came from a big family, there were eight of us, and I didn't like to be crowded, I guess. My mother and father were both from Doghole Bay, and they moved away from there when the mines came in, and the miners, and there was so much liquor and fighting. I didn't marry until I was older. I liked to be alone, to take life by myself, do what I wanted and go where I wanted. I traveled all over. I went with the York boats to Fort Nelson, and Fort York, and over to the east side of James Bay, where they speak differently. There were Aishkimawek there too. Eskimos. I had a good life, I liked to travel."

I said I understood that, certainly.

He said, "Then I came home and I met this woman and so we married. It was time to get married. We were a long time together and didn't have a child.

"At the time . . . " What time? I wondered. What were the dates, here? Where was this woman from? In the legends, the story always begins — almost inevitably — with the description of a still lake in the summertime. The wind is always still. The lake is shining. It is as if we begin our youth in this way, and move on to winters and storms.

"There was a writer here at the time. He liked for me to help him, translate for him, tell him the legends. Just like you. You'd like to hear a legend. But I am not telling you a legend now."

"No, not a legend," I said.

"He took them back to the university where he was and he would put them together. This is how he made his living." He shuttled the wooden oblong through the fine threads of polymer. "That's how a lot of white people make a living that come up here."

I said, "I work for *Wawatay*, that's an Indian newspaper."

"Yes." He nodded his head. "So my wife and this man became attracted to one another. Also, he liked to drink. He thought this made him good friends with Indians, drinking with them. We were sitting up in the Ministry cabin one evening, and everybody got drunk. They woke me up the next morning and said I had killed him. He was dead in the bathtub. I guess I had hit him in the head with a cant-hook. I hit him a lot of times. I didn't remember it. There was a trial . . . " He shrugged. "They decided nobody knew who did it. But sometimes when my wife is mad at me she yells at me. She says I killed him."

He was impelled by this story. He must tell it. I must listen. I must sit here, dumb and receptive and listen to this terrible tale. An unprintable tale. I must listen and nod and indicate, somehow, *I understand.*

I said, "This must be hard."

He repeats himself: "The courts couldn't decide who killed him." He wove, shuttled, threaded. His hard long hands as strong now, at perhaps fifty-five, as they were twenty years ago, but knobbier. They seem to be carved of wood. "But I must have. I got drunk so I wouldn't remember."

But he got off. Outside the hot wind continued sandblasting the walls of the house, and the entire village.

I said, "You got your revenge."

He said, "I am raising his daughter. My wife had a baby afterwards. It was his baby. That's the only child I will ever have, I think. It appears that way. I am doing my best to raise her well, as a Indian, even though she's half white."

I sat there, stunned. I thought about the silent, resentful woman, the contemptuous girl. The house without laughter. This is the price. There is always a price. Every time he looks into the girl's eyes, the white man who thought knowledge was the accumulation of data, looks back.

This is a dramatic story with a dramatic outcome.

What this man is telling me is that there is no action for which there is not a price. There is no blamelessness.

There is no solution to some things. There are some rages for which there is no peace, some slights and insults for which there is no forgiveness, there are family relationships which cannot be repaired, and marriages which engender such fury that there is no hope of reconciliation this side of the grave.

He is saying there are things that have to be lived with.

The girl was suddenly outside the window, blowing soap bubbles through a plastic hoop. She dipped it into the brightly colored glass jar, which sported the picture of a clown, and blew softly. The bubbles foamed into the window and sparkled across the floor.

"She will turn against me even more when she gets older," the man said. "Her mother tells her in secret every day that I am a bad man, I think. At least I dream about this. I always try to hold my temper, to be calm and reasonable, but I can't always. A man gets short-tempered sometimes. But I can see it in her eyes. 'He's not even my father.' So I have to raise this girl, and work hard for her future, even though she hates me more every day."

I wanted to say to this murderer, You're a good man. I wanted them all to let go of each other — the woman who has evidently based her marital career on both clinging and hating, the petulant, self-righteous girl. I wanted them to suddenly develop wisdom, courage, patience, forgiveness.

The girl blew her bubbles and, even though suppertime was coming, she wasn't going to bring in any of the dry wood stacked outside the door. If her father insists she bring it in, then the father is a cruel taskmaster. If the father brings it in himself, the girl will see him as weak and contemptible. If the father simply packs up and leaves, he will be a Deserting Dad who has abandoned a young girl and her mother. If he stays, there are only years of misery for his old age and in the end the young girl will leave, and her mother with him.

"Eh, my daughter," says the Wise Elder. "Come here, say hello to me."

The girl slid into the door, clutching her bubbles. Her father is trying to get her attention. The girl has learned that her attention and her approval are very valuable things, and she is determined to parcel these out sparingly. I could barely stand to watch this; what the old man wanted what we all want, was that they see him as a decent human being, a man worthy of respect, dignity. A murderer, a man who gave way to passion and brought death. The woman gave way to passion and, willy-nilly, had life brought out of her. The old man reached out to the girl nonetheless and gave her an affectionate hug. The girl sidled away again. She tossed her head in a cute, arrogant way. She looked at me.

She said, "You white people think you know everything."

I said, "We don't. The elders, though, they know a great many things."

"Like *what?*"

"That there is a price for everything."

Young people don't like to hear this. I didn't even like hearing it myself, much less saying it. Maybe I was growing up, or old.

The radio suddenly came on. Cat Lake had a one-watt FM station and "Jingle Bell Rock" suddenly burst out of the transistor. The girl left.

I sat and drank tea for a long time in silence, watching him thread the brilliant filaments of the gill net, repairing and repairing the big light-washed weaves into a whole. The girl blew resentful bubbles out in the yard. Her mother would cook hostile meals, maybe, and make spiteful beds, haul in petulant buckets of water and stitch begrudged moccasins and then go to her mother and recount long resentful stories.

The woman came back and offered me a plate of hot bannock with butter and jam.

"The newspaper pays if you reporters stay in somebody's house, don't they?" she asked.

I said they did.

"Well, if the plane doesn't come for you, you can stay here."

I thanked her, in reality thinking I would rather spend the night in the fuel shed than stay here, and ardently wished the wind would die down and Matt Mitchell would come and rescue me.

The wind roared outside and as I finished the bannock, wondering how the man was weaving the strands, the chief of Cat Lake came striding up to the door, his nylon jacket rattled by the wind.

"Hey! You the *Wawatay* reporter? David called, he said Matt Mitchell is coming for you! Go down to the dock, hurry."

We were the last to leave; all the other airplanes had gone — the firefighters' planes, the Northern Patrol plane. The Cherokee Stretch 206 came booming down the rigid wind, expertly flown, and the sun was beginning to melt into volcanic pools on the horizon. We had maybe thirty minutes to get back to the water base in Sioux Lookout before dark. Small planes that land on water can't fly in the dark. But here came the night.

I stood out on the bouncing dock and grabbed the line that Matt threw to me, and, helped by the Chief, dragged the Cherokee in close enough to leap onto the pontoons. It seemed odd to be drawing in this enormous plane, just the two of us, with one 3/8-inch line, but a plane on pontoons is very moveable. The door flew open, I threw my bags in, and then leapt up to the copilot's seat.

I waved to the Chief.

"Thank you!"

The Chief waved cheerfully.

"No problem! No fire, no problem!"

"Right!" I bellowed.

Matt Mitchell was, like most pilots, a man little given to chatter or social amenities. He bent to his instruments, a big, paunchy guy with a lock of black hair flapping over his wrinkled forehead.

I said, "Matt, are we going to get out of here?"

He said, "I think so."

He turned the plane out into the lake, forcing his engines against the beam wind. We heaved and leapt over the high whitecaps on our big silver-shoe pontoons. As soon as he managed to get far enough out on the fifteen-mile stretch of the lake, he turned downwind and revved engines and off we went. We seemed to struggle up out of the water. It was a much heavier plane than the one I had come in on, and we were not knocked about by the gale-force wind so much, but it was still a shaky ride. The sun fell into its lake of fire, spreading orange and vermillion all over the south-west. I could smell forest-fire smoke, and had no idea where it was coming from. Everywhere.

At blue dusk we drifted down onto Abraham Lake. It was dim, at the point where one can barely read newsprint, can barely tell where the dark water separates itself from air, when the docks are indistinct, the spruce forest melts into dreamy deep greens. When the pontoons touched down and a white wake foamed up behind them, the plane settled and quieted, I started breathing again.

There stood David on the dock, waving.

"I *told* you I'd get you back today!" he said, triumphantly.

I said, "I was never so glad to see anybody in my life."

"What was the story?"

"Not much. I can't even use her name. Small fire, it was out pretty quick."

"Come on back to the house, let me and Margaret get you a brandy and some supper."

"Thanks, it's good of you, but I think I want to just get back to the cabin and die."

I sat staring gloomily at my wood stove that night. Every evening, nearly, in the north, is glossed with a light chill, and a small fire makes the place a little brighter. Loons started up like something being frightened out of its wits right at the lake-edge, fifty yards away. They always made me jump.

The story I had heard there in Cat Lake deeply depressed me. It almost made me believe in the impossibility, under some circumstances, of doing the right thing. I watched the cat at the window. She was staring out at something that excited her, something she wanted to kill.

I had left Sergeant Preston in a burst of bad temper I could probably never retract. Sometimes, alone with ourselves, we simply don't like ourselves. We think about the things we have done, and they are so heavy and unlike our true selves, we hope, that they seem the actions of villains, of evil people in melodramatic tales. Things that cannot be undone.

Then I thought about me and the Chief of Cat Lake drawing in that great airplane to the dock, fetching it in on a 3/8-inch line, a great dense machine bouyant as a hot-air balloon as it rolled on the sprays of the whitecaps. It had weighed tons, with its steel and plexiglass, its big pontoons and weight of fuel, cargo, seats, engines, propellers. Yet it was so light, because it stood on water in its big shining shoes.

Me and the Chief of Cat Lake pulled it in, hand over hand, and it came to us like a wonderful catch, easily.

I thought, maybe some day I will figure out what this means. How one moves always on water, bouyant, alive with weightlessness. Then I will be an elder.

But I decided not to hold my breath.

# 64.

I eventually found the resources, or the mental Zen, to remain at a typewriter keyboard long enough to make a playable play. It was from sitting and typing all those stories, I suppose, for two years at the *Wawatay* newspaper offices. The patience that machines demand. The no-time time of waiting for planes in bad weather, of learning to listen to elders. To slow down and focus; it hadn't come easily.

Then there was funding to pay for the actors and the set designer and a person to make up the costumes, a producer and a director. Live theater was coming to Sioux Lookout.

This should not have been such an unusual thing; but we are all losing our common human ability to produce our own entertainment and dance, sing, tell stories, whistle, do voices, invent jokes, and/or play some kind of instrument. Every normal average person used to be able to produce at least some of their own entertainment. They did parlor games, told riddles, sang songs in harmony, even a badly played guitar was welcome. But we have changed from a people who could produce their own everyday amusements to consumers; passive consumers. We no longer put up with badly played guitars that require somebody in the house to tune the thing in order to sing along with it. We sit passively, limply, and consume, without effort, the finest guitar playing on earth.

But here were actors, live ones, who were going to come to Sioux and memorize homemade dialogue and put on costumes out of the Goodwill store.

The actors burst into town like a circus. They put up anywhere — just offer a bed, a room, a garage! — and threw down their sleeping bags. It seemed as if they were made of steel springs. They swept into our lives with crazed enthusiasm, snatching up the script, flinging themselves into early morning aerobics in the high-school gym, and the ones who were lucky enough to stay in the hotel jumped up and down on the beds. Ellen Sands, from the Kettle Island reserve, opened her mouth and sang long, gorgeous notes.

They were entranced with Sioux Lookout. It was out of a movie, they said. There were loggers, and miners, and prospectors with long white beards. Bush pilots looking just as bush pilots should look, wise native elders and strong young Ojibway hunters, charming Métis maidens, and indigenous women of beauty and talent and spirit.

They made me see the north all over again, as if it were perfectly new, and as entrancing as the first time I arrived in my city dress boots.

Graham Greene did amazing things with his long pony-tail. If somebody had the audacity to fart in public, he grabbed it and made it wave as if he were in a sudden gust of wind, and made stage wind noises. Doug Rodgers kept pestering Doris for new phrases in Ojibway.

"Hey Doris!" They were running in a circle in the gym, limbering up. "How do you say, *give it a big long suck* ?"

And she would shout something at him, god knows what.

She came up to her marks on stage, she bent over the script, memorizing, out at my cabin. She was staying with me, and so the place was often full of actors. The Toronto ones helpfully carried water from the lake, and the native actors approved and applauded, saying "That's not enough! Get more!" until I was awash in lake water.

Doris and Graham had been raised in native communities. They never shirked work or were without some clever solution for the thousand small problems that faced a theater company traveling about with sets, props and personal baggage on small planes through the north. Doris took on the task of acting with intense concentration and focus, quick to pick up hints from the other actors as well as instructions from Keith. Graham had that rare skill called "field expedience." His energy inspired people, he seemed to sweep other people along with him, telling jokes in the meantime. Most of the jokes were on himself. He was by far the most skilled actor in the cast; his ability to become somebody else was magical.

Graham paced around the high-school gym with his copy of the script. He was the protagonist.

"Let's see, let's see, I must seek out the *motivation* of my character. He's an asshole, right? Simple. I can do assholes."

Then he stopped joking and got serious.

Doug practiced his rant. He delivered his crazed, let's-mow-down-the-forest speech at top volume, the veins stood out on his neck.

"I like this, I like this," said Graham. "I get to watch Doug's veins pop out every night."

Rick Gorrie, the stage manager, and Keith began to construct a papier-mâché caribou hindquarter. I was riveted by all this; a common artifact of the north was turning into a stage prop! Then they made a plywood airplane nose and propeller, which would just peek out behind the sets. The actors tried on the Salvation Army costumes. Graham sat with a fedora on his head and a bowling jacket, writing notations on his script.

I listened to them speak their parts, and then crept back at night and changed things.

Keith said, "It's a very good script, very playable. At some point, you *must* stop."

"Okay, once again," said Graham. He walked up to his mark and said, "Ah, this is news. I know how to handle *news.*"

At the pub, where everyone repaired every night, I asked him, "Do you speak Iroquois?"

"Huh-uh. It's about disappeared. They're teaching it on the reserve school now but it's damn near too late. I hope people up here get wise to this. It's so *cool* to walk down the street and hear people just walking along, speaking Ojibway! It sounds like they've got to be talking about *wise* stuff, you know, discussing the fate of humanity or something. Of course, he's saying 'Did you forget to turn off the caribou stew, darling?' and she says, 'Why no, didn't *you*? I was skinning the beaver.'"

One night we walked out of rehearsal and wild, violent waves of northern lights were tearing across the summer sky, it was a light show, a ghostly armada in full sail, which then disappeared and was replaced by star-bursts.

Doug said, "This is unreal. People *live* with this."

Graham said, "I want to get up to a northern community."

I said, "So do I."

# 65.

My chance to go back to North Spirit Rapids came that fall.

I had been offered a three-month contract with the CBC to work with the radio station. Nathan said, go ahead, we'll hire somebody, you need to get laid back. He said this drinking his tenth cup of coffee for the morning and lighting two menthol cigarettes at the same time.

In North Spirit's crisp fall weather, I happily moved into a little cabin on the river. I didn't have to write anything, just do reports! Yes, yes, yes. I was making very good money, the newspaper had not collapsed without me. The actors were rehearsing down in Sioux, and soon they would begin their winter tour. I would have liked to remain in the north forever, and drift happily through life under the sign of the Bear's Head, loose as a head of a cotton grass in a high wind.

I rolled in a fifty-five gallon steel drum for a stove. This was a marvelous invention. I had seen them before and now had one of my own. It was set up on end with five empty Carnation milk cans for legs. Damon Crow, my neighbor, hammered a hole in the front end for a damper, into which another Carnation can just fit. To damp the fire, you shoved the Carnation can into the hole. The chimney pipe rose out of another hole in the flat top of the steel drum, and went on up through a hole in the roof. Milk and fire; it was a rich and vivid heating device.

I wrote my reports back to CBC by the light of a kerosene lantern. When people walked in, the entire cabin jiggled and scraps of curly moss fell out of the mill sidings that made the ceiling. The moss got into the reports mailed back to Toronto. I have no idea what my supervisor thought they were. He never asked.

I sat up late on my plank bed reading *The Idiot* by candlelight. I have always had trouble sleeping and this awful tome of Dostoyevsky was a perfect soporific.

There was almost no furniture other than a handmade plank table and three chairs, also a plank counter and shelves. I found I could surprise myself and live comfortably under all sorts of circumstances except loud noise. The one great discomfort of my life had always been boredom. And now, after a number of years in the north, I found that I was rarely bored. People played cards, they fell into deep conversations about dreams, or, lacking anything else, one could always drift off into a silent, meditative no-time. I could sit still for long periods, watching the fire.

Television had arrived in North Spirit, along with the radio pick-up on the microwave, and I found that the dances at the log community hall had ceased to exist. The hall sat empty and the children seemed to forget how to dance. The dances had stopped as suddenly as if they had been declared illegal.

I drifted from the Bay Store to the radio station and then to the bluff. My time was loosely organized around being with people and being alone. A cool fall snow drifted through the air and settled onto the water and the granite. As I passed houses and cabins, I often saw the pale erratic flashes of television light.

I walked down to greet the rising stars at the lake-edge, whoever they were. I thought, perhaps lady adventurers live under the sign of the Bear's Head.

The movements of the seasons in the north are theatrical and grand. The signs of seasonal change filled me with wonder and pleasure as I walked to the river for water, saw poplar leaves cast south-eastwards by the fall wind like the coins of gamblers, lemon-yellow in the fall. One night a wolf stood on the far shore watching in the window with a look of amazement and curiosity, and then ducked her head and trotted on, solitary, purposeful.

I had a great deal of time to think and ponder things. I was not the same person I had been four or five years ago. I realized I would have to face the solitary life of a writer sooner or later. How easily a life of movement and action had swept away good intentions to sit alone and work out the massive structures of language that constitute storytelling on paper, the narrative, the dialogue. How much easier it had been to tell stories, or to listen to them. It was so much simpler to get on a plane and fly into the reaches of Anishinabe-Aski, to a distant village, where some striking event had taken place, some human or natural drama, to ask and take a few notes.

The time was coming when I would have to leave and live quietly and begin the struggle to put these things down on paper. Just as the stories of the north were appearing on paper at *Wawatay* for the first time.

It was as if I had lived through a certain measure of the dance which had begun when I first boarded the DC-3 for North Spirit, and it was now bringing itself to a close. The pattern had been danced through.

The northern boreal world was unique and unlike any other on earth, still undisturbed, with deep linkages to other sub-arctic cultures and its unbroken chain of story-lives going back into the pre-Columbian past. The forests are as yet uncut, the greed of great cities for water and power has, as yet, dammed up only a few of its rivers. It has not been trampled by gold-seekers and ideology-mad politicos and marked by the uncounted deaths that has made Siberia a land of tears and terror and pollution. It is still clean and mostly aboriginal and the call of the wild is a melody arriving from inside us, out of our own distant past. Somewhere in the world there are rock paintings created by the ancestors of each one of us, and there are songs behind the dancing figures, and thoughts behind the songs. It is a past to be reckoned with, replete with action, violence, wars, discord, resolution, and courage, star-legends with episodes following one on the heels of another. At the end, someone turns into a chickadee or a star, the characters become something else and fly away, escaping the net of the narrative.

It was time to bend to the page and tell these tales. It was even more imperative now because of the arrival of the hypnotic drug of television. The interesting doings of white star people, the often wildly inaccurate news reports delivered in smooth professional voices, the voices of gods who were beyond doubting. The world in the south had moved on without me for years now, I didn't know what political events I had missed, what changes had occurred in fashions. The seasons would move in their long circle perhaps one more time, I would see the play through its tour in the northern villages, and then I would leave the north and go somewhere warm.

# 66.

I stood at the airstrip shack with Emasiah, waiting for a plane. It was arranged that Graham would stay with the Half-A-Days down with the River People, to visit, and see what this part of the world was like, since the play took place in the north, and the audience was to be these people.

It was a long, slow, smoky November. Graham got off a Twin Otter and, after I took him to Agamatin, walked for a long time by himself, watching, listening.

Later he said, "My reserve must have been like this a long, long time ago. This is cool."

I said, "I'll take you around visiting."

We stopped at Damon Crow's house, and I employed as much of the Anishinabe language as I had at my command, which wasn't all that much, even after seven years.

The Crow house was a neat, new, log cabin in a grove of poplars.

I walked in without knocking.

Graham said, "Hey, maybe they're kissing in the back room or something."

Damon Crow rose up from his chair. He had been cleaning a .30-30.

I said, "This man is an Iroquois person [Nodaway]. He has come up from the south to visit."

Damon said, "A Nodaway! Well. It's good you have come."

Graham said, "What's he saying, Jiles?"

I said, "He says it's nice to have you." I said to Damon, "Yes, he says he's happy to be here. He will be in the play that's coming."

Damon said, "Did he come by plane? From the Nodaway reserve?" Damon was speaking slowly and carefully for my benefit.

Graham said, "Is he saying something about me? Translate, will you?"

I said, "He's asking about Iroquois people. They call you guys Nodaways."

Graham said, "I'm Oneida."

"Same thing."

"Oneidas and Iroquois are not the same thing."

"Yes, but there's only one word for all Six Nations."

Nodaway actually means "enemy person." It was because the Six Nations used to range north to the Ojibway Nation in the seventeenth century and they had vigorous and often fatal disagreements about the trade routes. But I thought it best not to tell Graham this.

Damon said, "What's he saying?"

I said to Damon, "He says he's Oneida."

Damon said, "You said he was a Nodaway."

I said, "Oneida is kind of [like, resembling] Nodoway." I wanted to scream.

I said to Graham, "And he wants to know how you got here. I'm going to tell him you came by airplane, but they have a weird word for airplane here, it's not the same word I learned from Nathan." I said to Damon, "You understand *pimisewin*?"

Damon said, "Yes, I understand that word. We don't use it here though. Why do they call you 'Little Shabby Sioux?'"

I said, "It's complicated."

Graham said, "What's he saying? Give me a break, or a clue, or something."

"He wants to know how come people call me 'Puanets.'"

"What does that mean?"

"It's complicated."

Damon said, "What is this play?"

I said, "Well, it's like amateur night. . . . " And then language failed me. Every Halloween most of the villages had amateur nights, and they were great successes, with people in bum costumes, and people who could juggle things, and pilots in drag with enormous brassieres stuffed with fruit, throwing apples and oranges to an appreciative crowd. "Well, I don't know. An amateur night."

Damon said soothingly, "I understand."

Graham said, "That's okay, I'll just sit here in total silence while you guys chat it up. Never mind me."

I said, "He says he has some fresh caribou for sale. Would you like some? He has a loin."

Actually, I made this up, but he was cleaning his rifle, wasn't he?

"Yes. Good idea."

I said, "Damon, do you have any meat?"

"Yes, yes, I just got a caribou. Perhaps he would like some. All those Nodaways have to eat down there is hominy-corn soup."

So that went off okay.

# 67.

A young woman stood at the door of the cabin. She hung on the door frame and stared in, waiting for me to notice her.

I said, "*Pindiken.*" Come in. I looked up from my messy report. It was one of the little girls who had labeled every object in my cabin five years ago, now nearly grown, a young adult. Long grown-up hair spilled down her shoulders and she wore a semi-rebellious teenager jean jacket with sayings and signs written on it with bleach and a matchstick. STOP and WILD THING.

It was snowing outside. Snow was building, and North Spirit Lake was booming with new-freeze noises, deep, alarming cannon shots.

She said, "You will come. Celeste asks you to come."

"Is something wrong?"

"It is the give-away for the baby."

Of course. It was the one-year anniversary of the baby's death, and on that day the mourner gave away all the dead person's things, that had been carefully saved. There would be a feast, many other gifts would be given. I must go.

I walked up to the Hill, Agamatin, with my hands tucked in the pockets of my red down jacket. I looked out over the reaches of North Spirit Lake, now gray with forming frazil ice, and the song of the wind was the music of millennia upon millennia of the presence of the Anishinabek, with all the losses and the griefs, tribal clashes, marriages made in hell, happy families, spring spawnings, joyous drumming.

I thought of Pawakan, who mourns, and Mikinak, who will laugh at anything. The flags tore out sideways in the blowing snow: the Canadian flag, the flags of the Anglican church and the Gentlemen Adventurers Trading into Hudson's Bay.

The house belonging to Celeste and her husband sat down near Chebui Nayaushe, Ghost Point. It was a new cabin, built in the new style of fresh yellow logs, large and comfortable. There were lots of people arriving; talking, determinedly cheerful.

I walked in, and Celeste turned to me and smiled and grasped my hand in a fierce grip. There were many young matrons there, women in their twenties, with babies on their laps. They turned to look at me, smiling. The husbands, fathers, male relatives nodded. The wood stove crackled.

"It is good that you are here," said Celeste. She looked pretty in a big pink and white maternity sweatshirt. She was expecting again. I wanted to hug her, but it wasn't done.

She said, "Sit here, beside my mother."

I hadn't seen Celeste's mother since the baby died. She was a big woman, and she took my hand in her large one and patted it with her other hand.

Across the room I saw Nathan's mother, Mrs. Nanokeesic. Of course she would be here, as the feast-master. She nodded cheerfully to me, her headscarf a brilliant blaze of orange and blue and tan.

I struggled desperately against tears when Celeste began handing out small dresses and T-shirts, rattles and baby shoes to the other women. She smiled, laughed, her girlfriends made frantic jokes. One was not supposed to be sad. This was a kind of supplication to fate, this ceremony, a display of courage and generosity, an appeasement of whatever cruel dark things lived in the spirit world and might come back a second time. She smiled and handed me a package of baby diapers. I stared at them. What would I ever do with them?

"Take them, take them," whispered the young woman on my other side. I smiled and put them beside me.

A great deal of food was handed around: caribou, rabbit soup, tea, cake, Jell-O, more than I could possibly eat.

The lamps glowed against the snowy dim day outside, I choked down cake and Jell-O. Celeste was distributing nylons now, and pocketknives for the young women's husbands. Thank god she had finished giving away the baby's things.

She said, "Puanets, this is for you. Because you were strong."

Everyone was looking at me and smiling, nodding. It was a splendid piece of beadwork, great blossoming flowers on a wine-colored velvet background. It must have taken her months. It was wiry, vital, and springing with life.

I was really having an awful struggle with tears.

I said, "Many, many thanks."

And the food of the dead was eaten, and the possessions of the dead were given away to start a new life elsewhere, the wind howled at the chimney top and made it hoot and sing, and then it was time to go home. And sure enough, with all that food and gifts and a strenuous determination to be cheerful, everybody *was* cheerful, even Celeste.

At the door, I shook hands with everyone I could reach. Mrs. Nanokeesic came up and I reached out my hand to her and she did the most moving thing. She took my hand in both of hers, and bowed and kissed the back of my hand. I stood open-mouthed in astonishment.

This gesture from an elder of such high status and respect overwhelmed me. I had no idea what to say or do. I was dumbfounded. Ojibway flew completely out of my head. I snatched for words, any word, some word, and then remembered something; *Gahkenah Ninakomenawah.* My deepest thanks, to all the people. *Kitche-migwetj, Nokom.* Thank you, Grandmother.

There must have been some other, more elegant phrase; but that was all that came to me.

The guests went out, off into the trails and paths of North Spirit Rapids, bearing away their gifts. Mrs. Nanokeesic walked away down the River path, disappearing into the spinning snow. Her bright headscarf was a trudging garden of fabric-flowers and it seemed to glow. She was the feast-master who distributed gifts, and so her hands were always empty of stuff; things; possessions. The opalescent snow boiled down from the sky, this meant easy traveling. It was some meteorological feast-master pouring her white rewards down on Anishnabe-Aski. It was Kushkudene-Keesis, the Freezing Moon. Legends could now be told again, the story roads were open. I slid down the path with my package of baby diapers and beadwork. The light had the resolution of some colorless gemstone. In snow-light like this human life flares out in rich tones, against the void.

# 68.

The log community hall in Muskrat Dam is jammed with kids in parkas and moccasins, the teenagers are curious and shy, the elder women watch with iron resolution. The Honda generator outside is very loud but nobody notices.

I sit in the rear, with my script, looking at all my scribbled rewrites which will never be spoken or reenacted.

The lights come up.

It is a radio station in a small community. Graham plays a young Indian man returning to his home village after several years in college, prepared to change everything that needs changing. I can hear Sarah laughing.

The recording machine records the wrong things and can't be turned off.

The bureaucrat has come to plan out the entire village, from birth to death. An old lady comes in with tipi poles and the bureaucrat is horrified at her idea of housing. She plays cards with the bureaucrat and wins.

A child confuses theatrical space with real space, leaves the audience, and goes up and sits down at the card table and picks up the cards.

Doug picks him up by the parka hood and deposits him back in his seat.

The audience breaks out in applause.

There were rustling noises, whispering, and these were increasing in intensity.

Suddenly the kids were leaving. A little crowd of them had gathered at the door, and one after another they were sliding out into a billow of steam, disappearing munchkins in parkas and puffy moccasins. Graham speaks his lines more loudly, Doris begins to make her gestures larger, but nothing subdues the noise of the kids, creeping to the door and then dashing out.

I whisper, "Sarah, what's happening?"

"They're all going home to watch "Hill Street Blues" on TV. Everybody's got a TV now, since they put up that satellite dish."

"What satellite dish?"

"Oh yeah, you've been out in North Spirit most of the winter. They brought it up on the cat train. Yeah. The kids watch it constantly. They're speaking English to each other all the time. The grandparents can't talk to the kids anymore."

"But the play's mostly in English!"

"Television is more exciting, I guess. I don't know what to do about it. Nobody does."

Soon the hall is empty of children, and then some of the young adults begin to creep away, apologizing to the people they stepped over. But the play is coming to its end, and the exodus stops when the fiddler lifts his instrument and breaks into "Ste. Anne's Reel."

And so the play is over.

Nobody dies.

No planes crash.

A shamanic voice does not speak in a rich dark whisper out of the choral power of Beethoven's Ninth.

All the children live.

There is no mercury in this river.

It is alright. A true theater will happen in good time. I put down the script. We had evolved out of a vast stream of people, who started to invent a world of the mind sometime back in the Ice Ages, out of clans and tribes that contained drunken husbands, corrupt politicians, thieves and liars, heroes and murderers and great leaders and heroines. Lady adventurers, and the storyteller who went out into the world, and the storyteller who stayed home.

They must have had a system, a hundred thousand years ago, like playing cards, graphic images of all human types, a boreal *commedia dell'arte*, that moved through the seasons with the constellations. These images worked only in movement, and they flew like ravens through linked tales, singing their bell-like xylophone songs of geological time.

What was left were the great flowing bulls; reindeer in blacks and reds with their heads in the air and their antlers laid along their backs as they crossed some Ice Age river, the calligraphic forms of horses streaming down limestone walls. Lascaux was in my time-stream, my ancestry, and Lascaux was the joy and the transport of stories. That's what lasts. It has lasted thirty thousand years.

# 69.

The frozen moose hindquarter was diminished somewhat. All the actors have had supper from it, except the fiddler, who is sleeping in the log hall, away from all the meat-eaters.

The little nursing station is lit by electricity. We shove two desks together, sit on chairs and play cards half the night, until everybody has dissipated the tension and excitement of performing.

Keith says, "Give me two. We found somebody to do the next play."

"Oh, good," I said.

"You can go back to poetry, Jiles."

"Right. Who is it?"

"A guy called Tomson Highway. He's terrific."

Graham says, "You know, I auditioned for that made-for-TV movie, the one about Riel? They wanted guys in the charging Indian troops. I got hired as an extra, and you got more pay if you could ride. The director says, 'How many of you guys can ride?' I'm going 'Me! Me! I'd never been on a horse before in my life."

Sarah's laughing, trying to pay attention to her cards.

"I stayed on the damn thing." Graham deals quickly and expertly. "My girlfriend is going, 'You're going to die for sure this time, Graham.' The director says, 'Okay guys! Some of you are shot and you fall off in this final scene!'"

Graham clutches his chest, cards and all, like he's been shot.

"Every guy in the charge goes off his horse like he's exploded! The entire Cree nation is *creamed* right there! I went off like a dirty shirt. Who's going to pass up the chance to make a great fall off a horse right in front of the camera?"

"I thought you didn't know how to ride," said Sarah.

"Right! Falling off was a *snap*. The director is running around yelling,

'Wait! Wait! We can't have everybody dying!' I said, oh no, no, certainly not. So we drew lots. I got one. I was lucky. I got to die."

"I still think that's pretty brave, falling off a horse and you don't know how to ride."

Graham said, "It's called employment. Whose turn to shuffle these cards?"

"Me," I said.

"Aha, the Little Shabby Sioux."

"Watch this," I said. "This is the country girl Missouri shuffle."

I did a fancy riff with the cards.

Graham said, "Hand me those cards."

He knocked them together and slapped the pack down on the desktop. He leaned toward them and gave them a lo-o-o-o-ng wide-eyed stare.

"*That's* the Oneida shuffle."

# 70.

It was late when Sarah and I walked back to the Winnepetonga house. It was Nemebini-Keesis: Red Sucker Moon.

She was telling me about a dream she had.

The Bow Paddler, the North Star, was rising in his luminous majesty over the reaches of the frozen Severn, over the uncut forests, over Anishinabe-Aski. Over one of the last great wildernesses of the world, and all its tall imperial animals, over the final lamps of the village, pulling behind him the cosmic vessel of the heavens and all its passengers, a canoe full of sparkling stories; thousands and thousands of stories, stories as many as stars in the sky.

There are too many stories to be recounted. There are stories of the north for other people to tell from their own viewpoints. I think of Nathan, Jeannie, Sarah, Elizabeth, Oldman Woman, David, Kathy, Piitonya and Tokyo, Mrs. Mindemoya and Chief Makepeace, Mrs. Nanokeesic and the people I had met as stellar figures rising in their own constellations in an impossibly long tale. The house of the storyteller is a place deep in the forest, a place everybody, at some time, rediscovers like an adventurer reaching for the jewel at the heart of the snow temple.

The Northern Cross flew steadily down the Milky Way, afire with gems and plumes. Oda-Ka-Daun plunged his heavy blade into the body of darkness. He was steering the universe toward the northwest now, and the road that is at the edge of our galaxy and which leads outward into the strange radio voices of time.

Where is he steering us? What river, what vessel? In the spring nighttimes, without electricity or politics, without human planning or intervention, in the roaring blue fires of remote suns, he speaks only to the old people.

*I am the Stern Paddler. This is my voice. Remember me.*
*This is the river of stars. Here is the time-stream.*
*Remember this. We are moving down a watershed of years.*
*We are moving in the dark, startling reaches of heaven*
*where things are reborn and reform.*
*You have always been on this journey.*
*Listen! You were born, you grew, you began to speak.*
*You were always in this current.*
*I am erratic, I change with the seasons,*
*But the Bow Paddler stays still.*
*Between us two are all the stories that the storytellers have*
*to tell.*
*They are gifted and strange, listen to them, they live under*
*the rapids.*
*In the legends, you are perfectly strong.*
*You learn the joy of silence and the art of noise.*
*You move over the still water with someplace to get to, some*
*place in time.*
*Coming home in the universe with blood on your hands.*
*In the legends, you are perfectly strong.*